MEXICAN HOMETOWN ASSOCIATIONS IN CHICAGOACÁN

✢

LATINIDAD
Transnational Cultures in the United States

This series publishes books that deepen and expand our knowledge and understanding of the various Latina/o populations in the United States in the context of their transnational relationships with cultures of the broader Americas. The focus is on the history and analysis of Latino cultural systems and practices in national and transnational spheres of influence from the nineteenth century to the present. The series is open to scholarship in political science, economics, anthropology, linguistics, history, cinema and television, literary and cultural studies, and popular culture and encourages interdisciplinary approaches, methods, and theories. The series grew out of discussions with faculty at the School of Transborder Studies at Arizona State University, where an interdisciplinary emphasis is being placed on transborder and transnational dynamics.

Matthew Garcia, Series Editor, School of Historical, Philosophical, and Religious Studies; and Director of Comparative Border Studies

María Acosta Cruz, *Dream Nation: Puerto Rican Culture and the Fictions of Independence*

Rodolfo F. Acuña, *In the Trenches of Academe: The Making of Chicana/o Studies*

Xóchitl Bada, *Mexican Hometown Associations in Chicagoacán: From Local to Transnational Civic Engagement*

Adriana Cruz-Manjarrez, *Zapotecs on the Move: Cultural, Social, and Political Processes in Transnational Perspective*

Marivel T. Danielson, *Homecoming Queers: Desire and Difference in Chicana Latina Cultural Production*

Rudy P. Guevarra Jr., *Becoming Mexipino: Multiethnic Identities and Communities in San Diego*

Lisa Jarvinen, *The Rise of Spanish-Language Filmmaking: Out from Hollywood's Shadow, 1929–1939*

Regina M. Marchi, *Day of the Dead in the USA: The Migration and Transformation of a Cultural Phenomenon*

Desirée A. Martín, *Borderlands Saints: Secular Sanctity in Chicano/a and Mexican Culture*

Marci R. McMahon, *Domestic Negotiations: Gender, Nation, and Self-Fashioning in US Mexicana and Chicana Literature and Art*

A. Gabriel Melendez, *Hidden Chicano Cinema: Film Dramas in the Borderlands*

Priscilla Peña Ovalle, *Dance and the Hollywood Latina: Race, Sex, and Stardom*

Luis F. B. Plascencia, *Disenchanting Citizenship: Mexican Migrants and the Boundaries of Belonging*

Cecilia M. Rivas, *Salvadoran Imaginaries: Mediated Identities and Cultures of Consumption*

Maya Socolovsky, *Troubling Nationhood in U.S. Latina Literature: Explorations of Place and Belonging*

MEXICAN HOMETOWN ASSOCIATIONS IN CHICAGOACÁN

✦

From Local to Transnational Civic Engagement

XÓCHITL BADA

RUTGERS UNIVERSITY PRESS

NEW BRUNSWICK, NEW JERSEY, AND LONDON

Library of Congress Cataloging-in-Publication Data

Bada, Xóchitl.

Mexican hometown associations in Chicagoacán : from local to transnational civic engagement / Xóchitl Bada.

pages cm. — (Latinidad : transnational cultures in the United States)

Includes bibliographical references and index.

ISBN 978–0–8135–6493–7 (hardcover : alk. paper) — ISBN 978–0–8135–6492–0 (pbk. : alk. paper) — ISBN 978–0–8135–6494–4 (e-book)

1. Mexican Americans—Illinois—Chicago—Societies, etc. 2. Mexican Americans—Illinois—Chicago—Politics and government. 3. Mexican Americans—Social networks—Illinois—Chicago. 4. Social participation—Illinois—Chicago. 5. Political participation—Illinois—Chicago. 6. Chicago (Ill.)—Emigration and immigration. 7. Michoacán de Ocampo (Mexico)—Emigration and immigration. 8. Transnationalism. I. Title.

F548.9.M5B34 2014

305.868'72073077311—dc23   2013027191

A British Cataloging-in-Publication record for this book is available from the British Library.

Visit our website: http://rutgerspress.rutgers.edu

Manufactured in the United States of America

Para Claudio y Macarena, por su infinita paciencia

CONTENTS

Preface   ix
Acknowledgments   xv

1 Migrant Generosity and
   Transnational Civic Engagement   1

2 The Transformation of Mexican
   Migrant Organizations   24

3 Genealogies of Hometown Associations   53

4 Migrant Clubs to the Rescue   81

5 Participatory Planning across Borders   108

6 Expanding Agendas and Building
   Transnational Coalitions   136

Notes   163
References   187
Index   211

PREFACE

This book follows the challenges and opportunities of Michoacán hometown associations (HTAs) in their efforts to influence the civil societies and governments of two nations—Mexico and the United States. The book is based on formal interviews and conversations with HTA leaders, government officials, and nongovernmental organizations (NGOs) engaged in transnational activities in Michoacán and Chicago. To show how the transnational practices of contemporary Mexican migrant organizations have changed, I also include a historical analysis of early forms of binational engagement among Mexican migrants in Chicago in the early twentieth century. The book draws largely from participant observation and collaborative activist ethnographic research conducted between 2000 and 2011 in Greater Chicago, southern Illinois, Los Angeles, Las Vegas, and nine municipalities in the state of Michoacán.

The idea for this project emerged in the summer of 2000 while I was working as a consultant for the Mexico-U.S. Advocates Network, a project of the Heartland Alliance for Human Needs and Human Rights. I arrived in Chicago after volunteering at the Tepeyac Association of New York, a highly visible migrant-led faith-based Mexican organization.[1] When I finished my graduate degree in New York City, I was looking for a job in immigrant advocacy, and Sergio Aguayo, one of my professors at the New School for Social Research, connected me with Susan Gzesh, a well-known human rights activist who was then the executive director at the Mexico-U.S. Advocates Network in Chicago. After learning about my work at Tepeyac, Susan invited me to help her implement a program financed by the MacArthur Foundation to increase the organizational capacity of HTAs from the state of Michoacán. I agreed and became fascinated with the world of Chicago-based Michoacán HTAs. After my contract expired I continued volunteering with the Federation of Michoacán Clubs in Illinois (FEDECMI) between 2001 and 2005.

In the summer of 2008, I accepted a teaching position at the University of Illinois at Chicago (UIC), and I reconnected with FEDECMI, enjoying access to its monthly meetings and events. FEDECMI also invited me to participate as an observer in two of its digital diaspora list-serves.[2] During the preparations for the Civil Society Days of the Global Forum on Migration and Development in the summer of 2010, a representative of Latin American HTAs in the United States asked me to write a position paper for the forum dealing with the empowerment opportunities of migrant-led organizations, focusing on the U.S. case. I prepared the paper with my colleague Gaspar Rivera-Salgado, a Oaxaqueño immigrant academic at the University of California, Los Angeles. The process of writing the paper played an important role in developing the thoughts and conclusions presented in this book.

Over the course of the fieldwork, five remarkable events occurred that illustrate the changing relationship of migrant civil society to state governments in Illinois and Michoacán. First, in less than a decade, the modest state migrant affairs office that I visited in Morelia in in 2001 had become the only state-level Secretariat for Migrant Affairs in Mexico, and its staff increased from two employees to over forty. Second, in 2004 HTAs collectively founded the National Alliance of Latin American and Caribbean Communities (NALACC), which included almost 100 Latin American HTAs and grassroots organizations among its membership and chose Casa Michoacán in Chicago's Pilsen[3] neighborhood as its national administrative headquarters. Third, in 2006 then Illinois governor Rod Blagojevich inaugurated the first Office of New Americans Policy and Advocacy and appointed José Luis Gutiérrez, a former president of FEDECMI, as its director. Fourth, Mexicans abroad were granted the right to vote in Mexican presidential elections in the summer of 2006, and one year later Michoacán migrants living abroad became the first Mexican citizens allowed to vote for a governor in the state elections in 2007. Finally, in 2006 the city of Chicago was among the first in the United States to host a mass protest against the Border Protection, Anti-Terrorism, and Illegal Immigration Control Act, with the participation of HTA members in leadership roles.

Organization of the Book

The introductory chapter presents an overview of the social impact and visibility of Mexican migration to Chicago in the last two decades and the historical presence of Michoacán migrants in the Windy City. I introduce the reader to the world of Mexican HTAs in Chicago by including a brief narrative of a monthly meeting at FEDECMI's headquarters that illustrates the overlapping collective identities and agendas among migrant club members. This chapter defines key terms and outlines the book's goal: to advance the theoretical study of *transnational citizenship* and *civic engagement* by examining the evidence offered by migrant-led organizations such as HTAs, federations of migrant clubs, and larger migrant-led Latin American immigrant coalitions. I familiarize readers with the multiple arenas, networks, and geographies in which migrant civic engagement takes place in Chicago and Michoacán, such as families, sports clubs, museums, political parties, cultural groups, churches, prayer groups, labor centers, Latino and non-Latino grassroots organizations, and other civic institutions.

Chapter 2 explores the transformation of Chicago-based Mexican migrant organizations from the early mutual-aid associations of the 1920s to the creation of Mexican HTAs with binational agendas in the early 1980s. The historical analysis of Mexican migrant-led organizations in Greater Chicago traces continuities, similarities, and differences between contemporary Mexican HTAs and early twentieth-century organizations. Using primary and secondary archival sources to map the historical evolution of Mexican migrant organizing, I show that contemporary HTAs established in the 1980s are not an entirely new phenomenon. Each Mexican migratory wave had organizations with unique transnational agendas, but early Mexican migrant organizations did not engage in simultaneous practices of civic binationality at multiple geopolitical scales as their contemporary counterparts have done in the last two decades.

In chapter 3, I focus on the emergence of HTAs as a result of increased economic globalization and south-north human mobility, briefly introducing the main push-and-pull factors that produced the settlement of thousands of Michoacanos in the Chicago metropolitan area. I include the significance of rituals, celebrations, and topophilic attachment for explaining solidarity ties among HTA members and how participation in HTA activities serves as an important vehicle for integration to U.S. society. This chapter also addresses the challenges that women face to acquire leadership roles within HTAs and the elusive incorporation of U.S.-born youth in transnational activities. The chapter demonstrates that participation in HTAs does not come at the expense of engagement in U.S. civic life, but rather reinforces civic engagement in the U.S. context.

Chapter 4 analyzes the last two decades of the discourse on migration and development, applying a political economic analysis of family remittances and migrant views on the political and economic significance of collective remittances in rural Michoacán. This chapter demonstrates that praising remittances became the preferred mantra of international finance institutions, and offered Mexican politicians and subnational governments a positive narrative to interpret the increasing cash flows sent by vulnerable workers living across the border in the United States. After a decade of implementing programs to leverage remittances toward development purposes, these programs have advanced without much planning and without clear rules about how to transform philanthropic organizations without any prior experience in job-generating projects into successful social entrepreneurs. The examples offered in this chapter show the disconnect between ideals of cooperation in international institutions, sending states, and migrant organizations for rural development.

In relation to the contexts that triggered the political visibility and recognition of HTAs in local state governments on both sides of the border, this section pays special attention to important crossroads in the contemporary political history of Michoacán. These include negotiations to formalize cooperation agreements during state governments led by the Revolutionary Institutional Party (PRI) in the late 1990s, the consolidation of the organization after the triumph of opposition presidential candidate Vicente Fox in the 2000 presidential elections, and the impact the first opposition government in Michoacán had in increasing the visibility of binational organizations in Chicago. I argue that in Chicago and Los Angeles, Michoacán HTAs and other federations of migrant clubs experienced a visible scaling-up of their activities after the triumph of the opposition in Mexican home-state governments.

At the end of this chapter, I analyze the experience of the Three-for-One matching-fund program in the state of Michoacán as a heuristic device to focus on the debates on migration and development in Mexico's neoliberal state. I show that the developmental impact of collective migrant contributions is minimal for Michoacán and for the Mexican economy in general; however, the high visibility of migrant projects in local, national, and international policy-making circles opened a window of opportunity for HTAs to advocate broader policy changes for community development and migrant political rights at subnational, federal, and international scales. The evidence offered confirms that at the subnational level, states are interested in maintaining economic attachments of emigrant populations and have decided to create innovative state-society partnerships to reduce conflict and keep loyalties intact.

In chapter 5, I analyze the role of Michoacán HTAs as agents of social accountability and participatory governance in the state of Michoacán. I show specific mechanisms that HTAs use to increase transparency and governance by promoting potentially efficient models of state-society cooperation for participatory planning, migrant rights advocacy, and electoral engagement across borders. The chapter describes practices of extraterritorial citizen participation in rural communities within municipalities and explores the possibilities for creating synergistic interactions between HTAs and other agents of public accountability within and outside the state government.

Mexico's submunicipal rural governance regimes are seldom analyzed because they tend to be isolated from decision-making and oversight in municipal governance. The chapter provides an answer to several questions: Do HTAs constitute opportunities for state-society power sharing or are they merely legitimizing government decisions? What are the main challenges faced by HTAs in the state of Michoacán to increase the levels of "empowered participatory governance"? What are the tensions between market-based membership and nonmarket membership? Does one easily lead to the other?

The intervention of HTAs in state development plans illustrates the many hurdles that migrant leaders must overcome to regain their voices as full citizens while living thousands of miles away from their hometowns. It also demonstrates that the relationship between the state government and the Michoacán migrant community has shifted from pompous discourses that praised their economic contributions to the state via individual family remittances, to the inclusion of migrant leaders in policy decisions affecting the everyday lives of migrants and their family members on both sides of the border. Still, there is great inequality between the resources that state actors have compared to those of civil society.

Chapter 6 addresses the expansion of Michoacán and other Mexican HTAs networks across the United States and Latin America through the creation of national alliances and coalitions to advocate for migrants' political, economic, and social rights in the United States, Mexico, and Latin America. I examine the organizational challenges, sociopolitical agendas, dual citizenship practices, and scaling operations of HTAs, placing special emphasis on the evolution and expansion of their networks to create a fledgling migrant civil society across borders. I also describe the strategies that migrant-led organizations are using to increase their voice and empowerment in global and local advocacy arenas, such as the spring 2006 immigrant mobilizations, the Latin American Migrant Summit of Morelia, the Global Forum on Migration and Development in Mexico City, and the People's Global Action for Migration, Development, and Human Rights in Puerto Vallarta.

In this final chapter, I illustrate the pathways of synergy that migrant civil society has taken in the last decade to work simultaneously in different national spaces to advocate effectively for public policy changes. The chapter demonstrates that in a difficult environment to attract the attention and increase the civic engagement of disadvantaged minority groups, one of the most important gains for this new cohort of Mexican binational migrant activists working in HTAs and other migrant-led membership organizations is their capacity for self-representation. Mexican HTAs in Chicago provide empirical evidence that contemporary citizenship has become pluridimensional, multiscalar, and fluid, resulting from interactions with different organizations and state policies in more than one nation-state through practices embedded in an unequal global economic policy dominated by a dual discourse centered on liberal democracy and market fundamentalism.

ACKNOWLEDGMENTS

This is a story about migrant lives and their relationships to their governments and villages of origin, and I am indebted to all those who allowed me to get close enough to understand their binational struggles. They may not agree with all my interpretations, but I hope that our mutual efforts to bring visibility and recognition for their contributions to Mexico and the United States will eventually lead to greater social justice and democratic governance.

My first thanks goes to those who guided this project from its inception. My great gratitude goes to Saskia Sassen and Gil Cardenas because they provided unconditional support and wisdom when I first presented them with the idea of studying Mexican hometown associations (HTAs) in Chicago. I am also grateful for the time and effort they devoted to guide me through my graduate school years in Chicago and Notre Dame and, most important, for all the feedback and opportunities that I received during my tenure as a graduate research assistant at the Institute for Latino Studies at the University of Notre Dame.

The Institute for Latino Studies always offered a stimulating intellectual environment to develop my initial work on Mexican migrant organizations, and I enjoyed many fruitful conversations with all the staff, research assistants, fellows, and visiting scholars who provided valuable insight during the initial stages of fieldwork and data collection. My special gratitude goes to María Elena Bessignano, Allert Brown-Gort, Caroline Domingo, Virgilio Elizondo, Phil García, Guillermo Grenier, Dan Groody, Edwin Hernández, Amelia Magalamba, Tim Matovina, Renee Moreno, Sylvia Puente, Tim Ready, Georgian Schipou, and María Thompson. I am also grateful to my longtime friends and collaborators Luis Escala-Rabadán, Víctor Espinosa, and Gaspar Rivera-Salgado, whose work has been critical in filling many gaps in the world of Mexican HTAs. The time spent working and discussing each other's work in various seminars, workshops, and conferences was very valuable in enabling me to evaluate my work in a comparative perspective.

I also want to thank my dear friend and collaborator Jonathan Fox, who encouraged me to take a closer look at the world of Michoacano HTAs after reading my master's thesis. I will always be grateful for those words of encouragement during a lively Callejoneada Zacatecana at the First International Colloquium on Migration and Development in October 2003. While it took me ten years to complete the project, I enjoyed a thrilling ride finding transnational civic engagement here and there. I also wish to thank him for reading and commenting upon many chapters of this book and, above all, for pushing me to the finish line. I lost count of the many times he sent me "finish the book" reminders and was always ready to provide instant feedback every time I got stuck making sense of the collected data. I truly admire Jonathan's constant and unwavering commitment to nurture new voices and interdisciplinary approaches. I thank Susan Gzesh for her enthusiasm for this project, for her friendship, and for digging and sharing with me her notes on President Salinas de Gortari's visit to the University of Chicago and her very accurate memories of one of the first trips of Cuauhtémoc Cárdenas Solórzano to the Windy City. She even managed to convince John Coatsworth to search his personal archives on these visits and share them with me.

I also want to acknowledge the valuable help provided by a large number of migrants and their families who allowed me to take a peek at their binational lives in Chicago and Michoacán. They always received me with open arms in their houses on both sides of the border, and I will be eternally thankful for that undeserved gesture. The list is too long for me to acknowledge in this space, but my special gratitude goes to the families Balleño Zárate, García, and Moreno Liévanos for all their hospitality throughout many years. I am also grateful for all the time devoted by several members of Michoacano HTAs to talking to me about the activities of their organizations. I thank Carlos Arango, Lourdes Arreola, Rosa and Artemio Arreola, Gonzalo Arroyo, Yolanda Zoraida Ávila, Salvador Balleño, Rubén Chávez, Anita de la Cruz, Rosy de la Vega, José Díaz, Alfredo García, Arcadio García, José Luis Gutiérrez, Ramiro Izquierdo, Hugo Lino Espino, José Luis Moreno, Jorge Mújica, Raymundo Murataya, Reveriano Orozco, Alfredo and Consuelo Rodríguez, Raúl Ross Pineda, Mayte Ruiz, Agustín Sánchez, Rosendo Sánchez, Luis Soto, Gerardo Torres, Bernardo Villaseñor, and Pablo Vivanco. I also want to recognize the membership of clubs Venustiano Carranza, Chehuayo Grande, Las Cruces, Ciudad Hidalgo, Huandacareo, Jéruco, La Luz, Morelia, La Purísima, El Rincón de Dolores, San Bartolo, San Juanico, San Miguel Epéjan, San Rafael, Tzitzio, and Francisco Villa for all the wonderful events that I was honored to attend and for all the delicious food that you generously offered me and my family in Chicago and in your beautiful towns. I learned so much about the rich culinary culture and music of the state of Michoacán. It is always a pleasure to do research with a full stomach and listening to good live music.

In Michoacán, I thank the staff of the former Instituto del Migrante Micho-
acano (Institute for Michoacán Migrants) in Morelia, especially Eneida Reynoso
Acosta, Jesús Martínez Saldaña, Gonzalo Badillo, and Claudio Méndez, who provided invaluable information and logistical support during many field trips to
rural Michoacán. I also thank Paty Flores, the former research director of the
State Center for Municipal Development (CEDEMUN), and staff member Lupita
Márquez for her quick and efficient answers to all my information requests on
Michoacán municipalities and for their multiple invitations to observe the work
performed by CEDEMUN training staff at several sites. The staff at the Secretariat of Social Development (SEDESOL) in Michoacán also offered logistical
support during fieldwork and shared numerous documents related to local
Three-for-One projects with me. My gratitude there goes to Luis Gerardo Castillo Maciel, the assistant delegate for social and human development, for his
generosity in explaining to me the complex bureaucracy of any transnational
endeavor. Former Michoacán governor Lázaro Cárdenas Batel and former social
development secretary Graciela Andrade offered invaluable support and hard-
to-find government documents during the last stage of this project. In Chicago,
Roberto Joaquín Galíndez Gallegos, the SEDESOL representative in the United
States, always shared the most up-to-date official compilations of Three-for-One
project statistics and spent many long afternoons answering my pesky questions
about the nuts and bolts of this government program.

There are a few people who merit recognition for their valuable research assistance during this project: Joanna Schmit, for her bravery to drive treacherous
roads in rural Michoacán during my last field trip in the summer of 2010. I admire
her stoicism after listening to several unsolicited accounts of beheadings during
our interviews with HTAs' parallel committee members; Carlos Enrique Tapia,
for securing interviews with municipal staff members; and Vanessa Guridy, for
sharing her current research data on HTAs in Waukegan, Illinois. I want to thank
my dear colleague Gustavo López Castro from the Centro de Estudios Rura-
les at El Colegio de Michoacán (COLMICH) in Zamora, who always provided
an institutional affiliation, shared his vast knowledge of Michoacán migrants,
offered me unrestricted access to a superb specialized library, and, most recently,
offered institutional support to publish this work in Spanish. During my many
visits to COLMICH in the last decade, Sergio Zendejas and Gail Mummert also
provided invaluable tips and resources to develop this project.

A good number of institutions helped me and this project stay afloat since
2003. Fieldwork research in Michoacán and Chicago was financed by the Institute
for Latino Studies, the Zahm Travel Fund, the Phillip Moore Fund, and the Kel-
logg Institute at the University of Notre Dame. I also received external support
through research assistantships, seminar invitations, and conference attendance
travel grants from El Colegio de la Frontera Norte; El Colegio de Michoacán;
Enlaces América; Institute for Mexicans Abroad; the Mexico Institute at the

Woodrow Wilson International Center for Scholars; the Michoacán State Congress; the Chicago Council on Global Affairs; Tufts University; the University of California, Santa Cruz; and the Center for Latin American Studies at the University of Chicago. Most recently, a conference grant from the Katz Center for Mexican Studies at the University of Chicago, a faculty fellowship from the Institute for Research on Race and Public Policy, and the Under-Represented Faculty Recruitment Program research fund at the University of Illinois at Chicago (UIC) made it possible to complete the final draft and most of the revisions.

The final manuscript benefited from the careful reading of Laura Carlsen, who graciously agreed to help me to get rid of most of the Spanglish. Many changes were also made after receiving detailed and valuable criticism from colleagues. I cannot wait to return the favor. Thanks to Frances Aparicio, Iván Arenas, Judith Boruchoff, Katrina Burgess, Lauren Duquette-Rury, Víctor Espinosa, Adrián Félix, Nilda Flores-González, Lorena García, Shannon Gleeson, Luin Goldring, Patrisia Macías-Rojas, Cristóbal Mendoza, Juan Mora-Torres, Amalia Pallares, Stephanie Schütze, and Adriana Sletza-Ortega. At Rutgers University Press, I am particularly thankful to Leslie Mitchner for her support and valuable suggestions throughout this project. I would like to thank my reviewers, Michael Peter Smith and Nestor P. Rodríguez, for their very thoughtful comments and detailed criticism. As usual, all the remaining errors are exclusively mine.

I would also like to thank my colleagues and most recent friends at the Latin American and Latino Studies Program at UIC for providing the most wonderful climate to develop my work. It is a true joy to share the workplace with such a terrific group of publicly engaged colleagues: Salomé Aguilera Skvirsky, Chris Boyer, Simone Buechler, Ralph Cintron, Nilda Flores-González, Elena Gutiérrez, Alejandro L. Madrid (now at Cornell), Joel Palka, Amalia Pallares, Cristián Roa de la Carrera, María de los Ángeles Torres, and Javier Villa-Flores.

Thanks are due to the following publications in which portions of an earlier draft have appeared: *The Latin Americanist* 55.4 (2011) and *Latino Studies* 11.1 (2013), and the books *Rallying for Immigrant Rights* (University of California Press, 2011) and *Marcha! Latino Chicago and the Immigrant Rights Movement* (University of Illinois Press, 2010).

And last but not least, there are those who are closest to me. I thank my husband and cheerleader, Claudio, for his companionship and moral support throughout this long journey. I thank him for his professional pictures of many field trips and for his kind words of encouragement to finish this book when frustration took over my energy and focus. I also thank our beloved daughter Macarena, whose gentle but persistent reminders to finish this book contributed to the final delivery of the manuscript that you are about to read. Her frequent questions *¿mami, ya terminaste tu libro?* followed by *¿cuándo vas a terminar tu libro?* definitely kept me going.

MEXICAN HOMETOWN ASSOCIATIONS IN CHICAGOACÁN

✣

CHAPTER 1

MIGRANT GENEROSITY AND TRANSNATIONAL CIVIC ENGAGEMENT

Uptown, Chicago, December 18, 2010. Fifty members of El Rincón de Dolores hometown club have gathered with friends and families for a *posada*, a traditional Mexican pre-Christmas celebration. In a small party room adjacent to the pancake restaurant of Hugo,[1] a former club president, they're preparing to sing the verses that reenact Mary and Joseph's pilgrimage.

Each member has brought a dish for the potluck. The event includes a raffle to collect funds to finance a computer center with free Internet access in the Catholic parish of the village of El Rincón de Dolores, Michoacán. After singing, families line up for the buffet as members of the Mexican consulate prepare PowerPoint presentations in Spanish on the basics of opening a U.S. bank account and diabetes prevention. Next a club member who volunteers for ARISE Chicago, an interfaith worker center that provides legal support and training to low-wage immigrant workers, gives a basic training session on worker rights and distributes a questionnaire to collect data on safety and health violations in the workplace.

After the presentations are over, kids jostle to break the traditional treat-filled piñata.[2] Hugo tells me during dinner that he has been following the alderman's race and donated money to the campaign of an openly homosexual candidate whom he admires because he has seen him doing volunteer work to benefit the ward, such as sprucing up the parks. The candidate has shown interest in the work of the Rincón de Dolores Club to help Mexican migrants navigate life in the city and the suburbs. Hugo tells me that he is dissatisfied with the work done by the incumbent and wants to see some change in the ward office.

Ciudad Hidalgo, Michoacán, May 2, 2003. It is 5 P.M., and migrant leaders representing Michoacán hometown associations (HTAs) from Alaska, Arizona,

Indiana, Michigan, Nevada, and Texas are ready to discuss the last-minute details of the inauguration of the Third Binational Forum of Michoacán Migrants in the elegant municipal hall. This is the first time that the forum has been held in Mexico, and local and state authorities want to participate in drawing up the final agenda. The first discussion addresses the issue of national anthems. During the Second Binational Forum held at César Chávez Community College in East Los Angeles, California, both the Mexican and U.S. anthems were sung, and the two flags stood side by side on the podium. U.S. migrant leaders want to repeat a similar opening in Ciudad Hidalgo, but Michoacán local and state authorities are uncomfortable with the proposal. In a fourteen-to-nine vote, the planning committee decides against using the U.S. national anthem and flag. The migrants in the room, some of them holding dual citizenship, are disappointed, but they decide to let this one go.

The forum activities begin at the John Paul II Youth Center, a new community space financed with the collective remittances of Michoacán's migrant HTAs from California and Illinois. On the inaugural podium, migrant federation leaders rub shoulders with mayors, state legislators, the governor, and the general director of the recently inaugurated Institute for Mexicans Abroad of the federal Ministry of Foreign Affairs. The migrants chose Ciudad Hidalgo, a municipality then governed by the National Action Party, because Chicago-based migrant HTAs had a good experience collaborating with municipal staff to fund several projects, including church renovations and faith-based initiatives, using collective remittances.

During the inauguration, the conveners offered several welcoming remarks. In his speech, Francisco, a migrant leader from California, took the opportunity to manifest his disagreement with the war in Iraq and congratulated Mexico's official position against the invasion. "I applaud Mexico's position against the war because we do not want a green card tainted with blood." Salvador, a migrant leader from Chicago, said he believed the Iraq war was morally justifiable, but he respected Mexico's official disagreement with the invasion.[3] In his opening remarks, Lázaro Cárdenas Batel, the first governor of the opposition in the state of Michoacán, also weighed in on the Iraq war. "Migrants left because they could not find a good job in Michoacán. Migrants like their country, sing the national anthem, and have established HTAs since 1962 to contribute with the development of their communities of origin. Many Mexicans from Michoacán are fighting now in Iraq and some have died to make the United States a stronger nation so I believe that we should respect the ideological differences about the war."[4]

These two examples from both sides of the border give an idea of the dynamism of a new kind of civic involvement. Profoundly and proudly binational and bicultural in nature, innovative forms of citizen participation are changing the lives of migrants, their families, and their communities. These efforts challenge traditional political, social, and institutional spheres across borders and unpack practices of transnational migrant civic engagement demonstrating the process through which migrants transition from being *ni de aquí ni de allá* (neither from here nor from there) to being cultural, political, and social citizens of both societies. By taking a close look at the history and the character of the organizational nucleus of HTAs, we can understand the ways in which new forms of migrant civic engagement have transformed state-society relations using multiple identities, affiliations, and sociopolitical repertoires to demand the inclusion of migrants as members of two nations: Mexico and the United States. Contrary to some previous claims that HTAs' translocality is inherently circumscribed to local scales (Fitzgerald 2004; Waldinger and Fitzgerald 2004), this book documents how HTAs from Michoacán demonstrate migrants' capacity to engage with both nation-states *simultaneously* at several scales, from the most local micro level on up, including state, federal, and international scales.

At the outset of the third millennium, Mexican migrant HTAs emerged as one sector of Mexican civil society in the United States with a visible impact and the potential to promote civic engagement in more than one national space. The evidence presented in this book shows that contemporary HTAs have been an increasingly powerful force for social infrastructure support and public policy changes in their communities of origin, as well as for labor and immigrant rights advocacy in the United States. With few exceptions, most pioneer studies of non-indigenous Mexican migrant transnational engagement have not mapped the multiple layers of formal and informal interactions that migrant organizations sustain in the private and public spheres on both sides of the border. To fill this gap, this book addresses the dynamics of interactions between HTAs and non-profit organizations, grassroots organizations, churches, labor unions, Spanish-language media, worker centers, established Latino advocacy organizations in the United States such as the Mexican American Legal Defense and Educational Fund (MALDEF), and municipal and state governments in Mexico and the United States.

The Chicago metropolitan area has the second largest Mexican immigrant population, after Los Angeles. By 2010, the two million Latinos in Illinois, of whom 79 percent are of Mexican descent, comprised 16 percent of the state's total population.[5] As a result of this temporary and permanent Mexican exodus to Chicago, Mexico ranks as Illinois's third largest international market for inbound travel, contributing approximately $103 million to the state's economy.[6] Along with this growth in travel, trade and investment between Illinois and Mexico have also increased. In 2012, the total Illinois-Mexico trade totaled $15.5 billion, and Illinois ranked sixth among the fifty U.S. states for exports to Mexico. Besides, Mexico is now Illinois's second largest export market, and Mexican firms employ 1,543 Illinoisans at 138 different locations (State of Ilinois Trade Mission 2013).

With a 2009 total population of more than eleven million, Mexican migrants in the United States now exhibit a wide range of strategies to facilitate migrant incorporation into their new communities. The vast majority of migrants from Mexico

(64 percent) came to the United States in the 1990s or later. Naturalization rates for Mexican legal permanent residents have been rising steadily since the late 1990s in the aftermath of the 1996 tightening of immigration laws, and they increased substantially since 2006, despite the high increase in the citizenship fees, which went from $95 in 1998 to $675 by 2007 (Jiménez et al. 2008).[7] Today, more than two in ten Mexican immigrants (23 percent) are U.S. citizens, although naturalization rates vary widely across counties and cities (U.S. Census Bureau 2010).

MEXICAN STATE–DIASPORA RELATIONS

In the late 1980s, the Mexican state changed its policy on incorporating emigrants. When former president Carlos Salinas de Gortari realized that sympathies toward the opposition had grown among migrants living in the United States, he decided to move from a "state introversion" to a "state extension" model of greater engagement with the immigrant community abroad.[8] In 1991, Carlos Salinas met with Chicago mayor Richard M. Daley and the Mexican expatriate community in the West Side neighborhood of Little Village, the Mexican capital of the Midwest.[9] Since then, the Mexican government has implemented new programs and policies to incorporate the Mexican diaspora, which must be analyzed from different angles. Only a few studies have addressed the structure of changes in Mexican policy toward emigrants, but these tend to overlook the important role that migrant civil society has played in opening new dialogue channels with authorities at different levels of government.[10]

Many questions remain unanswered. For example, what are the dynamics that enable migrant-led philanthropic organizations to transform their charitable missions and become increasingly involved in multiple social agendas, including advocacy efforts to defend migrant rights and increase the political power of migrants across borders? To what extent have migrant HTAs been able to make citizen demands on subnational governments outside clientele and corporatist channels? In other words, how does migrant civil society expand in more than one national space?

Through a detailed exploration of community organizing efforts that build migrant civic engagement and transnational leadership, this book addresses the challenges and opportunities that migrant organizations face in building sustained cooperation with governments and civil society institutions in host and sending states. This exploration sheds new light on practices that mutually reinforce transnational citizenship, paying close attention to rural and urban development inequalities that prevent a larger expansion of transnational civic engagement practices in Mexico and the United States.

This book presents an in-depth account of a successful case of migrant civic engagement, tracing the organizational history and activities of the Federation of Michoacán Clubs in Illinois (FEDECMI). FEDECMI is an exemplary model of transnational civic engagement in two states—Michoacán and Illinois—and, more recently, across other Latin American countries through alliances and coalitions with other Mexican and Latin American migrant groups in the United States. Based in Chicago's Pilsen neighborhood, FEDECMI has been involved in building migrant civic participation and leadership in development issues for more than a decade in rural Michoacán and has organized migrant rights campaigns in Illinois and across the United States. A strong membership base of more than thirty autonomous HTAs spread across the Chicago metropolitan area makes up the core of the organization.

Many of its members also belong to the Michoacán Binational Front (FREBIMICH), a nonpartisan political organization with several chapters across the United States that began in 2004. One of the most visible achievements of FEDECMI is the acquisition of a building to serve as the headquarters for Casa Michoacán, a migrant-led community center that provides space for FEDECMI's hometown clubs, several local migrant advocacy grassroots organizations, a liaison office of the Secretariat of Migrant Affairs in Michoacán, and the National Alliance of Latin American and Caribbean Communities (NALACC). In this space, legal permanent residents and U.S. citizens of Mexican descent obtain referrals to Illinois social services, and any Mexican migrant, regardless of his or her immigrant status, has access to free tutorials to obtain a high school certificate, work-training courses, and online college courses financed by the state of Michoacán, among other services.

Also known as *clubes de oriundos*, or migrant clubs, Mexican HTAs are among the best-known migrant-led organizations. HTAs bring together migrants from the same communities of origin. Mexican HTAs are a paradigm for civic binationality, performing important roles to defend migrant human and social rights. HTAs often begin as informal associations, such as soccer clubs, mutual aid societies, or prayer groups, but over time many have not only become formal organizations but have also "scaled up" to form federations that represent various communities of origin from the same sending state. Sometimes the clubs create larger coalitions, including federations of clubs from different states.

Migrant organizations are still overlooked in the literature of migrant transnationalism. Few studies have approached them as an important variable to explain migrant civic engagement and incorporation in sending and receiving countries (Pries 2008). Instead, most work on transnational spaces has focused on individual political and social practices using survey research, state behavior toward diasporas, and changes in culture and norms within transnational families. However, the binational activities of HTAs to improve community development in sending communities and defending migrant social and political rights in receiving societies have not received the same level of attention.[11]

The Chicago metropolitan area has the second largest concentration of Mexican HTAs in the United States, with 270 registered by the Mexican consulate.

These organizations represent a third of all Mexican hometown clubs in the United States and Canada. Located in central Mexico, the state of Michoacán has the largest number of HTAs in Greater Chicago, with fifty clubs. Few Mexican HTAs become chartered as formal nonprofits in Illinois and so are often not included in official state registries. For example, in the metropolitan Chicago area, there are 205 Latino-led and Latino-serving organizations formally registered according to the Chicago Community Trust, but very few are Mexican HTAs or federations (Alejo 2008).[12]

THE REPERTOIRES OF CIVIC BINATIONALITY

In the past two decades, Mexican migration to the United States reached an unprecedented peak. Today, one in ten Mexicans lives in the United States, and this new reality offers challenges and opportunities for the development of migrant organizations interested in participating in the public arenas of two societies. Since the late 1990s, several researchers have correlated the expansion of migrant organizations to the political will of the Mexican state to encourage the creation of new migrant HTAs after realizing that loyalty to communities of origin was very high among HTAs from Zacatecas, Guanajuato, Jalisco, and Puebla (Alarcón 2002; Goldring 2002; Moctezuma Longoria 2011; Smith 2006).[13]

According to Robert Smith's "instituted process framework" (2003), once the Mexican government realized the potential of migrant clubs for contributing to the construction of public works in rural Mexico, the consulates sought to capitalize on migrant philanthropic organizations primarily devoted to supporting charitable projects in communities of origin. This focus on the role of the nation-state is definitely a step forward from the initial globalization framework that identified global capitalism and its structures as the main cause of transnational practices, without considering the power of nation-states for modeling behaviors of migrant organizations in an attempt to find support for a state's neoliberal agendas to manage and take advantage of international human mobility.

However, the most comprehensive approach to incorporate all actors is to analyze the multiple scales in which state-migrant relations take place. This work is inspired by the scalar analysis previously done by Michael Peter Smith and Matt Bakker in their study of transnational political citizenship practices in California, in which the authors emphasize the importance of studying "the interplay of multiple actors and structures operating at different spatial scales and the outcomes of this coproduced reality" (2008: 19). However, while Smith and Bakker focus mostly on the individual practices of HTA leaders, my work's central locus is the practices of organizations as they relate with municipal, state, and federal governments within two states: Illinois and Michoacán. Core questions include: Why do migrants from Michoacán appear to be more successful in organizing transnational organizations in Chicago than migrants from Zacatecas or Guanajuato, despite their similar

profiles? Why do some Michoacán HTAs decide to finance community development projects in communities of origin, while others focus more on social incorporation in Chicago? Why do they equally emphasize hometown, national, and
pan-Latino identities in the activities they perform?

Recent accounts of post-1965 Mexican immigrants in Chicago have focused
on labor relations in the service sector (Gomberg-Muñoz 2011), the precarious
nature of low-wage jobs in light manufacturing, and the social construction of
illegality as a powerful deterrent for civic engagement (De Genova 2005). In
these ethnographic narratives, we learn that Mexican immigrants are well aware
of the conditions of exploitation they face in the workplace and how they lead
everyday acts of resistance on the job. Post-1965 Mexican immigrants in Chicago
are not merely passive victims of capitalist economies; they have developed a
strong network of migrant-led organizations that has empowered them to speak
for themselves and make demands as transnational citizens, navigating a complex web of relations, selecting best strategies to advocate for their needs, and
encouraging the civic engagement of all migrants, regardless of their immigration status in the United States.

Grassroots migrant organizing covers several arenas, from labor coalitions
to faith-based initiatives and translocal public work committees to build infrastructure in communities of origin. Migrants who participate in these efforts
are frequently involved in more than one organization, but not all migrant-led
organizing includes binational advocacy activities. Therefore, migrant-led HTAs
and their federations are considered the paradigmatic case of civic binationality.
Social scientists in a variety of disciplines have sought to understand transmigrant activity and produced many descriptions defining transnational migrant
networks, circuits, and social fields.[14] What many of these social networks share
is their struggle for social justice with heterogeneous strategies and different geographical scales of action, creating a complex web of relations that form what
Colombian scholar Arturo Escobar calls "meshworks"—self-organizing networking groups that form in unplanned directions and include diverse elements.
Meshworks "exist in hybridized forms with other hierarchies and meshworks;
they accomplish the articulation of heterogeneous elements without imposing
uniformity; and they are determined by the degree of connectivity that enables
them to become self-sustaining" (Escobar 2003: 610–611).

Embedded in complex meshworks in multiple cities and states across borders,
migrant practices of civic binationality represent public actions of individuals as
they interact with and participate in organizations, associations, and institutions
of society in more than one nation-state. This activity is focused in three arenas:
government structures, the economic sector, and civil society. In the U.S. context,
the last arena has been dominated by a host of voluntary and nonprofit ethnic
associations, including faith-based organizations, worker rights organizations,
migrant-led Spanish-language media, and hometown clubs and federations.[15]

Recent scholarship on Mexican migrant organizations has focused on West Coast indigenous organizations. For example, Lynn Stephen's ethnography of indigenous migrants from the southern state of Oaxaca combines individual transnational experiences with the emergence of transborder organizations from two Oaxacan towns and the states of California and Oregon. Her work describes transnational citizenship practices among members of four grassroots organizations with significant indigenous Mixtec migrant membership, including transborder public work committees, farmworker centers, and the Binational Front of Indigenous Organizations.[16] Interestingly, Stephen's work documents a decade of mostly contentious state-society relations in the state government of Oaxaca dominated by more than eighty years of one-party rule, while my analysis of a mestizo organizing meshwork from Michoacán, a traditional sending state in central Mexico, documents the transformation of state-society relations from a contentious to a semicooperative model. This difference is partially explained by the democratic transition experienced in Michoacán since the late 1980s, which consolidated at the turn of the twenty-first century when an opposition party held the governorship for the first time.

According to official estimates, between 2002 and 2010 Michoacán HTAs in the United States sent $14.5 million in collective remittances to finance 1,123 community development projects in marginalized villages in Michoacán through the Three-for-One Program, which provides municipal, state, and federal matching funds to channel collective remittances for rural development (SEDESOL 2010a).[17] These donations have effectively reduced the costs of infrastructure in many municipalities. The migrant HTAs have had the chance to participate in project selection and voice their opinion on the relationship between migration and development in city and municipal councils, state legislatures, the Secretariat of Social Development (SEDESOL), academic events, and various international meetings on migration and development.

Migration, Development, and Civic Engagement

Mexican organizing in Chicago in the 1990s included new actors: migrants displaced from rural areas who were eager to contribute to the reconstruction of their hometowns after decades of neglect as a result of neoliberalism and privatization policies. In the 1980s and subsequent decades, many rural migrants from Guanajuato, Jalisco, Guerrero, Zacatecas, Durango, and San Luis Potosí came to Chicago, fleeing the effects of state downsizing, the demise of state-led development, privatizations, neoliberal reform, and agricultural modernization, and attracted by the promise of better salaries in Chicago's workforce.[18] Some found jobs in the service sector and light manufacturing, thanks to networks of family and friends. Decades after they settled, many kept in touch with their hometowns, attending town festivities to visit friends and relatives, and many were willing to lend a hand as part of their *faenas*[19]—voluntary work by community members to solve common problems such as school reparations, street cleaning, water well maintenance, and other shared necessities. For some groups of the most recent Mexican migrant middle class living in Chicago, their first volunteering efforts were aimed at addressing the needs of Mexican rural towns abandoned after decades of neoliberal reforms and unequal competition for staple products brought by the North American Free Trade Agreement (NAFTA).

The general view among some academic sectors and the public is that outmigration should be good for emigrant-sending countries because it functions as a safety valve to prevent social unrest by reducing unemployment and mitigating poverty due to the remittances sent by migrant workers that contribute to the survival of families and the financial stability of sending nations. In 2007, family remittances sent to Mexico reached $27 billion, according to the Banco de México. Despite their recent drop after the U.S. economic recession, family remittances have a significant impact on alleviating poverty in sending regions. According to official data reported by the Banco de México, the state of Michoacán received $2.5 billion from family remittances in 2006—more than any other state in Mexico. Although this amount represented just 13.2 percent of that state's GDP for that fiscal year, it is equivalent to what the state usually receives from federal expenditures and revenue sharing (Tépach Marcial 2011).[20] During the period 1980–2009, remittances to Michoacán increased by 1,035 percent, from $186 million in 1980 to $2.1 billion in 2009 (Navarro Chávez and Ayvar Campos 2010).

In the past two decades, the Mexican government has tried to incorporate the migrant community living in the United States through programs designed to preserve their loyalty to their hometowns and reconnect them with their roots. Among the most successful, the matching fund Three-for-One Program has been praised as an innovative model to channel collective migrant remittances to thousands of rural communities to build basic infrastructure and finance microenterprises. One decade after the initial implementation, the program has stimulated a vigorous discussion that offers insights into the role of organized migrants and their collective remittances in rural development and the political feedback effects of these new engagements to improve the quality of democracy in Mexico.[21] Yet the effects of the Three-for-One Program remain highly concentrated in few states. For example, in 2007, 59 percent of the projects and 54 percent of the funds have been allocated to just three states out of the thirty-one included in the program: Jalisco, Michoacán, and Zacatecas, the three states that concentrate the largest networks of HTAs in the United States (Aparicio Castillo, Maldonado Trujillo and Beltrán Pulido 2008).

The impact of Mexican migrant collective remittances and the fertile area of transnational community development have produced important contributions to public policy design. There have been many studies on family remittances for development purposes, but those analyses frequently apply a state-centered framework (Iskander 2010; Merz 2005). After the publication of Dolores Byrnes's *Driving the State,* which documents the emergence of Vicente Fox's plan to encourage migrants to invest in maquiladoras in his home state of Guanajuato, few subsequent publications have discussed the role that family and collective migrant remittances should play in the national development discourse from the perspective of migrant organizations.[22]

How can migrant organizations gain a voice in development after economic push factors have forced them to leave the country? What impact do migrants have on the political structure of sending communities? Is there any transference of political attitudes with potential democratizing effects in Mexican states with high rates of emigration to the United States? How can we begin to close the gap between the analysis of migration and development centered on monetary remittances and their economic spillover effects, to one centered on migrant empowerment experiences to improve their quality of life as a result of binational civic engagement?

Debates on migration have overwhelmingly focused on the impact that migration has on the nations and localities in receiving societies. Much less attention is paid to the effects of such movements in places of origin. In the last decade, as migrant family remittances to Mexico from the United States increased exponentially due to the massive exodus produced by free trade agreements and economic neoliberalization, emigrant-sending governments have tried to channel collective remittances to fund infrastructure projects with the goal of triggering economic development in rural Mexico and, eventually, prevent more migration. However, the economic impact of collective remittances has been rather modest, and the initial idea of financing job-generating enterprises instead of basic infrastructure has not materialized. After one decade of matching collective remittance funds with Mexican government funds through the Three-for-One Program to create sustainable development projects, less than 8 percent of projects financed with collective remittances of HTAs and entrepreneurial family investments can be categorized as "productive," and among those, less than 50 percent have survived more than five years.[23]

In May 2002, President Fox and President George W. Bush signed an agreement to implement the Partnership for Prosperity, an action plan to leverage private resources to promote economic growth in less-developed regions of Mexico. One of the objectives was to "foster an environment in which no Mexican feels compelled to leave his home for lack of jobs or opportunity" (Partnership for Prosperity Executive Group 2002: 2). The initial agreement was mostly a pledge with few commitments. Among the few concrete proposals to address the migrant-development connection with specific budgets was an Inter-American Foundation grant for $2 million (to be matched by the private Mexican foundation Fundamex) to ninety communities in twenty-one Mexican states with the highest rates of poverty and migration to the United States (Inter-American Foundation 2006).

A decade later, the only program that reached institutionalization was the Three-for-One Program, supported by the altruistic donations of Mexican HTAs. The rest of the initiatives to increase public-private cooperation to improve economic development in regions of high out-migration have for the most part stalled.

Between 2002 and 2012, Mexican HTAs in the United States and Canada financed more than 18,573 community development projects in rural Mexico (Gobierno Federal 2012). The investment in rural development transferred via collective remittances sent by HTAs quadrupled in this period, going from $8 million in 2002 to $33 million in 2009 (SEDESOL 2010b). Although the total contributions from collective remittances represent less than 1 percent of the Mexican government budget in poverty-reduction programs, the direct participation of HTAs in public policy design opened a window of opportunity to express their views on the official discourse between migration and development. For the most organized HTAs, such as those from Zacatecas, Michoacán, and Guerrero, the Three-for-One Program offered a chance to voice their opinions on rural development and demand more transparency and social accountability in program implementation. They became watchdogs for the program, looking after its implementation through the many intervening federal, state, and municipal institutions.

By 2005, three years after the institutionalization of this program, Mexican HTAs from Michoacán and Zacatecas, along with Salvadoran, Honduran, Guatemalan, and other Latin American HTAs grouped in the National Alliance of Latin American and Caribbean Communities, issued the "Cuernavaca Declaration."[24] The declaration presented a heterodox vision of the debate of migration and development. Migrant leaders discussed the declaration with their organizations in Chicago, and members confirmed that their participation in the Three-for-One Program and other similar collective remittance schemes in the region was merely a small piece of a more comprehensive strategy to increase the shared responsibilities of *sending* and *receiving* nations to address migrants' rights without relying on labor exports and imports as the only solution to generate opportunities for growth or social development. In other words, HTAs conditioned their participation in the Three-for-One Program on the Mexican government's agreeing to cooperate with them in other areas that did not involve the transfer of monetary remittances in charitable projects. These responsibilities of the sending nation included government investments to increase HTAs' organizational development in the United States, strengthening Mexican state and federal laws to protect all international migrants living in Mexican territory, expanding voting rights to Mexicans living abroad, and creating new programs to reintegrate returned and deported migrants into their communities of origin.

To contextualize the philanthropic activities of Mexican HTAs to contribute to rural infrastructure, they can be compared to U.S. government and civil society contributions. For example, the economic investments of the United States Agency for International Development (USAID) to Mexico have been mostly concentrated in drug-trafficking prevention and combat through the Mérida Initiative, and few resources have been channeled toward rural sustainable development (Seelke 2009).[25] In 2009, Mexico received approximately $11.2 million in development assistance from USAID, equivalent to 0.01 percent from the total official aid Mexico received from the U.S. government (Wainer 2011). The amount provided by migrant HTAs is similar to that of private U.S. foundations. Between 2002 and 2007, they contributed between $30 and $40 million annually (Layton 2009).

Through their actions, Mexican HTAs have shown that there is no contradiction between active transnationalism and successful social and political incorporation of permanent immigrants in host nations, even among those who delay the decision to naturalize as U.S. citizens. HTAs' practices of civic binationality show simultaneous loyalty and commitment to two nation-states to address the political, social, and economic rights of all migrants, both in the United States and Mexico.

LOCAL CONTEXTS MATTER

While Chicago-based Mexican HTAs have incorporated binational agendas into their programs over the last ten years, few studies have addressed the role that local institutional environments in U.S. cities have played to facilitate or hinder the development of binational agendas among Mexican organizations. I argue that the local contexts in which HTAs have flourished in the Chicago metropolitan area are crucial to understanding the increased practices of civic binationality among HTAs in that part of the country.

What is the role that the context of reception—in this case, Chicago's civil society and Illinois government institutions—plays in encouraging or discouraging Mexican migrants to organize and become empowered and to make claims on behalf of group members on more than one geographical scale? How can migrants hold their subnational governments in Mexico accountable to address their needs across borders and implement proactive advocacy strategies to defend migrant rights inside U.S. territory?

Official data on the percentage of eligible Mexican permanent residents who had become U.S. citizens as of 2004 shows significant variation across states. In Illinois, 31 percent of Mexican legal permanent residents had become U.S. citizens by 2004, but in New Mexico, only 16.5 percent had done so (U.S. Department of Homeland Security 2005). Why is there such a variation among immigrants from the same country? Is there something particular in certain cities and states encouraging legal immigrants to become citizens faster? Part of the answer lies in the context of reception.[26] Some cities, counties, and states are more likely to support immigrant incorporation as a result of organized citizen demands. For example, in 2005 the state of Illinois enacted the New Americans

Initiative, a bipartisan program aimed at facilitating immigrant integration. Among other things, the initiative distributed resources among hundreds of community-based organizations that provide services to migrants to encourage legal permanent residents to acquire citizenship. Between 2005 and 2008, the naturalization rate for Mexican nationals in the Chicago area increased 173 percent, adding more than 35,000 new U.S. citizens of Mexican origin (U.S. Department of Homeland Security 2009).

Illinois state and local Chicago political activism on immigrant-related legislation is a new model in the national immigration debate. Since the late 1800s, states and cities have been excluded from making immigration policy that affects the entry of noncitizens and their continued stay (Motomura 1999). However, in the last two decades, economic, political, and demographic factors have combined to create the contexts in which state and local activism is currently emerging.[27] Immigrant integration is one of the most overlooked issues in U.S. governance and local economic development. Currently, there is no national integration policy, and local and state governments face the need to design their own programs to encourage immigrants to become civically engaged and participate more fully in their new societies.

Mexican migrant organizations have existed in Chicago throughout the twentieth century, with diverse agendas since the 1930s. They have organized in Communist organizations, Catholic groups, mutual-aid organizations, civic committees, and social justice groups, pursuing heterogeneous social agendas. In the 1970s, as a result of changing demographics among the Mexican community and the civil rights struggles, Pilsen became an important site of organization for the Mexican community. The Pilsen Neighbors Community Council, originally serving a Bohemian population, became a center for grassroots leadership following the Saul Alinsky model of neighborhood change.

Casa Aztlán, one of the pioneer Mexican community centers in Pilsen, was formed in the 1970s when the Howell Neighborhood House, a Bohemian settlement house, experienced a change in its constituents when the Czech population left the neighborhood and Mexicans became a majority.[28] The most visible Mexican leadership in this decade was a group that included several educated urban migrants. This wave of immigrants included exiles from the 1968 student movement in Mexico who came to Chicago with and without documents to escape from violence and persecution in the aftermath of the massive protests prior to the Olympic games. These organizations combined radical protest strategies and community organizing to defend the rights of Mexican immigrants to have access to bilingual education, decent employment opportunities, and political representation in the city. While some organizations made demands to the Mexican government to address the needs of those who were frequently arrested during the raids conducted by the Immigration and Naturalization Service (INS) in the 1970s, these demands were usually channeled through the Mexican consulate and the Ministry of Foreign Affairs (SRE) without direct demands to subnational governments in Mexican states.

In the 1960s and 1970s, a steady stream of new migrants from Mexico to Chicago produced different demographic dynamics than in California and the Southwest. In Chicago, there were comparatively fewer U.S.-born children of Mexican migrants in these decades, and a steady stream of newcomers predominated. According to many historians, post-1965 migration to Chicago represented many different Latin American countries, which suggests that the diversity of Latin American identities made it more difficult to identify exclusively with Chicano identity (M. García 2012; Mora-Torres 2006; Ramírez 2011).

In fact, the Mexican organizations established post-1965 frequently questioned the limitations of Chicano nationalism in its exclusion of immigrant rights, particularly the rights of the undocumented. For example, the Chicago-based Center for Autonomous Social Action—General Brotherhood of Workers (CASA-HGT) was a Marxist-Leninist immigrant rights organization founded by Bert Corona that systematically addressed the relationships between immigration, Chicano ethnicity, and the status of Mexican Americans in the United States.[29] Its original motto, *Sin Fronteras* (Without Borders), became part of the political repertoire that would enable subsequent Mexican organizations to begin a new era of advocacy for immigrant rights, including dual citizenship and binational organizing frameworks in the late 1990s (M. García 2012). In fact, Margo Delay, a former program officer at the Chicago Community Trust and the daughter of Bert Corona, was among the first supporters of Jaliscan and Michoacano HTAs in the late 1990s. Perhaps it is not a coincidence that the motto of the Federation of Michoacán Clubs in Illinois, formally established in 1997, used to be *Michoacanos sin fronteras por cambio y progreso* (People from Michoacán without borders for change and progress). Today, FEDECMI's new motto, *Abriendo fronteras, uniendo comunidades* (Opening borders, uniting communities), reflects its increased practices of transnational community building.

In the city of Chicago, Latino organizations and leaders have been politically active in protecting basic Mexican migrant rights, and while many battles have been lost, modest legislative gains have been obtained. More than a quarter century ago, Chicago joined other cities like Los Angeles, San Francisco, and New York as a sanctuary city—a city where an immigrant's basic human rights are protected regardless of legal status. The sanctuary city law was enacted by former mayor Harold Washington in 1985 and was aimed to "encourage equal access by persons residing in the city of Chicago, regardless of nationality or citizenship, to the full benefits, opportunities and services, including employment and the issuance of licenses, which are provided or administered by the city of Chicago."[30]

The administration of Harold Washington (1983–1987) produced important policies to encourage the empowerment of Latino immigrant communities. During his tenure, Mayor Washington established the Advisory Commission on

Latino Affairs, which had a broad-based representation of Latinos in the city, including various nationalities. He helped establish the Independent Political Organization in Little Village to increase access to electoral representation outside of the democratic machine (Pallares 2010). Mayor Washington chose Mexico City as a sister city and visited Puerto Rico, signaling his understanding of the immigrant nature of a growing proportion of his constituents. He also supported a community-initiated referendum asking the governor not to send the National Guard to Central America (Torres 2004: 92), showing sensitivity to the national sanctuary movement, which was supported by the Chicago Religious Task Force on Central America, a community-led initiative established in the city with active representation of Central American immigrant leaders from El Salvador and Guatemala in exile as a result of the Central American wars.

The state of Illinois has also enacted policies to facilitate the incorporation of Mexicans while recognizing their need to support families in Mexico. Among the most relevant, in 1995 Illinois enacted the Transmitters of Money Act, a state law to protect transmitters of family remittances from deceptive practices and abuses, legislation that later would enable Chicago migrant plaintiffs to lead a class-action lawsuit that accused Western Union and codefendants Money Gram and Orlandi Valuta, two other wire transfer service companies, of collecting millions of dollars in hidden fees. Western Union and the others eventually agreed to a $375 million settlement, which included the creation of a fund for migrant-led and immigrant service organizations (Avila and Olivo 2007). Mexican HTAs have since pushed Western Union to invest in rural community development in Mexico through matching funds programs in partnerships with HTAs across the United States while simultaneously encouraging Western Union to increase its grant-making efforts to fund migrant-led organizing efforts in the United States.

Acknowledging the discrimination experienced by Mexican immigrants and naturalized U.S. citizens of Mexican ancestry who came to Illinois and the Midwest in the early twentieth century, Illinois governor Pat Quinn signed Senate bill 1557 in the summer of 2009, which requires state elementary school history courses to include information about the Mexican repatriations during the Great Depression of the 1930s (Ngai 2004). Interestingly, during the Great Depression years, the city of Chicago did not experience a coercive repatriation program because Cook County officials denied the INS access to the relief lists. In that period, an estimated 20 percent of relief recipients were foreign born in Cook County, and Mayor Antonín Josef Čermák, the foreign-born Bohemian American mayor, refused to cooperate with the INS to facilitate repatriation of low-wage Chicago immigrants (Fox 2012).

Following that tradition of friendly attitudes toward immigrants, in 2011 the Cook County Board of Commissioners enacted an ordinance to terminate the county's cooperation with the Department of Homeland Security and U.S. Immigration and Customs Enforcement (ICE) to receive individuals picked up on federal immigration violations unless the federal government reimbursed the county for all costs associated with the additional detention. The ordinance was introduced by county commissioner Jesús García, a prominent foreign-born Mexican American politician who is a former leader of Durango Unido, a Chicago-based HTA established in the 1990s. Earlier the same year, Governor Quinn sent a letter to the Department of Homeland Security withdrawing from the ICE "Secure Communities" program, and the state legislature approved the DREAM Act, SB 2185, by an overwhelming bipartisan vote of forty-five to eleven. During press conferences to announce these new legislative measures, Mexican HTA leaders were frequently interviewed for local and national media to comment on the role that migrant-led community organizations played in the debates on the laws.

The rising power of migrant organizations has definitely contributed to the decentralization of Mexican foreign policy affairs. State governments in Micho-acán and other sending states have become less dependent on consulates and more dependent on civil society to mediate official relations with local authori-ties in Illinois to provide services for their citizens living abroad. This shift toward subnational government management of migrant affairs is a consequence of the difficulties faced by Mexican consulates to offer quality services to increasingly larger constituencies, especially in urban metropolitan areas like Chicago. For example, the Mexican consulate in Chicago offers services to Mexicans living in 126 counties: 60 in Illinois, 40 in Wisconsin, and 26 in Indiana. The total served population includes 1.5 million citizens in Illinois, 300,000 in Wisconsin, and 200,000 in Indiana (Embassy of Mexico 2013). One of the most sought after ser-vices has to do with documentation requests and consular protection. There-fore, the services offered by subnational state governments that establish satellite offices in Chicago's metropolitan area modestly alleviate the burden of civil registry requests and offer support for cultural and civic engagement projects requested by Mexicans organized in HTAs.

Since the inauguration of Casa Michoacán in 2004 in Pilsen, the government of Michoacán has shared office space with FEDECMI to offer direct services to Michoacán migrants such as high school certification and college education, work-shops for children on Michoacán culture, computing literacy, and work training. The office also serves as a liaison between Mexican municipalities and Chicago-based HTAs to facilitate cooperation to build basic infrastructure, and to match small migrant investors with the appropriate state agencies to encourage produc-tive investments in Michoacán. In 2011, the Casa Michoacán model was expanded to the suburbs, and a second Casa Michoacán now operates on the campus of Saint Francis University, a Catholic university sponsored by the Franciscan order committed to a partnership to serve the Mexican community of Joliet, Illinois. Institutional support for Mexican HTAs in Chicago and in Michoacán from dif-ferent government and civil society sectors has helped increase their capacity and visibility to effectively advocate public policy changes across borders.

FAITH AND MIGRANT CIVIC ENGAGEMENT

Faith and religion are important values in the lives of many Latino immigrants, and religious institutions consistently play a key role in the immigrant integration process. Foreign- and U.S.-born Latinos share, to a certain extent, a religious commitment shown through high levels of church attendance and volunteerism. For instance, in an analysis of the 2004 National Survey of Latinos, researchers found that churches were the largest single recipient of Latinos' volunteer time, thus playing a role in creating social capital and community bonding, providing a place to make social connections, gain skills, and receive encouragement to become involved in other sectors of their communities. Regardless of their country of origin, Latinos who volunteer regularly in church-related activities are significantly more likely to volunteer at nonchurch activities (Hernández et al. 2007). Therefore, for Latinos, participating actively in a church is correlated to civic engagement in different spaces, such as school or tutoring programs, neighborhood organizations, business or community groups, and HTAs.

Religious congregations play a key role in the development of HTAs. In Chicago and other cities with a large Mexican immigrant presence, several enabling environments exist in congregations to support the moral and social projects of HTAs. For example, religious pluralism in the United States is shaping in particular ways the mobilization of migrants in the public sphere as different theological traditions embrace civic engagement differently.[31] In the late twentieth century, the United States experienced the Latin Americanization of U.S. Christianity, especially Catholicism, with the incorporation of practices and symbols crossing diverse national ethnic practices and rituals in many U.S. states.[32]

In Mexico, religion plays a central role for civic engagement. Some quantitative studies estimate that Mexican citizens tend to trust in the church more than in political parties, unions, or the Congress (Ablanedo Terrazas, Layton and Moreno 2008). In a recent survey to understand philanthropy patterns among Mexicans, 39 percent of those interviewed claimed membership in a religious congregation, and 32 percent said they volunteer regularly in church-related activities (Layton and Moreno 2010). In the state of Michoacán, an estimated 38 percent of the population belongs to a congregation and attends mass at least once a month (Cleary and Stokes 2006).

In the Chicago metropolitan area, countless Latin American immigrant congregations diversify Chicago-area Christianity in new ways, including new rites and symbols that increasingly link spirituality with political action. In response to the Theological Reforms of Vatican Council II (1962–1965), many Chicago-area clergy have learned Spanish and sought to identify with the life and struggles of Mexican immigrant parishioners in the areas of liturgy, popular piety and devotion, and, more recently, political activism to defend immigrant rights. The commitment of the Chicago Catholic Church to the plight of immigrants is related to the social justice heritage with worker rights, as expressed in John Paul II's 1981 encyclical, *Human Work* (Kniss and Numrich 2007).

In Chicago's suburbs, some Latin American priests were assigned to immigrant congregations in the late 1960s, promoting the creation of mariachi masses, shrines to the Virgin of Guadalupe, and Christian Base Communities.[33] In the 1970s, Mexican migrants living in Sterling, Rock Falls, Aurora, Rockford, Elgin, and Moline organized around the Catholic Church of Saint Mary's, forming a lay group called Movimiento Apostólico, whose primary mission was to focus on reflection and action, as evidenced by the group's bilingual monthly newsletter, *Las Razas Unidas*.[34] Editors of the newsletter used this free publication to teach topics like labor rights and U.S. history and government. *Las Razas Unidas* was also used to advertise the Mexican Independence Day Parade[35] and the campaign platforms of democratic candidates during election times. The newsletter reported extensively on the grape and lettuce boycotts of farmworkers in 1974.[36] As for their actions in Mexico, there is not much evidence of binational activities other than a clothing drive for the victims of an earthquake in Puebla in 1974.

These and other Christian Base Communities later formed devotion groups to bring their hometown patron saints and virgins to their new churches and founded formal HTAs to build basic infrastructure in communities of origin. The first HTAs in Chicago were from migrants from Michoacán (1960s) and San Luis Potosí (1970s), and the first activities they sponsored were *posadas*, mariachi masses for the Virgin of Guadalupe celebrated by the archbishops of their home state in their new parishes in Pilsen, Irving Park, and Aurora, Illinois. During the initial stages of an HTA, members frequently bring their priests from their rural parishes to baptize their children, offer mass in Spanish in a Chicago Catholic church, and bless their newly purchased houses. The priests bring news about their communities, along with requests to support church-related or social infrastructure projects.

In 1994, a group of women of the hometown club of Uruapan, Michoacán, actively participated in the rescue of the Mexican church of Saint Francis when the Catholic hierarchy closed it to comply with a policy requiring the consolidation of dozens of former parishes. To prevent demolition, Mexican immigrants occupied the building until the cardinal acquiesced to reopen the church.[37] Thus, Mexican migrant affiliation to Chicago churches has served as a venue for cultural reproduction, ethnic identity contestation, and migrant incorporation into the host society.

Religion is central for the emergence of HTAs, and these organizations have devoted a great deal of energy to establish Mexican rites and symbols as important pieces in the migrant repertoire for visible civic engagement. Devotion groups cooperate with HTAs in Chicago to build new migrant spaces of spirituality, and these efforts led to the construction of a shrine for the Virgin of Guadalupe in Des Plaines, which is the only replica of Mexico City's Cerrito del Tepeyac. In the suburb of Melrose Park, Saint Toribio, the "migrant saint," now shares space in Our Lady of Mount Carmel, an Italian ethnic church, thanks to efforts of Jaliscan HTAs and the Scalabrinian order.[38] In the vast majority of Mexican HTAs, Catholic rituals and masses are widely practiced by Mexican migrants and constitute an important way to integrate into their new societies. Many HTA members mention their hometown churches and their new churches in Chicago as important places to help them fulfill their aspirations.

In many conversations with Mexican government officials at municipal, state, and federal levels, they often expressed their frustration when HTAs choose church renovations as the first charitable project to build trust among members. However, according to many HTA members and leaders, rebuilding their parishes in home communities means to give back to local patron saints who helped them keep faith alive during difficult times in the United States or as they crossed the border.[39] Organizing a fund-raiser to improve the hometown church offers a bonding experience and builds social capital to gain trust among community members and leaders. In Chicago, Catholic and Evangelical congregations offer a convenient space to meet other immigrants and find solutions to problems they face to incorporate into the host society. Through partnerships with Catholic churches, many HTA leaders have used the pulpit to encourage civic engagement among congregation members in the struggle for comprehensive immigration reform, voter registration drives, and naturalization campaigns. They have also encouraged many priests to incorporate patron saints and rituals representing Mexican Catholic practices into everyday mass repertoires, thus effectively transforming the character of contemporary Catholicism in Chicago.

INCREASED VISIBILITY OF CHICAGO'S MEXICAN HTAS

Concurrently with U.S. cities and state policies to address immigrant integration, the Mexican government has also developed new mechanisms to encourage subnational governments to address the needs of their constituents in the United States, in the absence of comprehensive immigration reform. In the first decade of the twenty-first century, the Mexican government created institutions and mechanisms for the migrant community living in the United States. During the administration of Vicente Fox, Chicago and other cities witnessed the emergence of paradiplomatic activities in which Mexican state governments cooperate with HTAs. Today, there are twenty-two state offices representing Mexican subnational governments in U.S. territory, and eight of those (36 percent) are in the Chicago metropolitan area. The offices are located in Chicago neighborhoods with a significant presence of Mexican migrants from various states: Pilsen (Michoacán), the Near West Side (Guanajuato), and new suburbs with high concentrations of Mexicans such as Melrose Park (Jalisco) and Stone Park (Durango).[40]

Illinois government officials have formally recognized the contribution of migrants to U.S. society through culture, history, music, and traditions, thus increasing the visibility of Mexican HTAs in Chicago. During the bicentennial celebrations for Mexican Independence, Mayor Daley declared 2010 the "Year of Mexico" in Chicago, and the city celebrated its Mexican heritage on September 16 by lighting up the buildings across the Chicago skyline with the colors of the Mexican flag—a tradition that began in 2005 thanks to the efforts of several migrant-led organizations, including the umbrella organization of HTAs, the Confederation of Mexican Federations (CONFEMEX).

Migrant participation in ethnic enclaves and networks in the United States that have a significant concentration of Mexican migrants seems to be correlated with a higher propensity to establish migrant HTAs. The three states with the largest concentration of Mexican-born migrants—California, Texas, and Illinois—are also the three states that together account for the vast majority of Mexican HTAs in the United States and Canada: 69 percent of those registered with the Mexican consulate (Fox and Bada 2011).

Comparative research on HTAs has shown small progress due to the scarcity of large-scale databases of informal organizations. Survey research has found that Mexican migrants do not participate in high numbers in HTAs. Evidence is still inconclusive, but different sources find a rate of participation between 6 and 14 percent in different national surveys (Suro 2005; Waldinger 2007). However, when we compare the rate of Mexicans participating in U.S.-based HTAs with survey research on the social capital of Mexican citizens living in Mexico, the distribution is remarkably similar. A recent representative survey of urban and rural Mexicans found that only 4 percent of the population declares membership in social clubs, nongovernmental organizations (NGOs), and private assistance organizations (Layton and Moreno 2010).

Some analysts believe that Mexico does not provide an enabling environment for formal nonprofit organizations due to many obstacles to obtain tax-exempt status and because Mexicans are highly skeptical regarding the use of their monies. In the United States, there are approximately two million civil society organizations compared to 8,500 formally registered in Mexico.[41] In fiscal year 2005, the state of Michoacán had approximately 600 formally registered civil society organizations, including ninety social cooperatives. In comparison, by 2003 the Chicago metropolitan area had 6,472 nonprofits reporting to the Internal Revenue Service (IRS), which represents 66.3 percent of the total IRS-reporting nonprofits in the state of Illinois (Lampking and Waringo 2003). From this vast nonprofit universe, less than a third engage in advocacy, and only 22 percent promote positions on policy issues (Grønbjerg and Child 2003). Considering that not all nonprofits are required to report to the IRS, researchers estimate that there are at least 29,000 nonprofits in Illinois, and this number excludes many HTAs since very few register as nonprofits.[42] In any case, while participation in Mexican HTAs might be considered low, Mexicans in the United States participate in civil society institutions at higher rates than Mexicans in Mexico, though below the levels of Anglo-American involvement. For example, recent surveys report that, on average, Anglo-Americans participate in 2.8 civil society organizations, Mexicans in the United States in 2.0, and Mexicans in Mexico in 1.4 (Castañeda 2011; Moreno 2005).

In the midcensus of 2005, the state of Michoacán had a population of 4.2 million living in the state and at least 1 million Michoacán-born citizens living in the United States and other countries (CONAPO 2010). In the metropolitan area of Chicago, migrants from Michoacán represent the largest concentration of Mexican migrants and 15 percent of the total population (IME 2011). Their community includes legal permanent residents, naturalized U.S. citizens, and undocumented migrants.

The Michoacán HTAs in the area have increased their visibility through participation in complex "meshworks" as described above, made up of contacts, alliances, and coalitions with the Mexican consulate, the state of Illinois, Latino and non-Latino NGOs, churches, the state of Michoacán, cultural organizations, Mexican NGOs, unions and worker centers, individual philanthropists, and private foundations.

The simultaneous affiliation of HTA members with U.S. and Mexican civic institutions shows flexibility in the construction of multiple and often overlapping collective identities across two nations. Many Michoacán migrants living in the United States identify as migrant workers, Michoacán voters, Mexican citizens, naturalized U.S. citizens, Latin American and Latino immigrants, Guadalupano Catholics, and Evangelical Christians, conceiving of those particular affiliations as complementary rather than conflicting. Yet the nation-states to which these migrants belong do not always embrace these practices, as shown above in the example of the singing of the national anthems. Nevertheless, Chicago HTA members are embedded in multiple networks and geographies in which migrant civic engagement takes place in Chicago and Mexico, such as families, sports clubs, museums, political parties, cultural groups, churches, prayer groups, labor centers, Latino and non-Latino grassroots organizations, and other civic and advocacy institutions. As their visibility and influence increases, these organizations demand more immigrant-sensitive services from local, state, and federal governments in their two countries and advocate for humane public policies to address human mobility in Central America and other Latin American countries with large populations living in the United States.

METHODOLOGY

This research focuses only on first-generation Mexican migrants because previous studies show that this group is the most likely to preserve a close relationship with the sending country (Smith 2002). So far, the few studies that have explored the transnational practices of the second generation conclude that there is not yet strong evidence that transnational practices will be maintained by the children of Mexican migrants, at least not with the same intensity (Kasinitz et al. 2008; Levitt and Waters 2002).

In ten years of fieldwork, I observed activities organized or attended by Michoacán HTAs in the Chicago metropolitan area, Los Angeles, Las Vegas, Morelia, Ciudad Hidalgo, Zacatecas, Puerto Vallarta, and Mexico City. Between the fall of 2001 and the summer of 2011, I observed fund-raising events for development projects in several Chicago suburbs, seven annual celebrations of Michoacán week in the Midwest that included an array of cultural events, seven annual FEDECMI gala dinners, four inaugural blessing masses for Chicago's Michoacán week, four binational forums of Michoacán migrants, the first meeting of Chicago-based Mexican HTAs, and a national convention of the Chicago-based March 10th Movement.[43]

In the state of Michoacán, I conducted four extended field trips in the summer and winter months to attend multiple community meetings in fifteen villages where migrant-funded development projects were implemented. I also made several short trips to visit historical archives and attended specific international migration and development events in Mexico City, Puerto Vallarta, and Michoacán, including the First Latin American Migrant Summit in Morelia; the Fourth Forum of People's Global Action on Migration, Development, and Human Rights in Mexico City; and the Civil Society Days of the Global Forum on Migration and Development in Puerto Vallarta.

My theoretical approach while analyzing my field notes gives special emphasis to the extended case methodology proposed by Michael Burawoy (1991). This approach posits that every social situation is unique, and emphasizes paying attention to its complexity, its depth and thickness, but treating its causality as multiplex, involving a connectedness of elements, connecting the social situation to its causal context of production. In analyzing the ethnographic data collected through multiple observations of HTAs' microprocesses, I unveil the macroforces shaping transnational and translocal connections, constructing linkages between micro and macro forces and processes. Ultimately, the application of the extended case method to my research subject allowed me to address previously formulated transnational theory "not [as] discovered but revised, not induced but improved, not deconstructed but reconstructed" (Burawoy 2009: 13).

For processing and analyzing the historical collected information, the evidential paradigm methodology and historical microsociology (Ginzburg 1989; Morawska 1985) were useful for finding clues of transnational life prior to the massive technological transformations that have facilitated the more intensive transnational connections that researchers have mapped for different migrant nationalities in the contemporary period (Basch, Schiller, and Szanton Blanc 1994; Levitt 2001; Smith 2001).

To address the political and social dimensions of migrant-funded projects in the state of Michoacán, I analyzed available databases on the federal matching fund program that were established in the state since 2002. These databases contain baseline information on all projects that were funded between 2002 and 2010, but unfortunately, they do not provide the exact location of the HTAs that donate funds, arguing confidentiality protection. The Mexican Freedom of Information Act, the so-called Instituto Federal de Acceso a la Información (IFAI), allows anyone to request specific information on any federally funded program, but not everything that is legally sanctioned in Mexico works efficiently. I requested this information multiple times using different official channels, and I only obtained partial results, along with many excuses for not disclosing the information. Therefore, the lack of a complete visual map to illustrate the ongoing relationships between communities of origin in Michoacán with places of residence in Illinois and elsewhere is one of the important gaps that remain in this text.

CHAPTER 2

❦

THE TRANSFORMATION OF MEXICAN MIGRANT ORGANIZATIONS

On June 2, 1928, Mexican presidential nominee José Vasconcelos gave a speech at Jane Addams's Hull House on Chicago's Near West Side. Vasconcelos's appearance was sponsored by the Ignacio Zaragoza mutual aid society.[1] The meeting did not attract a large crowd because the play *Don Juan Tenorio* was being held simultaneously somewhere else. Only fifty people from different mutual aid societies showed up to listen to Vasconcelos, disappointing the organizers, who were expecting that more of its eighty members would be in attendance.[2] Vasconcelos spoke about Mexico's corruption, nepotism, and patriotism. He encouraged Mexicans to return to Mexico and to keep paying close attention to postrevolutionary politics, arguing that good Mexicans should escape the poor labor conditions they face in the United States: "Mexicans, let us never forget or cease to show interest in our country and in the land in which we first saw the light of the day. For if we are here working hard and suffering, it will not always be so. We are but the children of Israel who are passing through our Egypt here in the United States, doing the onerous labors, swallowing our pride, bracing up under the indignities heaped upon us here. If we expect to return and escape all this, as all good Mexicans ought to, then we should show interest in the affairs of our country from this Egypt of ours" (qtd. in García 1996:144).

In 1929, Mexican migrants in Chicago organized committees in support of presidential nominees for the newly formed National Revolutionary Party. Some Chicago committees supported Mexican presidential nominee Pascual Ortiz Rubio, who ran against Vasconcelos and eventually won the nomination. Ortiz Rubio visited Chicago in 1930 to address the Mexican community and thanked his supporters (Año Nuevo Kerr 1976). From California to Kansas City, migrant organizations pressured the Mexican government to grant absentee voting rights to

Mexican citizens living in the United States (Santamaría Gómez 2001). Never before had migrant organizations displayed such high levels of political organization over Mexican elections.

Chicago's Mexican community had to wait almost sixty years to host another presidential candidate. On Saturday October 28, 1989, Cuauhtémoc Cárdenas Solórzano of the National Democratic Front (Frente Democrático Nacional) visited the historic Mexican community of Pilsen on Chicago's Lower West Side. He had just lost his first bid for the Mexican presidency, nearly defeating the ruling Revolutionary Institutional Party (PRI) candidate. In his speech, Cárdenas Solórzano encouraged Mexicans in Chicago and throughout the United States to join the democratic struggle to change a country with so few job opportunities that millions are forced to emigrate every year: "I would like to invite Mexicans from both sides of the border to begin a massive mobilization to defend the vote. The communities in Chicago need to be well organized to demand your right to vote absentee before Mexican consulates and all political parties, including the official one."[3] As the speeches of Vasconcelos and Cárdenas show, Mexican citizens living in Chicago represent Mexican politics in different ways, including claims of inclusion as voters while simultaneously serving as constant reminders to politicians of the major political and economic problems that have forced them to work in Chicago and elsewhere in the United States.

Cárdenas Solórzano's visit to Chicago was coordinated by the United Network for Immigrant and Refugee Rights (Red Unida por los Derechos de Inmigrantes y Refugiados) with the support, among others, of the University of Chicago, the University of Illinois at Chicago, and the Twenty-Second Ward. According to Carlos Arango, the lead organizer of Cárdenas's meeting with the community, more than 1,000 people attended the event. Cárdenas walked from Zapata Park—the popular name of Harrison Park—to Benito Juárez High School, and several neighborhood residents joined him.[4] The city council recognized him as an honored guest, and the same weekend, Amalia Hernández's folk ballet troupe made its third visit to Chicago since 1959, performing at the Auditorium Theater downtown. Her show was well attended and garnered rave reviews from the *Chicago Tribune*'s dance critics.

Mexican migrant organizations in Chicago have been engaged in transnational practices with the Mexican state and presidential candidates since the early twentieth century. However, they did not follow the same trajectory as their counterparts in Texas, California, and other areas of the Southwest. In the Southwest, the formation of a Mexican American identity developed much faster among the second generation. In the Midwest, the transition from a Mexican immigrant identity to a Mexican American identity took a more oscillatory path.

In Chicago, renewed migration from Mexico in the 1940s, coupled with rising prejudice and discrimination, helped establish a distinct Mexican immigrant consciousness that lasted for two decades after the Great Depression. During the first half of the twentieth century, Mexican migrant organizations focused mostly on mutual aid solidarity and cultivating a sense of pride and belonging to an "imagined" Mexican community through the re-creation of cultural practices aimed at recasting their "Mexicanness" from abroad. Consular offices and the occasional visit of political candidates heavily mediated the negotiations of early organizations with the Mexican government and their engagement with Mexican national politics.

Topophilic identities refer to cultural attachments to specific aspects of place.[5] Yet, early Mexican organizations were not as closely identified with a particular region or locale in Mexico as they are today. This stems from the precariousness of the Mexican nation-state in the postrevolutionary era and the low density of geographically defined social networks, which led to migrant organizations that were based on more national than topophilic identification.

Today, the ethnic identities of Mexican migrants are not only manifested through a nation-state allegiance but also as a sense of belonging that primarily resides in their *oriundez* (attachment to birthplace). As Yi-Fu Tuan (1974) vividly shows, most human beings exhibit a sense of topophilia in their lives. Their appreciation of landscapes is more personal and longer lasting when it is mixed with the memory of human incidents. In fact, local patriotism, the idea of attachment to a *pays*,[6] or home region, rests on the intimate lived experience of place because of its historical continuity and representation by a physiographic unit (a valley or a coast) small enough to be known personally. This attachment to birthplace partially explains why Mexican migrants organize around caring for and investing in a particular locale. Their topophilia is tied to natural landscapes that remind them of childhood memories, peculiar smells, valleys, mountains, and foothills.[7]

The transformation of Mexican migrant organizations and the emergence of hometown associations (HTAs) began in the 1980s, when the Mexican-born immigrants became the largest foreign-born population in the United States, with 2.2 million immigrants. The city of Chicago and its metropolitan area has experienced a steady expansion of the Mexican-born population since the 1980s. During the 1980s, the Mexican population there reached 2 percent of the population, with more than 150,000 immigrants. In the following decades, the Mexican-born population more than tripled, reaching more than half a million persons by the year 2000, without taking into consideration the decennial census undercounts in all these periods (Paral 2006). Mexicans in Chicago came to represent the second largest Mexican immigrant community in the United States.

HTAs became increasingly visible during the 1990s, which coincides with the rapid population increase of the Mexican foreign-born. By 2010, Mexican immigrants represented 47.5 percent of Chicago's total population of Latinos of Mexican descent (a mix of legal permanent residents, citizens, and those who are undocumented), which partly explains the interests of keeping the constant connections with towns of origin (American Community Survey 2010). This new demographic—aided by transplanted spatial patterns from their villages of origin, along with economic and political pressures to decentralize government functions in Mexico—provided the impetus to create new organizations with transformed cross-border agendas in the 1980s. Thus, while contemporary Mexican HTAs retain mutual aid solidarity practices and the patriotic engagement of early twentieth-century associations, they have added several new dimensions to their agenda: a direct involvement in the design of public policies and legislation related to migrant affairs, a philanthropic loyalty with community development in their towns and villages, and an increased advocacy to recover the migrant's voice in the public affairs of sending municipalities and states.

EARLY TWENTIETH-CENTURY MIGRANT ORGANIZATIONS IN CHICAGO

Mexican HTAs in Chicago emerged in the late twentieth century, but they certainly were not the first civic organizations formed by Mexican migrants. Mexican migrants established mutual aid societies in the early twentieth century that were quite similar to the voluntary associations of European migrants. As Liz Cohen documents in her study of Italian workers in Chicago, soon after Italians settled in Chicago neighborhoods alongside their *paesani* (villagers), they organized around the spirit of *campanilismo,* or loyalty to their communities of origin. These Italian HTAs had actually been transplanted from Europe to America and were the social centers of men's lives, a substitute for their hometown piazza. While in America, Bohemians, Poles, Jews, and Italians joined with their compatriots soon after arriving to ensure themselves a proper funeral, daily companionship in a lodge hall, picnics, dances, and feast days while in a foreign land (Cohen 1990). As time elapsed, the smaller societies with narrow European orientations and purely local constituencies were not able to sustain themselves and decided to merge with larger fraternal societies organized around national identities rather than particular villages or regions. For groups with former ethnic rivalries, the consolidation of national societies drew people into more national ethnic communities. Even the Bohemians in Chicago—an ethnic group with one of the most successful HTAs in the area—eventually chose between two major national affiliations demarcating rival camps in the American Czech community.

Settlement houses, labor unions, and other institutions of the host society provided limited assistance to the first generation; therefore, those early immigrants devised internal strategies to fulfill the needs of unemployment, widowhood, burial, and social activities, encouraging a reliance on traditional forms of mutual assistance that were already well established in their homelands to fend off the nascent capitalism. The leaders of these organizations came from the small groups of skilled workers and intellectuals who received some training and education inaccessible to most peasants before leaving.[8]

In the United States, the vast majority of academic research related to immigrant organizing conducted in the early twentieth century led to a belief that immigrants in the United States lacked the necessary attributes that would lead to philanthropic activities and that assimilation to American society planted the seed for the creation of migrant-led voluntary associations (Moya 2005). However, voluntary associations, including hometown or village associations, were very common in many sending countries, and the evidence of organizational activities of some internal migrant groups prior to their international migration contributes to understanding the origins of migrant-led voluntary associations. Within Mexico, there is evidence that HTAs from rural communities flourished in Mexican cities since the mid-1940s as a result of internal migration from the provinces to urban centers. Village associations in Mexico City organized by indigenous and mestizo migrants from Oaxaca, Jalisco, and Puebla in the mid-1940s and afterward are well documented (Fitzgerald 2009; Hirabayashi 1986; López Ángel 2004). Historically, the persistence or disappearance of these organizations at different points in time is connected to differences in the context of migrant reception that could have encouraged or discouraged the vitality and survival of migrant associations over time.

By 1927, Illinois already ranked fourth nationally among all states in the number of Mexicans, who were concentrated in Chicago and its metropolitan area (Badillo 2006). Like many of the African American workers of the Great Migration, some Mexicans were hired to break steel and packinghouse strikes in the late 1910s and early 1920s, thus placing them often in conflict with European workers and decreasing their opportunities to build interethnic immigrant solidarity groups (Arredondo and Vaillant 2005).[9]

In Chicago, the social condition of Mexican laborers was similar to that faced by early European migrants. Mexican factory workers during the 1920s obtained slightly better pay and job security than their fellow countrymen in agriculture or on the railroads, offering them greater opportunities to form mutual aid societies, learn English, and educate their children. Their early economic stability allowed the more educated leaders among the Mexican migrant groups to establish mutual aid societies to improve their economic conditions. Similar to the European case, most leaders of the first mutual aid societies and fraternities came from the lower middle class, usually artisans or small businessmen. When the more educated middle-class professionals took control of the leadership of many ethnic organizations, they transformed the scope of their social milieu toward "high culture" activities such as symphony orchestras, glee clubs, and scholarly lectures, which eventually led to the withdrawal of the working classes. Many of these organizations were a vehicle to improve financial and social standing among ambitious newcomers who used the organizations for personal gain and status while simultaneously advancing and promoting political or religious agendas in the homeland.

The settlement of entire families in Chicago and the metropolitan area resulted in vibrant organizational activity. Most European and Mexican organizations modeled their first associations on a patriarchal approach to protect the family involving mostly men, but later they realized that involving whole families was the only means of survival for these ethnic institutions. Women and children provided the help and the audience for the organizational structure. By 1927, more than a third of these immigrants were women and children who had settled thanks to the social networks that slowly expanded between 1850 and 1930. The efforts of the members to educate the children of Mexican migrants were, in essence, very similar to the goals pursued by early southern and eastern European migrants: "to promulgate the idea of a home-country patria as a primordial, morally imperative, and exclusive symbolic community" (Morawska 2001: 193).[10] In fact, according to the historian Gabriela Arredondo, "in an ironic testament to the powers of nationalist sentiments, Chicago's Mexicans became Mexicans not while in Mexico but rather once outside of the bounds of the nation-state of Mexico" (2008: 172).

Founded in 1925 to protect the legal rights of Mexican citizens in the Chicago-Calumet area, the Confederation of Mexican Societies of the United States of America (Confederación de Sociedades Mexicanas de los Estados Unidos de América) was an umbrella organization of about thirty-five Mexican mutual aid societies that were active in the Chicago area and northern Indiana. To follow the rules and regulations of the mutual aid societies, its constitution forbade the discussion of any political or religious issue at any of its meetings or gatherings. Many Mexican Catholic organizations were members, but they had to refrain from discussing religious issues at the meetings. This alliance was short-lived because it was never possible to promote a formal merger among the many associations. According to its vice president in 1926–1927, the confederation "broke up due to the efforts and jealousness of some of the smaller society officers and leaders."[11]

There were seventeen visible Mexican organizations in the mid-1920s and early 1930s in Chicago, ranging from literary clubs, religious associations, cultural organizations, sports clubs, and mutual aid societies (Gamio 1930). The leaders of these organizations did not live in the barrios and *colonias* where most Mexicans concentrated. In those years, travelers to the Midwest included a core group of professional and petit bourgeoisie. Due to their education, they became the leaders of the Mexican colonies or were appointed by the Mexican consulate to guide their fellow countrymen, who were largely rural peasants without much education and who originally came to the United States in search for work to feed their families (Durand and Arias 2008).

In the postrevolutionary period, the Mexican consulate in Chicago emphasized unity as its main organizational theme, but the results were rather modest because consular officials did not consider Mexican migrant organizations as their partners and instead pursued a clientelist approach toward migrant leaders.

Nevertheless, the role of the Mexican consulate in promoting a positive image of Mexicanness cannot be denied. Besides, the Mexican consulate was an important mediator to improve conditions for Mexican nationals and provided legal protection to some Mexicans living and working in the area when wage disputes were reported to the consular offices. In spite of this, many Mexicans did not trust their authorities due to bad experiences these workers had with authoritarian governments and politicians in their sending states (Arredondo 2008).

Despite the significant size of the migrant community and the organizations' great interest in promoting migrants' social adaptation in Chicago and the metro area, migrant leaders were not always included in the high-level consultations on immigrant incorporation organized by the Mexican consulate. For example, the Mexican Relations Committee, an ad hoc committee chaired in 1926 by Luis Lupián, the Mexican consul in Chicago, did not include any mutual societies as members. However, the Spanish Mission, the United Charities and Legal Aid Bureau, Loyola University, the University of Chicago Settlement, and the Migrants Protective League were among some of the institutions invited to participate.[12] While mutual aid societies offered important social services to incorporate the immigrant community into Chicago's social fabric, they were not sufficiently visible in formal immigrant politics, which prevented them from taking a more active role in the decision-making processes regarding immigrant incorporation in Chicago's political landscape.

Regional Diversity within Mexican Migrant Organizations

Cultural and class divisions did not help to create strong organizations. Mexican immigrants at the turn of the twentieth century in Chicago represented a diverse mix of social classes. In addition to a small group of expatriate elites who frequently looked down upon Mexicans of different social positions, the lower and middle classes frequently clashed around looks, language abilities, and unemployment status, especially among men (Arredondo 2008). In fact, some migrants who were highly critical of the elitist nature of the early mutual aid societies decided to form alternative organizations. Jesús García and José Anguiano formed the Cuauhtémoc Society in 1926 in East Chicago, Indiana (García 1996). This organization tried to provide alternative social outlets. They chose this name to recast their Indian past in opposition to the unifying mestizo ideals of other organizations. The Cuauhtémoc Society organized vaudevilles and other recreational activities that drew larger crowds because those events were more appealing to the working class than poetry readings. In the 1940s, this group was equally interested in promoting the commercial and industrial relations between immigrants and their new society as in promoting its mutual aid and patriotic objectives. Its first bylaws implemented geographical limits to the group's membership, thus restricting admission to all Mexicans living in a radius of twenty-five miles from Indiana Harbor. Years later, this organization had an open membership, and anyone willing to pay the membership fees was welcomed regardless of nationality or residence.

The membership lists of the Mexican Cuauhtémoc Society between 1926 and 1949 reveal the great diversity of the Mexican community. During those years, there were 658 regular members from seventeen different Mexican states. While other mutual aid societies restricted membership to males and Mexican citizens who had not naturalized, the Cuauhtémoc Society developed an open membership including males, females, and U.S. citizens of Mexican ancestry as well as members of other nationalities. As time elapsed, the organizers realized that the idea of returning to the homeland was not realistically feasible, and the survival of the organization was dependent on the membership, regardless of stripe.

From 1936 to 1949, most members of this society were blue-collar male workers, although women, many of whom were also in the workforce, represented 21 percent of the membership. Not surprisingly, an important share of the membership came from two traditional sending states, Guanajuato and Michoacán, which provided, respectively, 18 and 17 percent of the total membership of the Cuauhtémoc Society. Among Guanajuatense migrants, 22 percent came from the city of San Francisco del Rincón; and in the case of Michoacán, 21 percent came from the city of Zamora. Although most people coming from Michoacán came from the northern part of the state, their geographical diversity was impressive. For instance, the 114 Michoacanos registered to this association came from fifty different cities and towns, most of which were important urban centers such as Ecuandureo, Morelia, Yurécuaro, Sahuayo, and Uruapan. Other highly represented birthplaces were Zacatecas, San Luis Potosí, Nuevo León, Jalisco, and Durango as well as several places in the United States, which indicates that both U.S.-born and native-born Mexicans participated in this organization (see figure 2.1).

The diversity of the Cuauhtémoc Society was also manifest in its non-Mexican membership. From its records, it becomes clear that the society admitted people from different nationalities, such as Spaniards, Yugoslavians, Russians, Romanians, Italians, Austrians, Anglo-Saxon Americans, Bulgarians, Canadians, Germans, and Poles,[13] which contradicts earlier assumptions by historians who believed that Mexican mutual aid societies prevented people from other nationalities from joining these associations. The nationality restrictions might have been enforced during the 1920s but were relaxed in the 1930s and afterward as a survival mechanism. However, not all Mexican workers chose to affiliate with ethnic mutual aid societies. Instead, some Mexican workers decided to join American societies, such as the Express Workers Mutual Benefit Society in Chicago.

In the 1940s, other Mexican mutual aid organizations adjusted to the new reality of dwindling memberships as well. For instance, the Benito Juárez Society of East Chicago changed its bylaws in 1939, fifteen years after it was initially

Birth Places of Sociedad Cuauhtémoc Members in the United States 1937-1949

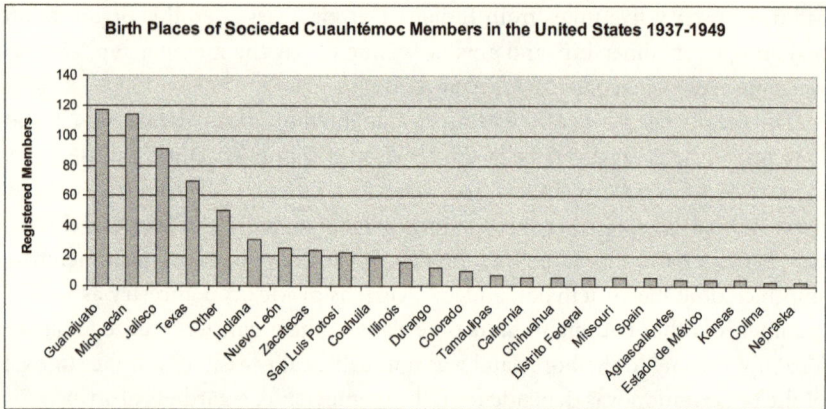

Figure 2.1. Birthplaces of Sociedad Cuauhtémoc members in the United States, 1937–1949. Source: Analysis of 656 membership records of Sociedad Cuauhtémoc.

incorporated in the state of Indiana. In the new statutes, the group pledged to keep strong ties with Hispanic Americans and Spanish people and accepted any Mexicans as members instead of only Mexicans who were not naturalized as U.S. citizens, thus transforming the exclusive national identity of the institution toward a more hyphenated American identity.[14]

Although a small number of athletic teams and mutual aid societies organized around people of the same village or from the same state, the majority of early Mexican migrant associations did not organize around topophilic identities during the first wave of immigration for various reasons. First, many migrant laborers harbored the hope of returning to the homeland after the turmoil of the Mexican Revolution. Second, for blue-collar workers in the steel mills, life in the United States was so hard that they tended to concentrate on how to improve their conditions in the new society and worried more about their children's educational opportunities.

Besides, the Mexican migrant population was so diverse in their regional origins that it was difficult to find enough people from the same village or municipality to start a migrant village association. Many migrants had lived in several places in Mexico before migrating to the United States due to the high social instability caused by the revolution, and this mobility diminished their attachment to birthplaces. In the 1920s, Robert C. Jones, in an unpublished manuscript on the religious life of Mexicans in Chicago, observed that although a very large percentage of Mexicans came from rural communities, many had lived in larger towns for varied lengths of time on their way north. From his observations, Jones realized that "unlike some other migrant groups, [they] do not have much of a tendency to congregate together on the basis of the old community groups in Mexico. Their old associations are very largely broken up and they feel the need of joining together with others for sociability and mutual aid."[15] Therefore, the social networks of the first wave were not geographically connected when compared to the social networks created at the end of the Bracero Agreements,[16] when chain network migration of large groups from the same rural towns increased considerably.

In addition to the high mobility pattern, it was common for migrants to work first in California and Texas after crossing the border. Eventually, beliefs and news about better wages in the Windy City subsequently drove some of these migrants to Chicago. Everyday life for Mexicans in Chicago was a lot different than the experiences Mexicans had in the Southwest. Before and after the Texas annexation and the Mexican Cession, many Mexican citizens had traveled to go to work in places like San Antonio, Los Angeles, Arizona, or El Paso. In those places, it was not difficult to find people speaking Spanish and some symbols of a shared Mexican cultural past (Mora-Torres 2006).

The early twentieth-century immigration of Mexicans to Chicago coincided with the new European immigration of Italians and Poles, as well as African Americans coming from the Deep South (Drake and Cayton 1945). In this diverse urban environment, language differences along with racial and residential segregation did not produce interethnic immigrant solidarity among these groups and accentuated national ethnic identity formations. Finally, in the 1920s and 1930s, during the time that the organizations were highly active, the Mexican state had recently finished a long period of civil revolution, and those in the migrant organizations believed that it was important to support the consolidation of the Mexican state. Therefore, the vast majority of the early organizations chose to defend the political positions of the Mexican government on religious freedom, sovereignty, and self-determination as their main mission. In choosing to emphasize their home communities over their national affiliations, according to available historical records, only two Mexican organizations followed a topophilic or HTA model in Chicago: the Sociedad Unida de Artesanos de Durango (Durango's United Society of Artisans), a secular organization founded in 1908, and the Comité Guanajuatense de Socorros (Guanajuato's Aid Committee), which was active in 1926.

For the majority of the Mexican community in Chicago that came from rural Mexico, patriotic attachments were primarily linked to their local communities before arriving in the United States. Rural migrants who faced Porfirio Díaz's policies reinforced their local and regional ties to survive, fostering what the U.S. historian Arturo Rosales calls a "*patria chica*" mentality, or what the Mexican historian Luis González y González calls *matria*, or "motherland," in his historical analysis of the San José de Gracia community in Michoacán (González y González 1995; Rosales 1978). However, when middle-class leaders began to encourage a sense of "Mexicanness" as the unifying element among migrants, a more cohesive national identity began to emerge. The process of identity construction was slowly developed in their new foreign environment in part because the formation of a collective consciousness among rural peasantry in Mexico was "closed-corporate" prior to their migratory experience. The collective image and solidarity of Mexican rural life after the Spanish conquest was anchored in three pillars, according to the classic study done by Eric Wolf: collective land property, the presence of a local patron saint, and the organization of local folk celebrations (Wolf 1957). Therefore, the collective "imagined community" for early migrant organizations was not anchored in following a national model of "horizontal camaraderie" à la Benedict Anderson (1983) but in cultivating a more vertical structure where patriotic loyalty and allegiance were the determining factors connecting members to each other and to the national body, as Claudio Lomnitz (2001) has argued in his revision of Anderson's imagined community for the Mexican case.

Class and labor divisions in early twentieth-century Mexico made it difficult to nurture a strong horizontally fraternal relationship between groups with essentially opposing interests, such as servants and masters, or peasants and landowners; however, many shared loyalty to the nation through the common elements of language and religion. Free and universal schooling was not constitutionally established until after 1917. Therefore, many early uneducated migrants in Chicago did not have the possibility of connecting with the members of the polity through an official foundational narrative or national civic instruction. For the middle-class leaders of early Mexican organizations, it was important to cultivate a strong nation-state allegiance while downplaying the topophilic sense of belonging that was common among rural migrants. Topophilic attachments were likely present among individual migrants because a significant number of early Mexican migrants to Chicago came as seasonal or temporary workers and eventually returned to their towns and villages of origin. However, the low density of the geographical social networks downplayed topophilic attachments and prevented the formation of organizations according to birthplace during the first half of the twentieth century.

William Thomas and Florian Znaniecki had already observed similar patterns of collective rural life in communities of origin in their explorations of Polish immigrants. In their classic study, they closely observed the lives of Polish peasants in their rural milieu as well as in their new dwellings in Chicago. They concluded that in Poland, the communities were reorganizing and moving toward nation-building, while in Chicago, disorganization and fragmentation were taking the lead, and institutional outlets for adaptation were slowly evolving (Thomas and Znaniecki 1927). Coincidentally, it was through practices of long-distance nationalism in America that they discovered their sense of Polishness, as members of a unified nation-state. For Mexican migrants in Chicago, their sense of membership in and belonging to a unified nation-state took a more oscillating path, with periods of high exaltation of Mexicanness as a reaction to prejudice

and discrimination by the host society, followed by a period of partial incorporation to a hyphenated Mexican American identity. Full incorporation would later
be thwarted by the massive flow of new Mexican migrants to the city during the
second half of the twentieth century.

EARLY CROSS-BORDER CIVIC PARTICIPATION

Mexican mutual aid societies that survived the Great Depression made attempts
to forge relationships with Mexico's government and civil society. In the 1940s,
the Mexican consulate constantly monitored the activities of Mexican organizations, requesting them to be registered officially, demanding their financial statements and an inventory of their properties. After the Depression, some
mutual aid societies were able to reorganize in spite of dwindling memberships
and kept providing services but did not solidify their connections with their
Mexican counterparts. For instance, in August 1940 the president of the Corporación Sociedad Amigos Mutualistas, with headquarters in Mexico City, sent
letters to all Mexican mutual aid societies through the consular networks asking to establish cross-border cooperation agreements with U.S.-based mutual
aid societies. Unfortunately, there is no evidence that the Mexican consulates
distributed the request among the intended organizations.

According to the correspondence of the mutual aid societies from East Chicago and Gary, Indiana, it is clear that direct, unmediated relations with institutions based in Mexico did not extend beyond emergency fund-raisers for natural
disasters, help in the search for missing persons, and the occasional letter from
municipal authorities asking them to intercede with Mexico's federal government to obtain approvals for new Bracero contracts. For instance, the Benito
Juárez Society organized a fund-raiser for the victims of the 1943 cyclone that
affected the Mexican West Coast after consulate officials sent a formal letter asking for donations.[17] Existing records of several post-1940 organizations demonstrate that leaders were not actively seeking collaboration agreements with
Mexico's civil society. Instead, most outreach efforts to increase ties between
migrant organizations and Mexican civil society came from government officials
and leaders of Mexico-based organizations. The vast collection of letters inviting consular officials and local government authorities to attend festivals and
parades to commemorate Mexico's independence show that it was more important to convince local authorities to attend their events in order to gain more visibility and wider recognition in the host society than to increase direct ties with
civil society in the homeland.

As Rachel Sherman (1999) notes, for most of the twentieth century the Mexican state followed a "policy of introversion" or limited inclusion when dealing with the incorporation of the Mexican diaspora in the United States as full
members of Mexican society. Therefore, the engagement of mutual aid society

leaders with Mexico's public affairs was commonly in response to invitations to events organized by the Mexican government to give migrants a chance to rub shoulders with political figures and make them feel as important members of Mexican society, at least during those brief events. In 1947, President Miguel Alemán invited all Mexican organizations in the United States to visit the homeland and meet with former expatriate leaders who had returned permanently. In a letter sent by a former member of the Benito Juárez Society to a mutual aid society member in East Chicago after the event, he congratulates the gesture of Mexican organizations to visit the homeland to honor "our very worthy and well loved" president, Miguel Alemán.[18] In the 1950s, there was the Patronato Pro-Juventud Mexicana en el Extranjero (Mexican Youth Abroad Sponsoring Committee) in Mexico City, whose mission was to offer annual cultural tours of Mexico to a select group of second-generation migrants. The Patronato sent letters to the Mexican consulates to ask for potential candidates for the tour, and the consulates distributed those invitations among the leaders of mutual aid associations. Since the numbers of sponsored children were limited, the consulate encouraged all mutual aid societies to organize fund-raisers to sponsor the cost of sending Mexican high school students to study summer courses at the National Autonomous University of Mexico.

Few archives exist on the early civic participation of these associations to improve the well-being in their communities of origin. From visits to three municipal archives in Michoacán with large migrant populations living in Chicago, I was only able to find evidence of individual requests to municipalities, asking varied services related to the register of deeds (marriage licenses, birth and death certificates, land titles, and so forth). Those documents were necessary when migrants decided to become U.S. citizens, which comes as no surprise since one of their primary concerns at that time was managing to incorporate into their new host society. However, other archives show evidence of early cross-border participation. In 1946, the Benito Juárez Society organized a fund-raiser to cooperate with the creation of a children's musical band in the northern city of Matamoros, Tamaulipas, after the municipal president of that city approached them asking for help.[19]

Due to the existence of alternative support networks in Mexico, mutual aid societies were not a common phenomenon in Mexico, and the mutualist organizations in the United States could not forge strong alliances with similar organizations in Mexico (García 1996). However, there were a few interactions, especially to show solidarity during moments of crisis. For example, in November 1932 Trinidad Jiménez, the secretary of the Miguel Hidalgo mutual aid society of Gary, Indiana, wrote a letter addressed to the Ministry of Foreign Relations in Mexico City stating that most members of this society had been repatriated and the society had to be dissolved. He requested help to rescue the funds of the organization because they wanted to donate them to the Mexico City orphanage.[20]

The mutual aid societies and patriotic committees were interested in the political affairs and debates taking place in the homeland. In 1935, just six years after the end of the Cristero War, the Pro-Mexico Committee of Alton, Illinois, sent a letter to the general consul of Mexico in Los Angeles to declare the committee's solidarity with the government after a group of women in Chicago—supported by Spanish priests—had made hostile declarations against Mexican institutions and the government. In the letter, the committee members said that the Mexican Colonia in Chicago respects the religious beliefs of all individuals but that they were not going to allow any interventionist remarks against Mexican laws and institutions.[21] This expression of secularism was largely due to the scarcity of Mexican-led faith-based organizations. In Chicago, Mexican religious associations took longer to solidify because the Catholic Church did not provide enough support for the adaptation of Mexican immigrants in Chicago in the early twentieth century. In fact, during the Cristero War, the absence of organized supporters of the Catholic movement in Chicago was noticeable.

The absence of community-based organized support for the Cristero War is surprising considering the demographic profile of the population. For example, a 1928 survey of Mexican migrants in Chicago conducted by Chicago's Immigrant's Protective League found that almost two-thirds came from Michoacán, Guanajuato, Jalisco, and Zacatecas, central plateau states that had shown strongest activism to support the Cristero War (Badillo 2006). According to the historian Ann Martinez, the Mexican National League of Religious Defense did not have any chapters in the United States, despite the letter exchanges the league maintained with the U.S. National Catholic Welfare Conference and some Mexican ethnic organizations such as the Mexican Catholic League (Liga Católica Mexicana) in Laredo, Texas, and the Pro-Mexico Benefit Society (Sociedad de Beneficencia Pro-México) in Chicago (Martínez 2003; Slayton 1988).

To show the heterogeneity of the early Mexican organizations, the Mexican Popular Front (Front)—a Communist-leaning organization originally initiated in Mexico with several sections active in Chicago—was a transplanted socialist political organization from Mexico City called the Anti-Imperialist Popular Front (A-Front), whose members kept close contact and ties with Front organizers in Mexico City as well as with Cuban nationalists, Spanish Loyalists, and several Chicago-based multiethnic labor groups, such as the Illinois Workers Alliance of Cook County and the United Packinghouse Workers.[22] The leaders of the Front came from the working classes of Mexican immigrants who in many cases were already active in the local labor movement. The leadership was interested in providing basic literacy classes to uneducated Mexican immigrants and in creating a collective labor consciousness against U.S. imperialism. Since most leaders and members were foreign born and did not have more than a third grade education, it was important to focus their activities in literacy instruction in Spanish sponsored by the Mexican consulate instead of English-language courses, which were readily available for free at the settlement houses.

Besides its agenda to participate in the global struggle against imperialism and fascism, the Front demanded more attention from Mexican consular officials and was also involved in labor-organizing activities. For example, this organization asked the consulate to help the community to have access to libraries and to finance Mexican schools in Chicago to transmit the Mexican culture to the second generation. It requested that the Mexican government sponsor a scholarship program for young students to prepare them to become leaders in Chicago and in Mexico, and the Front successfully obtained Spanish-language textbooks for its basic literacy courses from the Department of Education in Mexico City. In meetings, members discussed the labor situation of workers in Mexico and Latin America, strike techniques, and the possibilities for organizing a Pan–Latin American umbrella organization. The topics included in their discussions strove to have a practical application in their everyday lives in the United States while at the same time they looked for resources in Mexico. For instance, when Refugio Román Martínez—a founding Front member—joined the Packinghouse Workers Organizing Committee, he tried to convince other Front members to sign unionization cards. Martínez later became a visible political deportee during the Cold War (Bacon 2006, 2011). On December 11, 1948, Stanley Nowak, the national chairman of the New York—based American Committee for the Protection of the Foreign Born, sent an invitation to the Benito Juárez Society to participate in a fund-raiser dinner at the Congress Hotel in Chicago to prevent the deportation of two migrant workers participating in unions: Refugio Román Martínez, a staff member of the Packinghouse Workers Union, and Juan Díaz, a native of Spain and a member of the Food, Tobacco and Agricultural Workers Union.[23]

The Front activities in Chicago happened in the late 1930s, in an epoch when the University of Chicago Settlement House was providing space to several ethnic associations. It is no surprise that after several skirmishes with space administrators at the settlement house, the Mexican Popular Front was prevented from organizing its activities on university grounds. Despite the difficulties faced by different sections of the Front to pursue their agendas and anti-imperialist activities in Chicago,[24] they managed to organize some fund-raisers to benefit the A-Front, and they also collected money for Spanish workers. They also organized a fund-raiser to send representatives to the A-Front's international convention in Mexico City. The Front's initial activities in Chicago started in 1936 after an invitation from a Front group formed in Cleveland. One year later, the Front had been able to organize a second section at the Hull House, and a total of five sections were spread throughout Chicago. According to the historian John H. Flores, the Front leaders were able to "transplant the Front to Chicago by drawing on the institutional resources of the Chicago settlement houses"—basically by taking advantage of an initial positive reaction from the administrators, thus opening a window of opportunity to mobilize more resources from local civic institutions (Flores 2006).

Although the impact of the binational mobilization activities of Mexican migrants in Chicago has not been systematically measured, the existing records suggest that mostly the middle classes were engaged in those activities with moderate impact. The influence that early Mexican migrant organizations displayed in local or national policies in Mexico was quite limited because their binational advocacy was more discursive than oriented to tangible actions. While there are records and some published studies done on these early associations, they mostly focus on their activities within Chicago rather than on their binational connections. After all, assimilation into American society was the ultimate interest of the Hull House and other philanthropic institutions that supported many ethnic immigrant organizations.

While most mutual aid societies were recognized as independent civic organizations, there was a different system of migrant organizing that was entirely orchestrated by the Mexican government. During the 1920s, the Mexican Ministry of Foreign Affairs asked Mexican consuls in the United States to establish civic organizations to help them carry out their expanded duties with the expatriate community. As the Mexican *colonias* were growing larger in several U.S. cities, the Mexican consuls needed help to learn more about the challenges these communities were facing. For that reason, the Mexican government created the Honorary Commissions (Comisones Honoríficas), organizations generally appointed by the Mexican consul although the Mexican colonies were also encouraged to submit independent proposals (Valdés 2000). However, the Mexican consul always had to approve the organization and appoint its president, a permanent position. The members were allowed to elect a secretary, treasurer, board members, and other committee members to serve in these positions for one-year terms.

Considering the social and political unrest that Mexico faced in the 1920s and 1930s, the Mexican government established Comisiones Honoríficas in an effort to mobilize migrants' national loyalty, engage them in home-country politics, encourage them to return to their home states, and squash any political activity that would be deemed subversive. In fact, in that historical period, both the United States and Mexico exerted exclusionary demands on their immigrants and emigrants regarding their national commitments and showed little tolerance or protection for divided loyalties. Therefore, for the Mexican government, it was very important to keep track of the structure of these organizations and exercise as much power and control as possible. The consulates even administered the funds collected by these organizations.[25]

However, not all migrant organizations unconditionally agreed with the consulate's mechanism to encourage civic engagement. The instances of conflict seem to have been initiated by the most progressive organizations. In 1942, the mutual aid societies of East Chicago presented a joint petition to the consulate

demanding to be included in the selection process for the Comisiones Honoríficas. They believed that members appointed by the consuls were mostly incompe-
tent. According to existing records, the consul responded positively, promising to
invite representatives of the mutual aid societies to the next elections.[26]

The Demise and Transformation

The massive repatriation of Mexicans in the 1930s negatively affected the Mexican population in Chicago. As Gabriela Arredondo and Derek Vaillant (2005: 1)
remind us, the employment precariousness of Mexican immigrants exacerbated
their removal from Chicago and its metropolitan area:

> With the cooperation of the U.S. and Mexican governments, local civic organi-
> zations such as the American Legion of East Chicago rounded up hundreds of
> unemployed workers and their families and placed them on trains bound for
> the U.S.-Mexico border. Forcible and voluntary repatriation drives focused on
> workers who "looked Mexican" and often ignored the citizenship of those who
> had been born in the United States. Others, conscious of their bleak prospects
> and the hostile social climate, voluntarily accepted the free train trip south. In
> the decade of the 1930s, the Mexican population in the Chicago area was cut
> nearly in half. By 1940 an estimated 16,000 Mexicans remained within Chicago.

At the end of the 1940s, very few mutual aid societies survived as Mexicans
were slowly integrating into labor unions, learning English, and attaining better
positions in the industries after the Congress of Industrial Organizations (CIO)
encouraged foreign-born industrial workers to participate in American urban
politics (Glazer and Moynihan 1970). The Mexican mutual aid societies in Chicago
and its metro area could not survive because they were reluctant to merge with
similar societies to keep their financial viability. As their membership decreased
due in part to diminished migratory flows after the Great Depression and subsequent massive repatriations, these organizations were not financially sound to
pay out more than a few benefit checks before having to fold (Innis-Jiménez 2013).

The first cohort of Mexican mutual aid societies was highly dependent on the
ebbs and flows of the U.S.-Mexico migratory waves. In Chicago, the U.S. Department of Labor pressured the Immigration and Naturalization Service (INS) to
conduct deportation drives due to concerns about the decline in wages and
oversupply of workers in the steel industry, which declined from 90 percent
to 50 percent of capacity during that period and could no longer employ many
Mexicans. Most early organizations had operated for less than two decades when
the Great Depression hit the Midwest, and they had not consolidated as viable
nonprofits. The mutual aid societies were highly dependent on membership
dues to finance their altruistic activities, which included serving as important
providers of relief and emergency services to attend the ill and unemployed with

scarce funds during the Great Depression and they were not able to diversify their funding sources to keep up their basic operations.

For example, in 1943 the Benito Juárez Society asked the Cuauhtémoc Society to merge into a single organization. The leaders of the Cuauhtémoc Society rejected the offer. In 1956, the Benito Juárez Society made a second attempt to merge with the Cuauhtémoc Society, but the two societies did not reach an agreement.[27] It was not until 1957 that both societies and the Protective Society for the Benefit of Latin American People–which eventually became the Mexican Steelworkers Association—merged into the Unión Benéfica Mexicana (UBM).[28] In December 1958, a new Sociedad Mexicana Cuauhtémoc, under the leadership of the original founder, tried to reorganize, but the UBM filed a petition with the Indiana secretary of state to request the denial of the charter to the new organization. As a result, José Anguiano, the founding member of the Cuauhtémoc Society in 1926, was permanently expelled from the UBM on December 30, 1958, after four long hours of deliberation among sixty voting members. As their assets dwindled, the mutual aid societies evolved into different civic ethnic organizations. Fractures, social class divisions, personal rivalries among the leaders, and external forces also contributed to their demise and revealed the complexity of the composition of the Mexican community in the area, which was far from a homogeneous group. Paradoxically, the original aims of the Mexican consulate to ensure loyalty to Mexico among these groups had helped to glue them together in a way that created common links out of the differences within this nonhomogeneous group.

In the second half of the twentieth century, the Mexican organizations did not disappear completely but rather reorganized and eventually transformed their purpose to focus on the preservation of culture, political integration, and the incorporation of the second generation. The new organizations of this period, "unlike those formed in the late 1920's and early 1930's, were usually devoted to life . . . in the city, rather than in Mexico. In effect, those who had come in the first wave of immigration were now more American than Mexican" (Año Nuevo Kerr n.d.). Some male migrants began to lengthen their stay in the United States and brought their wives and children with them. As many Mexicans started to cross the path from sojourners to settlers, they slowly changed the profile of their social spaces. As they began to identify as Mexican Americans, they became interested in forging solidarities with other Latin Americans, such as newly arrived Puerto Ricans and Cubans, in the hope of establishing a strong Hispanic coalition to advocate for their rights as an ethnic group. Therefore, their transnational attachments to the homeland were transformed into new ethnic identities that became an important point of reference for their activities in the Chicago metropolitan area.

The Mr. and Mrs. Society and the Manuel Pérez Jr. Post 1017 are good examples of evolving organizations that formed in the postwar period and were struggling to keep their memberships active. Established in 1959 as a bowling league of young Chicagoans of Mexican descent, within one year the Mr. and Mrs. Society had become M & M Society, Inc., a philanthropic and charitable organization committed to the promotion of mutual understanding, assistance, and cooperation within Chicago's Mexican American community. In 1995, the organization celebrated its thirty-fifth anniversary, but only twenty-three members remained active. The Manuel Pérez Jr. Post 1017, an organization that also emerged after the Second World War, had only sixteen members left in 1996.[29]

The Juárez Club of Chicago evolved into a social club that published the *Crown*, a bilingual Pilsen-based neighborhood newsletter (mostly written in English, with some comments and announcements in Spanish) from 1938 until 1998, edited by Rubin J. Torres (Gellman 2005). In 1946, the club had approximately seventy-five members, and their activities ranged from organizing the float contests for the Independence Day Parade to staging bathing suit contests. In the pages of its bulletin, popular Mexican music albums received the same coverage as American ones. The *Crown* had a circulation of 1,000 and covered important news, especially anything related to the connections between the two countries.

Examples of postings include the misery and starvation in Mexico and the visit of President Harry S. Truman to Mexico. In 1976, the editors denounced a series that the *Chicago Sun-Times* ran on undocumented workers written by Roberto Suro. They applauded the decision of William Sotelo to write a letter to the editor in response to the series. In his letter, Sotelo explains that he had written many letters to the Mexican authorities demanding Mexican passports for undocumented workers. For him, this reflected "the ineptitude of the Mexican government in regard to its citizens abroad. . . . I am in favor of amnesty to these illegals, but it should be conditional—if within seven years they have not become U.S. citizens by justified means, their residence status should be revoked and they should be deported from the United States."[30] As observed in this comment, interest in full incorporation to American society through naturalization was an important condition for accepting Mexican undocumented immigrants as full members of the expatriate community.

The bulletin also dedicated space to explain the celebration of holidays such as Valentine's Day, Thanksgiving, Saint Patrick's Day, Christmas, Easter, Flag Day, and so forth. Among their social activities, the Juárez Club members organized Mexican patriotic festivities with similar organizations such as the Mexican Patriotic Committee, the Mexican Civic Committee, the Club Miguel Hidalgo, the Club 30, the Mr. and Mrs. Dance and Bowling Club, and the Necaxa Soccer Club. Once again, as happened to the early mutual aid societies, the organizations of the 1940s also wanted to keep their personality and independence and refused to merge into a single Mexican organization despite many efforts made by some community members to form one unified confederation of Mexican American clubs and societies.

In 1946, the Mexican United Club Council tried to unify some of the sports clubs with voluntary and religious organizations. Ciclistas S.A.C., the Saint Francis Crier, the American Legion, the Miguel Hidalgo y Costilla Club, the Saint Francis Girls Club, and the Wildcats of Saint Francis joined this council. The Wildcats had been in existence since the late 1930s and are believed to be among the first Mexican sports clubs who chose an Americanized name.[31] In fact, the post-Depression ethnic organizations linked sports with Mexican American identity in order to preserve ties among the second generation and demonstrate that ethnic solidarity, the foundation of their organizational support, and Americanization were not incompatible.

Due to the early influence of the Chicago Hull House, Mexican organizations experienced a process of ethnicization in which they became hyphenated American citizens concerned with preserving the culture and traditions of their homeland but at the same time actively interested in participating in local politics. In the 1950s, attention seems to have turned away from Mexico, and several of the organizations remaining from the late 1930s became integrated into mainstream U.S.-based charities, including voluntary and membership organizations.

For example, the Mexican-American Council of Chicago was created in 1951 as a membership-based organization focused on the integration of the second generation. At some point, some members wanted to change its name to the Spanish-Speaking People's Council because they believed that potential new members could feel alienated if they considered themselves real Americans and disliked the implications of the hyphenated name.[32] The name change never happened because most council members objected to it. In 1962, the Mexican American Democratic Organization of Chicago was organized to encourage political participation. In the 1950s and 1960s, there were other Mexican American ethnic organizations, such as the Illinois Federation of Mexican Americans, the Cardinal's Committee for the Spanish Speaking, the Mexican Independence Day Parade Association, and the Pan American Games Committee. By then, most organization had made the linguistic transition, and all their names were in English.

Despite numerous attempts of these organizations for preserving the loyalty of the migrant masses, they were only partly successful because many newcomers had loyalties to other ideals and institutions, such as unions and churches. Relatively low membership in fraternal organizations, mutual aid societies, and other national ethnic organizations is a historic fact for other ethnic groups as well. For example, the overwhelming majority of Romanians in America never joined any cultural or beneficial society. In Chicago, neither Mexican nor Italian mutual aid societies of the 1920s could register the vast majority of their immigrants. There is no reliable evidence of total membership among the early Mexican organizations, but my own estimates based on the membership of the Cuauhtémoc Society and the average membership of similar organizations in the area conclude that they could not have exceeded 10,000 members in the most optimistic scenario, representing less than 50 percent of the total Mexican population in the area. In the case of Italians, a survey of 3,000 families in Chicago in 1920 by the Illinois Health Insurance Commission found that only 57.8 percent of Italian American families sampled had some form of life insurance, and probably no more than half of these policies were held in Italian mutual aid societies (Bodnar 1981; Bodnar 1985).

Competition, conflict, accommodation, and assimilation—the four necessary steps that sociologist Robert Park devised to understand migrant adaptation to the new society—were not linearly followed by the Mexican community. While many stayed and settled in Chicago after the 1930s, others kept commuting back and forth during the Bracero era and after, which is contrary to the assumption of one-way settlement and assimilation. The classical assimilation process in the United States was mostly described using examples from European migrant communities that transformed into hyphenated ethnic Americans when their emigration flows to the United States considerably decreased. In the Mexican case, an intermittent flow of new migrant workers to Chicago after the Great Depression would guarantee the replenishment of a fresh ethnic identity for at least another fifty years.[33] Early observers were not able to predict the permanence of the Mexican migratory flows and the fragility of a homogenous hyphenated identity as they missed the interconnections among migration, development, Mexico-U.S. economic dependency, several peso devaluations, neoliberal reforms, and free trade.

THE REVIVAL OF MEXICAN ORGANIZING IN THE POST-BRACERO ERA

At the end of the Bracero Agreements in 1964, Mexican migrants continued coming to Chicago and its suburbs following a circular process that was, in part, encouraged by the relative geographic proximity with the homeland in comparison to transatlantic migrants. The constant exchanges of social and cultural remittances allowed the permanence of some cultural and organizational sites in Mexican neighborhoods. Over time, not all Mexican organizations evolved into mainstream philanthropies or social membership organization such as Rotaries, Lions, twist dance clubs, and Veterans of Foreign Wars (VFW) groups. Some groups decided to retain a migrant ethnic identity, while others acquired a new one forged through their participation in the civil rights struggle.

In the 1970s, the Mexican American Democratic Organization was active in Chicago. When the Chicano movement acquired national visibility, a few Mexican groups formed Chicago-based Chicano clubs. In the 1980s, through similar organizations with specific national or pan-ethnic identities, Mexican migrants were accessing social and political spaces through the display of Chicano, Latino, and Hispanic identities. They were actively promoting voting rights, combating discrimination, and fighting for social justice and better salaries in the United

States, but their concerns had largely shifted to the conditions that they experienced in the host society. As time elapsed, Mexican organizations started to form ethnic branches of mainstream voluntary and charitable organizations such as the Chicago Azteca Lions Club, the Licenciado Benito Juárez Lions Club in Chicago, the Chicago Mexican Lions Club, and the Azteca Lions Ladies Auxiliary, some of them still active under different names.[34]

In late July 1980, there was another effort to unify several Mexican organizations in a new federation in South Chicago. The Mexican Community Committee of South Chicago, the Mexican American Chamber of Commerce of South Chicago, the Club Patriótico Mexicano, the Club Social Latinoamericano, and League of United Latin American Citizens (LULAC) Councils 4003 and 313 formed an umbrella organization called the Federation of Mexican Organizations. Their principal mission was to promote social justice and access to services among the underserved Mexican migrant populations in South Chicago and elsewhere in the city. One of the purposes of the organization was to establish "a Mexican Federation similar to the Italian American Federation or the Jewish Federation" (Sulski 1980).

In the early 1980s, Mexican migrant communities in the Chicago metropolitan area reorganized to form new transnational social fields that connected their places of origin with their new communities of residence. As more Mexican migrants came to the city of Chicago to work in the service sectors and the manufacturing industries of the suburbs in the 1960s and 1970s, the density of people coming from the same village of origin grew considerably. These new migrants—especially the ones coming from the traditional sending areas in central Mexico—were bypassing the urban centers in Mexico and choosing Chicago and the metro area as their first or second destination after leaving their hometowns. Therefore, the majority of them had two frames of reference to define their national identities: the semihorizontal camaraderie stemming from rural hometowns where they were born, grew up, and went to school; and the more vertical attachments they felt toward the homeland. Similar to their previous counterparts from the early 1900s, the new Mexican organizations also tried to ban discussions of politics and religion in their meetings, but this time without much success because religious and political identities would now play a significant role in the formation of the new breed of organizations.

IRCA and the Formation of HTAs in Chicago

Between 1930 and 1960, the Mexican community in Chicago followed different paths of organization, creating diverse associations that catered to the needs of the first and second generation of migrants (Fernández 2005; Innis-Jiménez 2005). By the late 1960s, formal Mexican HTAs arrived to fill the void left by the early ethnic organizations when the contemporary (post-1965) wave of Mexican migrants started to settle. After the official end of the Bracero Program in 1964, many Mexican migrants continued to cross the border in search of work or family members with or without legal documents. Many of the founding members of contemporary Mexican HTAs came during this period and were able to regularize their status thanks to the Immigration Reform and Control Act (IRCA) of 1986, which offered an opportunity for legalization to millions of undocumented workers (Durand 1994).

In the late 1960s, along with the HTAs whose main activities focused on communities of origin, a new breed of Mexican organizations started to emerge in Chicago with the sole purpose of preserving the culture, the traditions, and Mexican holiday celebrations. For instance, in 1969, the Sociedad Cívica Mexicana de Illinois was established by a group of foreign-born Mexican migrants who wanted to preserve Mexican customs and traditions.[35] However, none of the newer Mexican social organizations were initially focused on improving the lives of their communities of origin in Mexico.

During the Mexican "stabilizing development" period (1950–1970), the Mexican-born population in the United States was the seventh largest foreign-born population in the country, with fewer than 600,000 immigrants by 1960. Just two decades later, the Mexican-born population became the largest foreign-born population in the United States (Gibson and Lennon 1999). The 1980s saw a dramatic increase in geographical networks density, and many small rural villages experienced mass migration of entire communities. Due to the high concentration of *paisanos* from the same village working in the same industries in Chicago, supporting the same soccer and baseball home-teams, and living in the same neighborhoods, the possibilities for organizing by topophilic identity became feasible.

Religious and spiritual attachments played an important role in the formation of the hometown clubs, as it was common for rural migrants to create prayer and devotion groups and committees to collect funds for bringing replicas of hometown patron saints and virgins to their new Catholic parishes in Chicago. After years of praying together, a sense of solidarity grew among members, and some leaders added new projects to their spiritual agendas. For instance, Salvador Balleño, the president of a pioneer hometown club from Michoacán, decided to create a reconstruction committee in 1986 to bring basic services to his hometown after reading the book of Nehemiah in a Bible study group in Chicago (Espinosa 1999). He was very moved by the story, in which the king of Persia grants his Hebrew cupbearer Nehemiah permission to return and reconstruct Jerusalem, the ruined city where his parents had been buried. Salvador wanted to follow this example and began making phone calls and knocking on doors to enlist the help of his *paisanos* living in Chicago, Carpentersville, and cities in Michigan, Texas, and California to discuss the construction of a new well to replace the one that had gone dry for three years in their hometown.

As the post-Bracero flow of migrants started to settle in Chicago, they established new organizations, but this time the unifying element was their village or town of origin, thus recasting their topophilic identities along with their national allegiance. Some of the early organizations in Chicago had their origins in soccer clubs or religious associations, such as the Club Deportivo Taximaroa from Michoacán, which formed in 1968–1969 (Badillo 2001; Pescador 2004), or the Club San Miguel Epejan, which started as a committee of Virgin of Guadalupe devotees in Aurora, Illinois. These organizations, along with the Club San Luis Potosí, organized in 1971 (Badillo 2001), are among the first HTAs of the post-1965 migration era in the Chicago metropolitan area.

By the 1970s, the fourth-largest urban Mexican American population was found in Chicago, after Los Angeles, San Antonio, and Houston. Their high numbers also helped to revitalize Mexican sports clubs in the area and encouraged the creation of larger athletic organizations. For example, the Chicago Latin American Soccer Association (CLASA), founded in 1967, now boasts 7,000 players, 340 teams, and 130 clubs in sixteen divisions that mimic the regional identities of famous Mexican and Latin American soccer clubs.[36] By the mid-1990s, there were already 6,000 Mexican soccer leagues across the United States supported by the Program of Attention for Mexican Communities Abroad (Thelen 1999). In the fall of 2000, as part of the celebration of Jaliscience migrant culture in the city, FEDEJAL, the Jaliscan HTA federation, invited Mexican anthropologist Andrés Fábregas Puig, the author of a book about *Las Chivas,* to offer a talk about the beloved *Chivas* team in a Cicero stadium (Fábregas Puig 2012).

The birth of HTAs in Chicago coincides with the renaissance of the cultural pluralism ideology in the American public discourse that occurred in the 1960s and was accompanied by its practical implementation in the legal system and public institutions. Local established nonprofit community service institutions offered a helping hand to some of the pioneer leaders of the new organizations who at times were simultaneously active in HTAs and in the more established nonprofit organizations. A good case in point is Gonzalo Arroyo, the first president of the Federation of Michoacán Clubs of Illinois, who in the late 1990s simultaneously served as executive director of Family Focus, a well-known family-oriented nonprofit community service organization in Aurora.

For hometown leaders and members, the friendlier local context of reception offered the opportunity to gather around difference and make identity claims salient in the public institutional and legal sphere, albeit marginally. HTA leaders were interested in re-creating the culture and values from the Mexican rural countryside that had been absent in the agendas of previous Mexican organizations formed by educated urban leaders from the middle classes in the late 1960s and 1970s. Thanks to the amnesty granted by IRCA in 1986, many migrants began returning to their communities of origin more frequently and gradually became aware of the economic disparities that many rural towns were facing due to economic restructuring. Each return trip from the United States meant facing the shocking reality that many of the comforts of modernity such as running water and electricity that they enjoyed on a daily basis were lacking in many of their communities. Many migrants still had family members living in Mexico and wanted to do something to improve those conditions.

Due to the relative prosperity in U.S. labor markets, some migrants had a modest surplus income to spend in the reconstruction of their small towns and villages. Once migrants felt more settled in Chicago, many organized weekly get-togethers to share a friendly soccer match, eat some homemade ethnic food, and chat about their towns' most pressing needs. At a time when the Mexican state was enjoying relative economic stability and a relatively peaceful environment, migrant allegiances turned to their villages instead of the "important national problems." The lack of effective electoral democracy, the growing social opposition to the North American Free Trade Agreement (NAFTA), and the conflict in Chiapas were not on the initial list of priorities for HTAs. Instead, HTAs were working to fight government corruption in their local villages and demanding more services and basic public infrastructure. Local problems in their new communities—including bilingual-bicultural education for their children and preventing gang violence—were among the causes that hometown members were pursuing in their new places of residence. The national allegiance to the Mexican state was thus renegotiated as their topophilic identities became the glue that held together these organizations at their initial stage.

There were some preconditions that facilitated the reemergence of strong Mexican organizations with a binational agenda. For instance, the reinvigoration and increased scale of transnational connections in the 1980s and 1990s were, in part, facilitated by the transportation and communication revolutions. Telephone connections were available in many Mexican rural towns by the mid-1980s, and information about collective needs spread faster. This and other technological advances, such as cheaper air transportation, fax machines, the Internet, and handheld video cameras, helped to coordinate infrastructure development plans between physically absent financial sponsors and local collective remittance beneficiaries (Bada 2003a, 2003b). Moreover, in the late 1980s and early 1990s Mexico experienced a process of economic decentralization that granted more decision-making power to municipalities but also put new pressures and challenges on municipalities that were used to a highly centralized federal system. As a result, newly decentralized local governments were given new responsibilities and resources to deliver and improve public services for small communities far from capital cities.[37] But resources were not always equally distributed, and many remote rural villages were frequently not included in the allocation of resources for basic infrastructure. Therefore, for municipal presidents interested in multiplying resources for building new basic infrastructure, it became a good idea to call their *paisanos* abroad and ask them for help.

In the 1990s, the Mexican Ministry of Foreign Affairs embarked on the task of reaching out to all types of Mexican organizations, including the more established national organizations such as the National Council of La Raza, the League of United Latin American Citizens, and the Mexican American Legal Defense and Educational Fund. Under this new strategy, the Mexican consulate in Chicago sent its staff to find out how the migrant communities were organizing at the grassroots level and invited them to participate in the new institutional programs designed to incorporate them as members of the nation with partial political rights because they were still not allowed to vote absentee in presidential elections. After preliminary reports from hired consultants, consulate officials realized that many sectors of the Mexican community had been organized by village of origin since the late 1960s and had been donating considerable amounts of money for development projects in their communities of origin, taking advantage of the National Solidarity Program (PRONASOL) started by President Salinas de Gortari in 1988.

Many Mexican hometown clubs in Chicago and the suburbs were familiar with PRONASOL and contributed money to carry out infrastructure projects to benefit their communities in the late 1980s. The PRONASOL was a government program established in 1988 by President Salinas de Gortari to increase social spending in projects for education, health, transportation, and regional development. Among its goals, the program fostered intensive grassroots activity across Mexico through direct participation of its beneficiaries in project execution and implementation (Bailey 1994).

Eventually, PRONASOL managed to coordinate some infrastructure projects with a few organized migrant groups in Chicago and elsewhere in the United States. Besides the small development projects organized and funded with the collaboration with municipalities through PRONASOL's International Solidarity Program, Chicago HTAs financed many reconstruction projects without government funds, using the networks they had through family members and municipal authorities, virtually without the intervention of federal and state governments (Iskander 2010). Thus, when the Mexican government established an outreach program to organize the migrant communities in Chicago and other places in the United States, government officials realized that once again, as had happened in the early 1900s with the Comisiones Honoríficas, many migrant groups were already organized. However, the active "extended incorporation" that the government carried out during the early 1990s was definitely instrumental in increasing the number of organizations interested in the development of their hometowns.

In the early 1990s, the consulates offered guidance for navigating the complex state and municipal bureaucracies to obtain the necessary government funds to rebuild their communities, many of which were impoverished and abandoned after two decades of neoliberal economic restructuring and blatant neglect from all levels of government. In so doing, the Mexican government tried to exercise some control over a population that, by their sheer numbers and undocumented status, was not easy to find or document. The main difference from the strategies followed during the early twentieth century was that the Mexican government did not ask emigrants to return to their communities after a temporary stay in the United States. Instead, the government asked them to invest their hard-earned money in the homeland. In fact, contrary to the limited engagement that the nationalist state had usually maintained with the diaspora, President Carlos Salinas de Gortari's neoliberal reforms (1988–1994) actually promoted and produced the conditions whereby HTAs were further encouraged to grow.

The move from a subtle incorporation as full members of the Mexican society in the early 1900s to an extensive incorporation at the end of the twentieth century marked a turning point in the understanding of the nation-state and the national identity. Like most states, Mexico historically rejected dual nationality, but thanks to a constitutional amendment to the Nationality Law that went into effect in 1998, Mexican migrants who had adopted a foreign nationality and the first generation born to Mexican nationals abroad were offered an initial five-year window to regain their Mexican nationality as part of the efforts made by the Mexican government to embrace migrants living abroad as members of the nation (Donner 1994; Gómez-Robledo Verduzco 1994; Vargas 1998). Thus, the possibility of retaining Mexican nationality rights after acquiring U.S. citizenship was helpful for increasing the civic participation of Mexican migrants in homeland affairs.

In 1995, the Mexican consulate in Chicago recorded thirty-five Mexican HTAs in the metropolitan area. By February 2011, the Mexican consulate listed 275 HTAs in its database, representing seventeen states of origin and the Federal District. The vast majority of the leaders and board members of HTAs are naturalized citizens or legal permanent residents. These associations are organized into eighteen federations and the Confederation of Mexican Federations. By the end of the twentieth century, topophilic attachments of Mexican migrants led to larger organizations but within the confines of states of origin. The success of nationally oriented confederations—located in Los Angeles and Chicago—has been modest, but member organizations are trying to increase visibility among larger diaspora charity networks from Latin America and elsewhere as well as among mainstream nonprofit organizations. The central objective of these organizations is to advocate public policy changes while fostering the organization of Latin American migrant groups to work for the development of healthy communities, both in countries of origin and destination. At this moment, Mexican migrant-led organizations hold great promise for increasing the quality and breadth of migrants' social capital while brightening the possibilities for the consolidation of a robust civil society where immigrants have direct representation in societies of Mexico, Latin America, and the United States.

CONTINUITIES AND CHANGES IN MEXICAN MIGRANT ORGANIZATIONS

Contemporary Mexican HTAs in Chicago appeared in the late 1960s and early 1970s to fill the void left by the disappearance of the mutual aid organizations of the early twentieth century. These new forms of migrant organizing kept the commitment to function as self-help groups as the mutual aid societies did, but their civic binationality became anchored to the local place of origin as a way to re-create a topophilic identity. Whereas prior Mexican organizations had mostly concentrated on addressing the needs of Mexican migrants in their new communities, and their connections with Mexican institutions—that is, federal and state governments—was minimal, contemporary HTAs decided to connect with communities of origin to bring development back while maintaining culture and traditions from the rural countryside.

The selectivity of Mexican migratory flows after the 1960s produced a large population of rural migrants with low levels of formal education who did not believe that their cultural, communitarian, spiritual, and social agendas were adequately represented in the existing Mexican civic organizations.[38] The local context of reception in Chicago and its metropolitan area allowed migrants a quicker access to relatively better-paid jobs in manufacturing and the service sector economy compared to rural migrants working in the fields elsewhere. In the favorable climate produced by the legalization program of 1986, migrant incorporation into churches and sports clubs offered the possibility to create independent topophilic organizations that were originally supported by philanthropic and civic institutions whose origins were frequently tied to nineteenth-century immigrant and religious philanthropies.[39]

Over time, local connections between rural migrants and small towns and villages expanded to the state and national levels, leading to the creation of practices of civic binationality in which HTAs pursued simultaneous agendas in two national spaces. While the binational connections of early twentieth-century Mexican migrant organizations in Chicago established an important precedent, cross-border connections were mostly conducted between the federal government and migrant organizations that, for the most part, did not incorporate topophilic attachment preservation as an important goal of their organizations. Although every migratory wave exhibits unique features to connect with the homeland, and early migrant organizations did not engage in highly visible practices of civic binationality, the study of early transnational connections of Mexican migrants is useful for understanding the roots of current practices of Mexican binational civic engagement and the transformation of migrant organizational identities throughout the long process of immigrant incorporation into U.S. society.

Compared to the early twentieth-century relations between Mexican migrants in Chicago and the Mexican nation-state, the new relationship between the Mexican government and its diaspora is not just different in density and scale but also in kind. The connections now include national government discourses welcoming all Mexicans living beyond the national borders and subnational discourses addressing more geographically intimate connections that go beyond the recovery of a migrant's political rights or the infrastructure needs of communities of origin. These days, Mexican HTAs and federations are demanding a change in state-society relations to incorporate migrant voices and direct representation in public policy decisions and new legislation affecting migrant lives on both sides of the border. In Chicago, HTAs have joined a long list of Mexican, Latino, and Mexican American organizations creating a diverse civil society that embraces an oscillatory mode of incorporation and refuses to accept a linear immigrant assimilation path.

꙰

CHAPTER 3

GENEALOGIES OF
HOMETOWN ASSOCIATIONS

Previous studies on transnational communities have addressed the multiple civic engagements of Zacatecan hometown federations in Southern California, the transnational lives of Poblano migrants in New York, and the transnational topographies of Oaxacans from San Juan Mixtepec across Mexican-U.S. geographies. These studies offer a clear picture of the different political and geographical scales in which transnational social spaces are created.[1] The majority of studies on Mexico-U.S. civic binationality conclude that the increased visibility of Mexican hometown associations (HTAs) and federations in the new millennium is the consequence of a drastic change in Mexico's foreign policy toward its diaspora first implemented in the late 1980s. However, the local and translocal institutional contexts that enabled the emergence of HTAs before the 1990s in metropolitan centers in the United States have been insufficiently studied.[2] When Mexico's federal government did not show much interest in addressing the needs of its growing emigrant population beyond offering consular services, Mexican migrants used their experience in rural organization to express solidarity, ease the shock of their uprooting, preserve their culture, and provide welfare services to those unemployed or temporarily disabled. They also exchanged tips to find higher-paying jobs, fought against inequalities in the workplace, and demanded the inclusion of their cultural symbols of spirituality at their new houses of worship.

In Chicago, Michoacán HTAs formed their first umbrella federation in 1997 with fourteen clubs, barely one year after Governor Víctor Manuel Tinoco Rubí visited them for the first time.[3] Before that, most HTAs had preferred to work in isolation or had directly collaborated with municipal governments or local priests rather than the state government, because political instability in the late 1980s and early 1990s produced several interim governors, and attention to migrant communities was not a priority for the state government.[4]

In 1999, a decade after the inauguration of the Federal Program for the Attention of Mexican Communities Abroad (PACME), the Mexican consulate in Chicago registered 125 hometown organizations in its database. One decade later, there were 275 Mexican HTAs registered in metropolitan Chicago, the vast majority interested in obtaining matching funds from the government to finance collective remittance projects in their hometowns. However, the origins of Chicago's HTAs are varied, and many came together to provide an opportunity for family social events and functioned as a bridge for social incorporation through sports, faith, and the celebration of holidays and family traditions, a process that Michael Peter Smith and Matt Bakker (2008) refer to as the second face of transnational citizenship. In this spontaneous process of formation, hometown clubs received support from settled immigrants, educational institutions, churches, nonprofit organizations, community colleges, local universities, and social service Latino organizations.

In this chapter, I suggest that participation in HTAs does not come at the expense of engagement in U.S. civic life, but rather reinforces civic engagement in the U.S. context.[5] In the following sections, I offer a roadmap of the multiple economic, social, and political factors leading to the emergence of HTAs among transnational Michoacán communities in Chicagoacán, including the role of economic liberalization, topophilic attachments derived from trust and friendships, spiritual needs, prior socialization experiences, and engagement with Chicago-based institutions. Finally, I also focus on the gendered division of labor among clubs and the challenges to engage the second generation in club activities.

LEAVING THE RURAL COUNTRYSIDE

Artemio Arreola works as a community organizer at a Chicago immigrant advocacy organization in Chicago's downtown. He migrated to Chicago from Acuitzio del Canje, a small rural town located 20 miles south of the state capital of Morelia in August 1989, and, as he tells it, "By September, I was taking a CTA bus to participate in the Little Village Independence Day Parade."[6] As the eldest child of a family of eleven, he got the chance to attend La Huerta, an agricultural self-sufficient high school in Morelia, while working part-time. Soon, he realized how expensive it was to pay for college and settled for a degree as a computer-programming technician. Now in his forties, Arreola has spent almost half his life in Chicago. He left his community in his twenties after repeated attempts to find job security, believing in the promise that getting an education was the key ingredient to leave backbreaking agricultural work behind. Before migrating, he was an active citizen, engaged with *cursillos* (Christian Base Communities), supporting teacher strikes during a brief stint as a middle-school teacher, and affiliated with the Confederation of National Popular Organizations (CNOP) when he worked as store manager for DICONSA, the state-sponsored rural store network.[7] Arreola was also active in electoral politics and ran in the state legislative primaries, representing one of the democratic currents within the Revolutionary Institutional Party (PRI) against the incumbent old rural bosses of his community, which effectively meant running against the political group of his father, an *ejidatario* (rightsholder of communal land) who returned permanently to Acuitzio in 1972 after several trips to California in the 1960s. In 1988, Arreola lost his bid in the state primaries in one of the first real electoral competitions.[8] As a result, he became an outcast in his family and decided to devote more time to his work at DICONSA. He sought to expand operations to sell fresh produce and other perishables, but after the mid-1980s, most rural credit state agencies disappeared, and he had to borrow money from a loan shark, with a 13 percent monthly interest rate.

Soon, he was paying too much interest, and the only way to repay the loan was to join a younger brother who already lived in Chicago. With the help of his brother, he found work on the night shift in a plastics factory in the suburb of Wheeling, where he met his wife, a U.S.-born citizen who grew up in Mexico City. Arreola says these were the worst two years of his life. He did physical labor and had to put up with a German supervisor who yelled at the Mexican, Guatemalan, and Salvadoran workers and refused to allow bathroom breaks, among many other abuses.[9] However, he noticed he had a union because he was able to read some English, and he carefully checked the deductions in his pay. With the help of a bilingual coworker, he went to the city Department of Labor and asked for help to find his union and learn about basic worker rights. Within a year, he was elected to represent his coworkers at his local, demanded a contract renegotiation, and requested translation of the contract into Spanish since 90 percent of the workforce was from Latin America.[10]

During his first five years in Chicago, Arreola had many doubts about staying because his life revolved around long hours of work, and he did not find purpose in his life until the day he was invited to attend a spiritual retreat in Spanish offered by a Polish Catholic church in Chicago's Ukrainian Village. During the retreat, one of the instructors said, "In the land of the blind, the one-eyed man is king." At that moment, he decided he was the one most able to fight for social justice in his new community. His decision to invite fellow Mexicans to form a club to finance infrastructure projects in Acuitzio would come almost a decade later, when the North American Free Trade Agreement (NAFTA) left many rural communities without opportunities to make a living from agriculture, as cheap imports of corn and wheat gradually inundated grain markets in Michoacán and state subsidies did not reach the poorest farmers in the 1990s.[11]

Arreola's life is somewhat typical among the most successful leaders and members of contemporary HTAs. They are usually the sons, daughters, grandsons, and granddaughters of migrants who came to the United States in the twentieth century to work on the railroad as braceros or came as undocumented migrants to work in foundries and factories. Some of these migrants brought their families and settled in Chicago in the 1960s, and others returned to their rural villages. Some of the pioneer HTA members of organizations created in the 1960s and 1970s first came to work as agricultural laborers in California but later made connections through friends and family networks to work in manufacturing, food services, and construction in Chicago suburbs.

In the late 1970s, many rural communities in Michoacán were uprooted when the government began an accelerated process of increased urbanization and economic liberalization. Out-migration was encouraged by the family remittances of those who left after the 1960s, which helped subsidize agricultural production and family reproduction but also financed more emigration.[12] In the 1980s, many rural towns in Michoacán received phone lines, television sets, satellite antennas, washing machines, refrigerators, in-house toilet facilities, and other comforts of modernity thanks to family remittances sent mainly from Mexico City, Tijuana, and the United States.[13] With these new technologies, households with domestic and international migrants were able to compare their lives as rural peasants with the glamorous life of soap operas and Hollywood movies portraying urban lifestyles, catching a glimpse of urban life and its many unaffordable amenities.[14]

In 2001, I traveled to Las Cruces, a rural village of fewer than 300 inhabitants in the municipality of Churintzio in northwestern Michoacán, and marveled at the Jacuzzis that HTA club members from Blue Island had installed during temporary returns to enjoy patron saint festivities.[15] While some club members had managed to bring their families to the United States and lived with their nuclear and extended families in Chicago, others were still planning to save enough money for a permanent return and invested their earnings in household amenities in Mexico. For example, Arcadio García's family was patiently waiting for him to return permanently, after twenty years of commuting to work between Las Cruces and Blue Island to save enough money to buy a plot of land and some cattle to maintain a livelihood in Mexico. His wife joined him in Chicago in the late 1980s, but could not endure life in isolation in an apartment building and went back. During my visit, Marissa, Arcadio's eldest daughter, showed me her favorite place in the village, a beautiful tree on the path to the cornfields. There, Marissa and her teenage female friends would reenact their favorite scene of the movie *Titanic*, pretending to be Kate Winslet, using the base of the tree as a ship's bow. The scene is a reminder of the power of mass media to make people in the rural South view their conditions of exclusion and poverty in an entirely different light. As Oscar Chacón (2011: 468), a Salvadoran American immigrant rights activist, explains, "The overwhelming dominance of U.S. communications networks in Latin America and the Caribbean have been delivering a daily invitation to people to come to paradise, namely the United States of America, where the good life is."

In the 1970s, when the Mexican economy attempted to integrate rural labor markets with urban economies, Michoacán peasants living in the countryside had few options: those with land were able to hold on to their *ejidos*, or small private property, for subsistence farming, while those without land became laborers in nearby semirural manufacturing plants that offered job opportunities to those displaced by the Green Revolution. However, manufacturing jobs rarely provided social benefits, job security, or stable salaries. Many worked by piece rate. Rosendo Sánchez, a member of Chehuayo Club, remembers: "I made good money by piece rate in an upholstery factory in 1978 in Morelia. I worked full time and finished middle school by attending night school for workers. However the salary was not enough to pay for high school without family support so I migrated and found landscaping work in Lake Forest. Supposedly, in a couple of years I would be able to save enough and return to enroll as a full-time student. I soon learned those were just rumors."[16] Despite less-than-dreamed-for conditions in the United States, for those with family networks, going to the United States became a feasible economic alternative to mitigate the effects of economic globalization. These migrants were the reluctant participants in a new global hyperspecialized division of labor, where peripheral economies exported cheap labor to boost stagnant productivity in industrial economies.

In the 1960s, 59.4 percent of the population in the state of Michoacán (1.1 million) was considered rural (Zepeda Patterson 1988). The lack of access to secondary education in the small rural towns throughout the state forced second- and third-generation children of *ejidatarios* to look for an education outside their communities as an alternative to work in the fields. Many were interested in becoming veterinarians or agricultural engineers to climb the social ladder without abandoning their rural lives permanently, but it was not until 1968 that Michoacán increased the number of high schools from three to ten across the state (Ochoa Serrano and Sánchez Díaz 2003).[17]

By the early 1980s, Mexico began to abandon the state-led model of industrialization through import substitution and the fledgling bourgeoisie began to push for a liberalized and privatized economy, firmly opposing populist politics as a means to fulfill the unfinished promises of the Mexican Revolution. Between 1970 and 2010, the percentage of the population working in agriculture in the state of Michoacán fell from 62 percent to 21 percent. This local process reflects larger national trends. Between 1994 and 1997, almost half (46.9 percent) of *ejidos* in Mexico had financial problems linked to agricultural production, and their dependent households had to diversify income sources (Aylwin 2003). According to the 2010 census, only 31.3 percent of the population in the state of Michoacán still lives in localities with fewer than 2,500 inhabitants (INEGI 2012). As a result of this increased urbanization, many of the state-sponsored mechanisms to support agricultural production were eliminated, forcing people to migrate to urban areas.

The demise of the rural sector led to population increases in medium and large-size cities as a result of migration, but few public resources were distributed to finance the much-needed basic infrastructure for localities that remained with small populations during the urbanization process. For example, in the 1970s, 20 million Mexicans (41.3 percent of the total population) lived in localities with fewer than 2,500 inhabitants. By 2010, 26 million Mexicans (23.2 percent of the population) lived dispersed in small rural localities with fewer than 2,500 inhabitants (INEGI 2011). The current average population size for these localities is 126 residents (García Espinosa 2010: 350). Thus, there is a simultaneous process of urbanization and rural isolation in which seven out of ten Mexicans (76.8 percent) now live in a city, leaving small rural villages with fewer resources to fend for themselves against economic liberalization, triggering processes of internal and international migration.

In the 1980s, due to the rapid growth of cities, 53.3 percent of the state population lived in regional urban centers, a phenomenon that produced the creation of shantytowns on the outskirts of the capital city. In an effort to retain the labor force in the state and avoid more migration to Mexico City, the federal government began to regularize irregular dwellings in Morelia. According to Juan Luis Calderón Hinojosa, who was a state legislator and candidate for the municipal mayoralty of Morelia for the National Action Party (PAN) in 2001, the urban revitalization project in Morelia failed because "we increased the number of schools and educated thousands who came to Morelia, but we failed to create jobs to retain them. Therefore, they were pushed to their second migration and left to the United States since migration to the city did not solve the drop in rural household income because of all the errors made by previous public policies."[18] In the 1990s, 38.4 percent of the population in Michoacán lived in rural communities with fewer than 2,500 people, and there were few urban centers. In 1990, there were only sixteen cities with more than 15,000 inhabitants; by 2005, the number increased to twenty-five (García Espinosa 2010; INEGI 2011). Yet urbanization did not provide enough jobs, and between 2005 and 2010 more than 100,000 Michoacanos left the state in search of better opportunities in the United States, making it the third largest exodus in the country for that period (INEGI 2011).[19]

In the 1980s and 1990s, after living one or two decades in Chicago, many HTA members gradually came to terms with the economic devastation of small-scale farming as a viable subsistence model, and few envisioned a permanent return to live off the land like many of their parents did during the Bracero Program (1942–1964). Some men brought their wives and started new families in Chicago, while helping their parents buy seeds and fertilizer for the annual harvest in Mexico so they could hold on to their cherished patches of land. Gradually, many Michoacanos began to postpone plans for a permanent return after bringing their nuclear families to Chicago. However, the settlement process in Chicago did not mean that they were no longer attached to their birthplaces, as several became interested in participating in the collective solution of their hometown problems, especially after finding modest income stability.

FINDING ECONOMIC OPPORTUNITIES IN CHICAGO

While changes in the economic structure of the Mexican countryside were occurring, the United States was experiencing a transformation of the manufacturing sector that had provided the working class with the basic means of survival at the end of the Second World War, thanks to a pact between the state, workers, and unions. This pact had established an increase in productivity in exchange for sharing a small fraction of the profits with workers. Economic development in the United States from Franklin D. Roosevelt's New Deal to the late 1960s was based on mass production and mass consumption, with an emphasis on the domestic labor market during the late Fordist capitalist era.[20] However, as competitive capitalism transformed to monopoly capitalism and U.S. corporations lost their competitive advantage to Germany and Japan in the early 1970s, low-skill jobs were increasingly exported to countries with surpluses of low-skill workers in peripheral regions of international capitalism, in the corporations' search of low wages and higher profits.

For Chicago's manufacturing sector, the decline of decent-wage blue-collar unionized jobs in manufacturing left workers without high school degrees without attractive opportunities and pushed many out to the illegitimate labor market, especially in the case of African American males. Between 1967 and 1987, Chicago lost a full 60 percent of its manufacturing jobs, and many industries relocated to the suburbs, attracted by tax incentives (Wilson 1999). Between 1969 and 1974, overall employment in the suburbs increased by 18 percent, comprising 220,000 jobs at a moment when Mexican migrants were arriving in great numbers and taking up residence in urban neighborhoods that whites had abandoned during ethnic succession processes or going to the suburbs in search of new manufacturing jobs (De Genova 2005).

While the agricultural peasant economy in rural Michoacán continued its march toward obsolescence in the new market economy, transformations in the manufacturing sector in Chicago offered possibilities for new migrants to take some jobs in light manufacturing in Chicago and its suburbs. In 1926, Manuel Gamio estimated that 20 percent of Mexicans living in the United States were born in Michoacán (Gamio 1930). By the early 1980s, Chicago's Mexican population had reached a critical mass, and the new global division of labor propelled an increased interconnection between long-term migrants and newer migrants from Michoacán, perpetuating a cycle that began early in the twentieth century.

At the beginning of the twenty-first century, the Mexican government estimated that 16 percent of Mexicans living in Illinois came from Michoacán—the largest share from a single Mexican state. Several domestic factors combined to produce the increase in migration and subsequent settlement among Michoacán migrants in Chicago and its suburbs: the reactivation of family networks from the Bracero period, the Immigration Reform and Control Act (IRCA) of 1986, the crisis of affordable housing and employment in traditional destinations in California, harsh penalties for undocumented border-crossings after the immigration legislation of 1996, and decreased circularity of migration due to increased smuggling costs.[21] The labor histories of three founding members of Michoacán HTAs formed in the 1970s, 1980s, and 1990s offer a human face to these seemingly detached processes of international globalization.

Anita de la Cruz was born in 1947 in San Miguel Epejan, a rural agricultural community of 555 houses that experienced the massive migration of its residents in the 1980s and 1990s to Aurora, Illinois. The community is now nearly a ghost town. According to census figures, 22 percent of houses are abandoned, but local residents estimate that almost half of the housing is empty. When I interviewed her, Anita was waiting to retire to be able to spend six months in San Miguel Epejan and six months in Aurora. She legalized her status through IRCA, and when we met in 2005, she was studying to pass the citizenship test since she had failed it previously due to her limited literacy, as she only completed three years of primary school. Anita came to Aurora in 1979 to join her husband after suffering the separation of her family for a decade during which her husband commuted back and forth between San Miguel Epejan and Aurora without her. Anita was close to her due date for their fourth child when they hired a smuggler in Tijuana to take her to the United States and her mother offered to take care of their first three children. As she recalls, "In one day, la migra [the Immigration and Naturalization Service] caught us three or four times. And there was one day that I will never forget because I was very close to my due date, swollen. I walked all night over a hill, then crawled through a tunnel; we were very close when la migra caught us again with their dogs. We came back to Tijuana's cantinas to find a new smuggler and failed again. It wasn't until somebody suggested we go to Colonia Libertad that we were able to cross and managed to get to Aurora."

Anita did not work right away. But she soon realized that her husband was living off loans from friends to send money to their children, and so she began looking for a job without telling him, since he did not want her to work outside the house. She eventually found a job in 1980, working the night shift in a Christmas tree and Halloween decoration factory, where 80 percent of the workforce was Mexican, mostly female. She stayed there for twenty-two years until the factory closed, firing all employees, and moved operations to Ciudad Juárez. After that, she found work in a multinational company that assembles mail order catalogs, but she had to accept lower wages. She is proud of the sacrifices she made for her nine children and the educational opportunities they had attending public schools, later serving in the U.S. Marines and the U.S. Army.[22] All her children are U.S. citizens. Anita wants to retire in San Miguel Epejan because she tells me that her neighborhood in Aurora has become unsafe and she misses the freedom she feels in San Miguel Epejan.

Pablo Vivanco is a founding member of La Purísima Soccer Club and a dual citizen. In his youth, he became alienated from Mexican electoral politics since the day his father arrived with his first electoral card and asked him to vote for Miguel de la Madrid Hurtado in the 1982 presidential election. His hometown did not have a high school when he grew up, and he only was able to finish grammar school. In 2005, 72 percent of the population fifteen years and older had not completed the nine years of mandatory basic education in Pablo's municipality.[23] La Purísima is a community in northern Michoacán with a long history of migration since the Bracero Program (Cockcroft 2005) and large concentrations of migrants in Bryant, Texas; North Hollywood, California; and Carpentersville, Illinois. Pablo's first labor migration was to Houston in the late 1970s to work in a screw factory when he was fifteen years old. He tried to cross without documents with fourteen close friends, but one of them died in the desert. He moved to Cary, Illinois, in 1983 to join his brother and worked as dishwasher in a restaurant. Later, a migrant from Guadalajara referred him to a better job working in landscaping and then in a paint factory in Carpentersville. He settled there at a time when there were very few migrants from his hometown. But he remembers that in 1986 many people from his hometown moved from California to Chicago, fleeing unemployment. "I was still single and had to host loads of *paisanos* in my tiny apartment because it was very difficult to find lodging for so many who came from California."[24] Pablo now owns a small highway construction company that offers employment to six of his coethnics from La Purísima. His wife works in a nearby factory that provides health insurance for the family. Multiple injuries to her hand suffered at the workplace left her with a permanent disability. She did not receive proper worker compensation; however, she cannot afford to lose her job. Their four U.S.-born children attend school and refuse to return permanently to live in La Purísima, despite annual visits and Pablo's subtle yet constant suggestions to resettle there. Their eldest daughter attends a community college in Elgin, Illinois.[25]

Rosa de la Vega came to Cicero, Illinois, in 1995 with a high school education and a degree in preschool art education to join her husband, who was a legal permanent resident working in construction. As a newly wedded nineteen-year-old wife, she was afraid of her mother-in-law and did not want to move to her husband's household in Álvaro Obregón, the municipal town center of her husband's village. She soon became pregnant, and her aspirations to become a teacher dissolved quickly as she found a full-time job as a nanny, making $80 working thirty-five hours per week—well below the state minimum wage. However, for Rosa, this salary was a small fortune compared to the $20 a week she made in her town washing and ironing to pay for school expenses. During her baby shower, she met other women from her hometown, and soon there were enough birthdays and baby showers to keep in touch with her *paisanos*. Thanks to valuable information that her social network provided, Rosa was able to take weekend courses in Spanish at Triton College on early childhood education and eventually opened her own state-licensed day-care center after her husband learned at the Casa Juan Diego youth center that she qualified for adjustment of status through section 245(i) of the immigration law. As news of the successes of HTAs from neighboring villages spread among former residents of Álvaro Obregón in Chicago and after the visibility of Federation of Michoacán Clubs in Illinois (FEDECMI) increased, her social group became interested in organizing fund-raisers to do church renovations for the town parish as they did not want to seem like the less organized transnational community and sought to imitate their peers. In a sense, they were transforming the traditional character of self-help among intimate social networks cultivated through rural childhood friendships and adjusting it to the peer pressure of being recognized as social benefactors both in the public arena of rural Michoacán and in their new social milieu in Chicago.[26]

As migrants from Michoacán diversified and dispersed in the United States, many found low-wage jobs in light manufacturing, the service sector, and the construction industry. Achieving their goals of saving enough money to return permanently was taking longer than expected. Wives and family members grew impatient with the long wait, risking dangerous crossings to reunite with their family. As the literature of migrant settlement shows, the goal of returning permanently begins to fade as wives and children join husbands in the United States. When a migrant family stays in the United States for more than ten years, their chances of returning permanently are drastically diminished, as grown children and wives refuse to return. But the *dream* of returning always lives on.[27] In addition, the lack of access to land for women became an extra anchoring device to the United States for those who joined their families. Without any direct ownership of agricultural lands, there were no obligations or desire to return permanently. Only a minority of women inherited land from their parents or husbands because land inheritance was traditionally reserved for men.

Creating Networks of Trust among Friends and Family

Most survey research finds that in general, there is a decline in trust among those living in the United States, but it might be that researchers have not developed adequate instruments to measure it more accurately.[28] For example, the vast majority of HTAs produce an increase in networks of trust among their members, but their operations are informal, and few decide to register as independent nonprofits or join the formally registered umbrella state federations of HTAs. For many HTA members, their decision to preserve informality is actually due to low levels of trust in government and its regulatory institutions; consequently, it takes a long time to build trust toward institutions in their new places of residence. In Mexico, strong, secular, and autonomous civil society institutions are relatively new, and civic engagement used to be traditionally tied to government-sponsored initiatives, which created a culture of skepticism due to the constant failure of government to deliver on its many promises.[29]

Michoacano HTAs' trust networks are quite interesting because they defy common expectations if we consider the low levels of trust among those living in Michoacán. In Michoacán, less than 25 percent of citizens believe that most people deserve to be trusted, regardless of their income level. The results come from a United Nations Development Program (UNDP) survey conducted in 2007, the year the federal government sent the federal army to this state in an action that is considered as the formal inauguration of President Calderón strategy to combat drug trafficking. The high levels of social violence and public insecurity are cited as one of the most common reasons to explain the lack of interpersonal trust. However, the modest use of social networks to identify and solve common needs does not extend beyond the nuclear and extended family members, and the number of people seeking help is higher than the number of those willing to offer help. Family social networks are mostly activated to solve urgent monetary problems and to find employment. Few people reach out to neighbors and friends to solve common needs because a large proportion finds it very difficult to reach common ground (UNDP 2008).

Therefore, despite their relative invisibility in the world of formal nonprofit voluntary associations, social attachments cultivated through HTAs play a fundamental role in incorporating recent migrants into their new societies, while simultaneously offering opportunities to remember and re-create the social world they left behind. As Anthony Giddens (1990) and other social theorists predicted, the expansion of communication technologies creates digital diasporas and Internet-based social networks that unite communities across borders, helping to reduce space-time distances, dis-embed social processes from a limited geographical area, and lift social relations out of their physical context. These new technologies of globalization lead to groups and organizations that are more informal, fluid, flexible, and, consequently, less visible.

As Jews, Japanese, and Chinese who migrated from the same town or province founded *landmanshaft vereins* (homeland societies), *kai*, and village associations,[30] social cohesion among Michoacanos from rural villages aided in the formation of *clubes de oriundos* anchored in common backgrounds that give rise to solidarity sui generis among fellow nationals, family, and friends—what Emile Durkheim would call "mechanical solidarity" (1984). Mechanical solidarity is expressed through contemporary Mexican HTAs in the moral rules that bind all members to pursue a common goal: improve the well-being of fellow countrymen and women in Chicago and of those left behind in rural Mexico. These informal associations fill the void left by the Hull House and other immigrant settlement houses after some of these institutions transformed their mission and devoted their energies to addressing the needs of refugees and other economically disadvantaged minorities (Wucker 2006).

Among the most widely recognized and successful organizations of U.S. migrant communities are the informal rotating savings and credit associations

(ROSCAs), commonly known as *tandas*.[31] Among HTA members, social bonding frequently begins in small *tandas* among friends and family. Later the *tandas* transform into funerary associations to provide emergency funds for widows. When HTAs organize a fund-raising event to finance a project in rural Mexico, they usually choose a community member with a good previous track record organizing *tandas* or social events to administer funds. Surprisingly, incidents of members stealing funds are rare, but when they do occur, they lead to the gradual demise of group cohesion, since the erosion of trust is not easily repaired.[32] The long-term success of HTAs and their eventual transformation into formal, non-profit, membership-based organizations depend on sustained mutual reciprocity and trust among members. After small migrant clubs evolve into formally registered federations of HTAs, they maintain the connection to member organizations through shared moral values of civic engagement and transnational moral communities,[33] where constituents are willing to subordinate their private interests for the sake of larger goals to benefit all Mexican and Latino migrant communities across borders, beyond their co-ethnic group.[34]

In 1996, after the implementation of highly punitive immigration laws in the United States, it became increasingly difficult for migrants, especially undocumented ones, to gain access to social services, educational opportunities, affordable housing, and English-as-a-second-language (ESL) classes in the Chicago metropolitan area. As welfare services decreased as a result of economic policies aimed at reducing the role of the state in addressing social inequality, private individuals or groups took independent action—spurred by motives ranging from self-help to traditional charity—to provide social services that were previously offered by city governments.

Many HTA members were able to advocate for community services thanks to their modest educational attainment. In a small survey that I conducted with sixty-six members of Michoacano HTAs between 2001 and 2003 in Aurora, Illinois; Los Angeles; and Ciudad Hidalgo, Michoacán, I found that members are more educated than the general Mexican migrant labor force in the United States. They tend to have an average of 10 years of education compared to 7.9 years of schooling then exhibited by the forty-four million Mexicans participating in the labor force in Mexico (Migration News 2007). Similar levels of educational attainment (nine years on average) were found in a larger survey of 150 Michoacano HTA members living in the Chicago metropolitan area (Andrade Ferreyra 2007). More schooling consequently leads to higher income, enabling participation in transnational advocacy activities. For example, the average annual income of HTA members answering the income question in my survey was U.S. $39,971, which is consistent with national averages. On legal status, only one member reported to be undocumented. The great majority are legal permanent residents followed by a smaller group of naturalized U.S. citizens who declare to vote in all U.S. elections. With one exception, all members were born in Mexico, thus confirming that this is mostly a first-generation phenomenon, at least for the case of migrants from Michoacán.[35]

In rural communities in Michoacán, participation in *faenas* (voluntary communal work) is widely expected as a mechanism to preserve membership, solve community problems, express solidarity, and be a good citizen. If a school needs painting, parents are expected to do it. If fall is around the corner, a volunteer public works committee is established to keep the communal water well free from leaves and debris. Among those with higher socioeconomic standing in the community, it is acceptable to pay someone else to do their *faena*, although people usually assign more value to donated labor than to paid efforts. When systems of voluntary work are no longer possible due to long absences, they are sometimes transplanted to self-help informal groups in the new host societies.

In his study of human solidarity and societal exchanges of services, Marcel Mauss (1990) finds that although the presentations and counterpresentations of gift giving and services take place under a voluntary guise, they are, in essence, strictly obligatory, and their sanction is private or open warfare. Rules of exchange, reciprocity, and generosity are quite similar in mestizo migrant communities from rural Michoacán.[36] For instance, it is customary that migrants who have been in Chicago for long periods of time help newcomers from their town by sharing their social networks and providing free or low-cost temporary lodging, job referrals, and addresses for social services agencies. The support, voluntary gift giving, and human solidarity bestowed upon disadvantaged fellow countrymen and women help more established migrants preserve membership in good standing in the hometown. News about whom to contact after arrival spreads fast across the border, and anyone who hides in Chicago to avoid helping newcomers is considered cheap or selfish. This becomes a moral obligation, and negligence can be heavily sanctioned by a jury of peers: few migrants want to become social outcasts for violating norms of reciprocity.[37]

Rural systems of reciprocity and mutual exchange are also reinforced through childhood friendships that become relevant to defining social position as a migrant in a new society and preserving the topophilic attachment to birthplace. For example, Rosendo Sánchez has lived in Chicago for thirty-three years and has a small circle of close friends that includes Serbians, Poles, and other whites. He mentions that the only Mexicans he considers his real friends are his childhood friends: "I left Chehuayo when I was eighteen, then came here and didn't have anybody to socialize. I felt very isolated. After a while, I reunited with a childhood friend here in Chicago and suddenly, more and more childhood friends came and we maintain this bond, which is different. I don't know how to describe it, but we grew up together, there is nothing that can erase this friendship, even if we don't see each other often." In their adaptation to new urban environments, migrants resort to their networks of trust, solidarity, and cooperation, challenging global trends of depersonalized relations and the increased coordination of nation-state regulations to preserve their socialization systems including the rise of government institutions and bureaucracies to channel migrant affairs.[38]

The membership of HTAs mirrors the structure of the Mexican migrant population in the city. A typical organization is composed of ten to fifty families that include dual citizens, legal permanent residents, and undocumented migrants. Those members with higher human capital—that is, those with higher levels of education and socioeconomic standing—tend to take leadership positions and volunteer more hours to organize soccer tournaments, plan monthly get-togethers, and make proposals to finance projects, while those with more unstable jobs and incomes are more likely to contribute with donated labor and volunteering in the preparation of fund-raising events. Attending events organized by the clubs unites recent and more established migrants and provides an avenue for socialization, bartering, and networking for new jobs.

HTA members usually share nationality, faith, and attachment to birthplace, but they have diverse interests and group affiliations.[39] In traditional voluntary organizations engaged in charitable welfare projects, it is common to find a great degree of socioeconomic homogeneity among members. For example, Chicago's first Rotary association was a group of successful attorneys and businessmen who transformed a friendship club into a social service organization to build public toilets for Chicago in 1905. The entrepreneurial spirit is still widely shared among Rotarians around the world. While some HTA leaders are small businessmen and have acquired a solid middle-class status, the average participant works in the blue-collar labor sectors that Chicago's racial hierarchy has imposed— namely, manufacturing, construction, and food services.

Robert Putnam (2007) argues that immigration and ethnic diversity produce increased social isolation, reducing social solidarity and social capital in the short run. However, he recognizes that levels of immigrant incorporation depend on the institutional contexts of reception, making it difficult to generalize his observations as a general trend across U.S. cities. For example, a closer look at the members-at-large of HTAs reveals social heterogeneity as participants belong to a wide range of civic and political organizations. In Chicago, HTA members belong to Parent-Teacher Associations (PTAs), block clubs, soccer leagues, Catholic and Protestant church congregations, neighborhood and ethnic chambers of commerce, anti-abortion groups, the National Rifle Association, labor unions, independent worker centers, and the Democratic and Republican parties. In Michoacán, members declare affiliations to their parishes, seed cooperatives, and the three main political parties. Despite all the challenges of historical racial exclusion, it is fair to say that after the civil rights movement, migrant ethnic attachments have strengthened the cohesiveness of America's communities, while not serving as a permanent barrier to modest upward mobility and incorporation, at least among some sectors of the migrant working classes. The growing diversity of interests and affiliations among members causes some conflicts within the umbrella organization as it becomes harder to reach strong consensus for the best political advocacy strategies, but it offers good grounds for leadership training.

SPORTS AND FAITH STRENGTHEN SOLIDARITY

Club Deportivo Taximaroa began in 1962 in Chicago's North Side as a soccer club to channel an ethnic rivalry with the Polish population. In the early 1970s, there were fifty families from Ciudad Hidalgo living on the North Side, all working in the hotel industry as maids, busboys, and cooks after successful referrals among friends got them invitations from business owners to come here legally by the end of the Bracero Program.[40] Organizing a soccer club was not an easy task those days because clubs needed formal registration to have the right to play in neighborhood parks and it took several years to collect the money to register with the National Soccer League.[41] Once the club won some tournaments, the organizers added children's teams and a marching band, first to honor the Mexican flag during Independence Day parades and later, as more members of the second generation joined, to honor the U.S. flag also. Ciudad Hidalgo's marching band is frequently invited to commemorate historical anniversaries such as Benito Juárez's birthday at Michigan Avenue's Plaza de las Américas and the closing ceremony of FEDECMI's annual cultural week, and to perform at various events in Ciudad Hidalgo, Michoacán. In the early 1980s, it was very difficult to find enough players to form a co-ethnic soccer club in Chicago suburbs with small foreign-born Mexican populations. Pablo, from La Purísima soccer club based in Carpentersville, remembers:

> I had to join a soccer club called Los Astros with people from several Mexican states because there were few Mexicans living here. This club disappeared in the 1990s when members joined soccer clubs with their own co-ethnics as Carpentersville received more Mexicans from several states. In fact, I did not like soccer because my favorite pastime was *jaripeos* [Mexican rodeos] but soccer was the only recreation when I came so I developed a taste for it and even became a coach, to have an activity to bond in our free time. We became members of the Elgin Soccer league and continued organizing to make sure there were enough funds to pay for referees and uniforms. Later, our club organized fund-raisers to finance a water well when we realized our municipal government would never start construction without the support of our remittances.[42]

For Mexican migrants arriving from the rural countryside, life in a big city was socially isolated, as it was difficult to find free time from work to find a sense of belonging. Soccer provided a bonding opportunity for single men because the sport was relatively affordable and pick-up games did not require too much organization or dealings with local authorities. After learning that group sports were actually regulated by the parks when non-Mexican groups asked them to leave the premises unless they showed proof of registration, migrants faced their first challenge of incorporation: registering their teams to gain formal access to parks and following and respecting predetermined schedules to use facilities. Many HTA members credit the successes of soccer leagues as their first training ground for organizing for a common goal. Janice Fine, in her research on independent worker centers, finds that soccer leagues and hometown associations have been important community institutions that frequently encourage immigrant participation in the worker center movement, facilitating interactions between labor organizers and ethnic networks at the workplace in North Carolina, Nebraska, and New York (Fine 2006).

When the single men participating in soccer leagues began to have families, they added women's teams, and women joined the soccer leagues to socialize with other families, and to prepare food and drinks after the game. Soccer clubs are still one of the most popular forms of migrant incorporation, kept alive thanks to the renewed sense of ethnicity that shapes social integration in Chicago.[43] When members see potential in a young player, they send him to tryouts with professional Mexican teams. José Ceja, a twenty-two-year-old Chicago native whose parents come from Huaniqueo, has played both with the Morelia Club in his parents' home state and with the Albanian Stars in the National Soccer League in Chicago.[44] He started his soccer training with the Tarascos, a soccer club affiliated with the Mexican league of Chicago's Latin American Soccer Association.

While soccer clubs offered a useful way to socialize within one's own ethnic group and later with other ethnic groups, faith and religion also provided an important vehicle to affirm ethnic belonging and to organize in Chicago. Although Americans remain far more religious than those in other industrialized countries, net church attendance has fallen by approximately one-sixth according to some observers,[45] thus bringing a decline in social capital. However, among Latino migrant groups, especially among groups coming from countries with inefficient provision of social welfare, the church represents a vital source of social services in times of economic need and embodies an institution that migrants trust across borders.[46] Among Mexicans, a significant amount of volunteer time and resources is devoted to church-related activities in both countries.[47]

As Liliana Rivera Sánchez (2005) explains, there is a tendency among Mexican migrants to preserve religious identities and beliefs, and these practices take on added meaning in the global context of accelerated migration—not only as a reactive response to the hostility confronted by migrants in their places of destination but also as an affirmative response based on a profound and sometimes dogmatic respect for their particular religious practices. Priests enjoy high levels of trust and credibility among HTAs despite complaints about isolated negative experiences with priests who run away with HTA funds or who do not offer itemized reports on the use of HTA contributions to patron saint festivities. In a recent national survey of Mexican HTA members, 40 percent of respondents considered the church to be the most important institution for providing public goods and services in communities of origin besides the municipal government. The next most important institution according to 23 percent of respondents was the local civil society.[48] Rural priests in Michoacán have also played the role of intermediaries in the emigration process, offering letters of reference to obtain passports in the 1940s or facilitating the work of *enganchadores* (middlemen) to make travel arrangements to work in the United States.[49]

Spirituality among migrants is rooted in their devotion to cultural and religious symbols that represent ethnoreligious communities, helping to create what Elaine Peña (2011) calls "devotional capital," similar to Pierre Bourdieu's conceptualization of symbolic capital. In Chicago, many migrants attend churches offering Spanish mass to ease the cultural shock. They find a sense of belonging among those sharing the same faith, and pray to find well-paying jobs. They often find both spiritual and practical guidance to access social services.

Religious performances are sometimes different in Chicago's Catholicism, as they tend to have the flavor of previous immigrant groups, such as the Irish, Italians, and Romanians who arrived at a time when the Catholic hierarchy supported ethnic national parishes.[50] Therefore, with the exception of Our Lady of Guadalupe Church in the South Side, Mexicans did not have an opportunity to shape their own ethnic parishes as their numbers grew.[51] For many rural Mexicans, their patron saints and virgins were not always represented in the public space of their new churches, and new arrivals from remote rural towns had to construct their devotional altars to honor particular virgins and saints in the private sphere of their homes until they were able to introduce them to their new parishes.

One of the most important religious symbols leading to the formation of devotional capital is the Virgin of Guadalupe. In Chicago, Guadalupanismo has spread to dozens of parishes across the metropolitan area, and the Virgin of Guadalupe now has a shrine in Des Plaines, Illinois, that is a replica of the one in Mexico City's Basilica of Guadalupe.[52] However, devotional capital is the product of a long struggle to find a permanent home for the Virgin of Guadalupe in local churches.[53] For example, when Anita de la Cruz came to Aurora from San Miguel Epejan, Mexican immigrants had to share the devotional space with the Romanian Catholic community, who did not accept them with open arms.[54] Josefina, a member of San Miguel Epejan Club, remembers that in the 1960s, the Romanians did not talk to them when they bought their first house on Pierce Street. She believes Romanians did not like Mexicans moving into the neighborhood, and they sold their houses. When Romanians left, Puerto Ricans and Mexicans moved to the neighborhood, in a classic process of ethnic succession.

In 1962, the first Guadalupano Club was established in Aurora by the same group of families that organized the Mexican Independence Day parade and beauty queen contest. Every week, club members would knock on doors asking for donations to organize a monthly mass to honor the Virgin of Guadalupe and an annual birthday party with *mañanitas* and *menudo* on December 12 in Saint Joseph Church.[55] A decade later, in 1973, Saint Joseph Church invited an Ecuadorian priest, Julio Armijos Suárez, to offer Spanish mass for the Virgin of Guadalupe on December 12 for the growing Mexican congregation.[56] After the successful organization of masses for the Virgin, the Epejenses who were members of the Guadalupano Club acquired a signed image of the Virgin in Mexico City's basilica and donated it to Saint Joseph Church. In the late 1970s, when rumors of the successful devotional capital among Epejenses from Aurora spread in the hometown, Juan Martínez, the local priest, visited the migrant community in Aurora and enlisted their help to rebuild the local temple. Between 1972 and 1983, the Guadalupano Committee from San Miguel Epejan collected U.S. $14,000 through canvassing and installing collection tins in Mexican supermarkets to request donations to rebuild the temple of their ancestors. With these practices, Mexicans were transforming the character of American Catholicism in Aurora while simultaneously revitalizing their faith in San Miguel Epejan.[57]

Although Michoacán HTAs have Lutheran and Evangelical converts among their members,[58] they have embraced a respectful ecumenism in their organizational structure. Despite their secular organizational character, faith constantly accompanies their advocacy work. For instance, during monthly assembly meetings at Casa Michoacán, HTA representatives hold hands at the beginning of the session and ask for volunteers to lead a prayer for a successful meeting. The volunteer leader of the prayer then adds a special dedication referring to their binational work. In a 2011 meeting, Alfredo, from San Juanico Club, said: "We dedicate this prayer to ask God to put an end to the violence in Michoacán and to end the suffering of our migrant brothers and sisters in the United States."[59]

The opportunity to use the public space of worship to spur civic engagement is frequently taken by HTA members. During the 2009 inauguration mass of the Michoacano cultural week at the Des Plaines shrine of the Virgin of Guadalupe, Artemio asked permission of the invited bishop of the Zamora Diocese to use the pulpit to address parishioners. He asked hundreds of parishioners to pull out their cell phones and dial their U.S. senators to demand legalization of all undocumented immigrants in the United States.[60] With the incorporation of faith to their lives and the transference of ritual and performances to their new houses of worship, Mexican HTA members reaffirm an ethnic identity that is profoundly tied to their membership in an ethnoreligious community that transcends borders and helps them carry out their transnational advocacy mission. The close interaction with priests through volunteering at their congregations serves to share their tribulations at the workplace and has convinced several congregations to take action on behalf of immigrant rights. Volunteering at their congregation frequently entitled HTA members to use church space for their fund-raising activities on behalf of communities of origin. Women were especially good at negotiating access to church space, as they were highly visible in the organization of devotional groups to honor their favorite saints and virgins.

A Gendered Division of Labor

Since the appearance of the first HTA studies, most ethnographies have characterized these organizations as male dominated (Goldring 2001; Zamudio Grave 2009). In fact, the most recent research of Mexican HTA leadership confirms this trend (Duquette 2011). Although men frequently lead HTAs, women are not officially prevented from joining or from participating in elections to leadership positions as used to be the case in similar traditional membership-based voluntary organizations such as the Rotary clubs, where it took a 1987 U.S. Supreme Court ruling before women could join.

Due to the gendered division of labor in Mexico, the negotiation with municipal and state authorities has been left to men in HTAs because land tenure was customarily reserved to males and most development-related community affairs are still addressed first by *ejidatarios* in rural communities. However, the appearance of HTAs in Chicago cannot be explained without women's acquiescence to allow men to participate in these organizations. In the United States, male domination is a naturalized social construction that transcends racial hierarchies producing a sexual division of labor into which Mexican migrant women are embedded.[61] As Pierre Bourdieu explains, this structural division of labor "extends to all domains of practice, and in particular to exchanges, with the difference between public, discontinuous, extra-ordinary male exchanges, and private, even secret, continuous, ordinary female exchanges, and to religious or ritual activities, in which similar oppositions are observed" (1998: 48).

Following Bourdieu's theorization, in the social organization of Mexican HTAs, women are entrusted with the gendered labor of preparing food, making decorations, handling child care, transmitting ethnoreligious values, and agreeing to allow men to go out some evenings to discuss strategies to convince authorities (in Chicago and Michoacán) to pay more attention to social inequalities in their hometowns and in Chicago neighborhoods. Meanwhile, most women are busy doing their double shift, selling Avon and similar independent entrepreneurial activities, working in manufacturing to help pay for household expenses while taking care of children, making sure their children do not face discrimination from their teachers, finding health care for family members, and many other gendered tasks that demonstrate the gendered division of civic engagement. Women take advantage of picnics and *kermesses* (fairs) to meet other women to compare the quality of schools and learn about the pros and cons of bilingual education in Chicago's public schools.

The issue of what some women perceive as excessive volunteer civic engagement among Mexican males in HTA activities is addressed in public spaces. In

2008, I attended a theater production in Spanish organized by the Zacatecas federation of HTAs, an organization with a longer history of female presidents than FEDECMI's. The play was a collection of short sketches, which had been written by HTAs families and U.S.-born youth members. In one segment, actresses dramatized the long absences of men to discuss club affairs with other men, while they were left abandoned, sometimes struggling to make ends meets due to excessive charitable contributions to club projects. The self-mockery had the audience in stitches and provides evidence of the power of art and self-representation to discuss gender challenges within their organizations.

María Zárate is a stay-at-home mom. She volunteers at her Evangelical congregation in Elgin and contributes with food preparation for fund-raisers to benefit La Purísima Club. She came to Chicago in the 1980s after marrying Salvador Balleño, a founding member of FEDECMI. She is very interested in passing the U.S. citizenship test and has taken it twice. She is very frustrated because she memorizes the questions, and the test administrator keeps asking them out of order. They have five U.S.-born children. María's training ground for civic engagement started when she had to defend her son in a Chicago public school. When José, Maria's eldest son, was in grammar school, he came home one day crying because his African American teacher did not allow him to say the pledge of allegiance.[62] José remembers that the teacher did not offer any explanation. She just said to him: "There is no need for you to stand up and recite. You can remain seated." María went to talk to the teacher the next day, and afterward she became an advocate for simultaneous translation during parent-teacher meetings and fought with administrators every time they threatened to cancel the budget for interpreters. She explains that she has always been very diligent attending parent-teacher meetings, asks her husband to volunteer time to do small repairs to the school, and is convinced that it is her right to have language accommodation provided to her children.[63]

During 2005 elections to renew FEDECMI's executive board, the organization inaugurated the first women's affairs committee. Rubén Chávez, the president at that time, told me that women's participation had not been well recognized, and this had to change. He said that they had failed to ask women their opinion about important decisions, and they were trying to address the power disparities produced by traditional roles:

> Women have always been very active. In my hometown, Francisco Villa, they participate in state-sponsored initiatives to grow vegetables, receiving training to optimize water for irrigation. They also attend work-training courses as beauticians, seamstresses, and artisans. The most important role that women play in HTAs is to help their husbands, to support their decisions. Maybe because of our culture, our traditions or because they have stayed at home, women's participation as leaders has been scarce. But now that our organization has grown, women are more active. They decided what food to prepare

for today's *kermess* and this is a change. Before, husbands used to ask women to donate a pot of *pozole*[64] without even asking if it was possible and they did not like that. We realize that this is wrong, and we are now asking them to decide what to do for fund-raising and how to do it and we hope to see an increase in their participation.[65]

Ana[66] belongs to the first small group of women to be elected to FEDECMI's women's affairs committee. She does not own land in her rural hometown and in Chicago works in a factory, helps her husband with his business, and takes care of her children. When I met her, she was finishing high school through an online program offered at Casa Michoacán in partnership with Morelia's Colegio de Bachilleres. She gets very excited when she lists the activities she volunteered for in Michoacán, including a malaria prevention campaign and cooking for a breakfast-for-all initiative. In her new position, she had many program ideas to increase binational engagement, such as health prevention courses, a day care cooperative, new work-training programs in her rural village, and a women's coffee club, obliging men to take care of children while women talk about women's issues. After announcing her platform in front of the mostly male board, the public reaction left her very disappointed: "Boo, get her out of here" was the immediate response. Ana explains this reaction as jealousy: "Men are very jealous. After they booed me, I told them that whenever they leave the house to play billiards or go out for a beer, nobody says a word."

FEDECMI elected the first female president in 2011, a working mother, after fourteen years of male presidents. While there are a few female HTA presidents in the organization, they are a minority, and their incursion in the male-dominated world is frequently due to economic power or family structure, as they tend to be small business owners, divorced, and/or single mothers in female-headed households. While FEDECMI has gradually incorporated ad hoc committees to address women's issues and male leaders constantly worry about the lack of female presence in leadership positions, there are structural barriers that are difficult to break.[67]

Younger generations of migrant women are changing the traditional gendered division of labor dynamics, but changes are very gradual, and it takes courage for wives to face husbands. FEDECMI has a public commitment to include more women in leadership positions and not just as staff members, but structural barriers are difficult to break in the traditional family dynamics of HTA members. Women's best weapons against gender discrimination have been their reluctance to return permanently to rural Michoacán, their eagerness to acquire U.S. citizenship, and the purchase of homes as a sign of their decision to plant roots in Chicago.

In the Chicago and Washington, D.C., metropolitan areas, Latino migrant women are taking the lead in the total number of naturalizations (Bada, Chacón, and Fox 2010; Jones-Correa 2009).[68] Dual citizenship allows women to bring their aging parents to visit grandchildren more easily and gives them more opportunities to have access to educational and training opportunities that are restricted to citizens. When retirement age gets closer, dual citizenship gives women freedom of mobility, allowing them to divide their time between Mexico and the United States and continue their civic engagement in two countries.[69] In some families that belong to HTAs, younger wives tend to have slightly higher education levels than men, and they are less afraid of taking the citizenship test, which is a de facto literacy test for many Mexican migrants who came after 1965.[70] In the 1970s and 1980s, citizenship status in the United States was of minor importance to receive social services, but this situation changed with the immigration laws of the mid-1990s, creating important distinctions between citizens and residents when it came to access to social services. The reduction of rights for legal permanent residents encouraged many Mexicans to seek citizenship, especially after the Mexican government changed the nationality law in 1998 and allowed Mexicans to acquire a second nationality without losing their Mexican citizenship.[71]

The lack of representation of female migrants has a powerful cultural reference related to rural origins. In the countryside, discrimination against women was exercised systematically on many fronts: excluding them from access to land, discounting their contributions to the family economy, blocking their access to education, using them as straw women to preserve fathers' rights to communal lands, steering them toward marriage and motherhood.[72] In this environment, it is no coincidence that the few female leaders who have managed to take a visible role in migrant organizations from Michoacán and other states are frequently divorced, single mothers, single business owners, or full-time workers doing double shifts, which has offered significant economic empowerment in their households.

Hybrid Traditions, Dual Belongings

One of the most important functions of Michoacán HTAs is the preservation of culture, traditions, and family values and their transmission to the second generation. For most Americans, a popular way to reflect on history is to look at their family's history. Historians believe that history as it is taught in schools does not engage most Americans, but people are deeply involved with other dimensions of the past. Almost every American regularly engages the past, and the past that engages them most deeply is that of their families (Rosenzweig and Thelen 1998).

Among Michoacanos, the meaning of family and past is in constant evolution after their arrival to Chicago, as their nostalgia for places, smells, and childhood memories gradually includes both reminiscences of past rural life and emotional attachments to their new urban dwellings. Nowhere is this constant change of emotional topophilic attachments more evident than among Michoacán migrants. They develop a dual meaning of home, which is now less a physical location than a mental construct, a place of dreams and memories, present even despite long absences.[73] The boundaries of family are no longer limited by physical place, since they can keep in constant contact with rural life through chat groups, instant video streaming, online local newspapers, and cheap phone calls. Because nonphysical family contacts can now take place virtually anywhere with the aid of Skype video, it depends on migrant families to make their own sense of place, virtually connecting their rural and urban attachments across borders.

In Chicago, the process of immigrant incorporation includes the gradual addition of ethnic traditions to the local culture. Historically, immigrant groups have offered their ethnic flavors to U.S. civic and festive holidays, sometimes helping to revive the public display of traditions, as when German and Irish immigrants became the main sponsors of the public centennial celebrations of U.S. independence in Chicago's downtown. For these immigrants, being ethnic was part and parcel of becoming American, and as they added ethnic aspects to quintessentially American celebrations, they carved out a niche for their cultures in their adopted land (Litwicki 2004).[74] During Fourth of July celebrations, many Mexican families from HTAs proudly display the U.S. flag outside their homes along with the Mexican flag, especially those living in mixed-status households with U.S.-born children, legal permanent residents, and undocumented migrants. Among those who still have not had a chance to become U.S. citizens, attachment to their adopted land is rooted in decades of permanent residence and socialization, positive and negative experiences of incorporation included.

In a globalized world with increasing inequalities, migrant socialization processes happen in spaces experiencing the constant movement of capital, goods, and people—the last in spite of national laws that severely restrict human mobility.[75] Rather than closed territories, places are revalued and provide greater security and stability to people's identities. Places utilized for celebrations of holidays and traditions provide shared experiences between people and the community over time in such a way that they enable a sense of belonging to a group (Crang 1998).

Hometown clubs have been indivisibly associated with the social infrastructure projects they develop in communities of origin as a way to preserve membership, place attachment, and belonging to those physical spaces, but many clubs also organize social and cultural activities that are not related to fund-raising for development projects in rural Michoacán. The misconception that HTAs' main purpose is to organize charitable projects has led some observers to even classify them into active and inactive organizations. An active club is given this status in governmental records or even in the records of the umbrella federations of HTAs when it pay dues on time or is actively organizing a fund-raising project.[76] However, the bonds of solidarity among club members do not disappear, and clubs continue their social gatherings for several decades, reinforcing the solidarity ties among members and organizing reunions of friends and family.

Social gatherings in Chicago parks, church basements, and other public spaces usually mark important traditions and celebrations in both Mexican and U.S. calendars for HTA members. Three Kings Day is celebrated with the traditional *rosca* (fruitcake) on January 6; they meet for tamales on February for Candelaria's Day, organize couples' dinners for Valentine's Day, and construct piñatas for Children's Day.[77] For Halloween, they celebrate with trick or treat for children while adults eat *corundas* (triangular-shaped tamales prepared with lard and soaked in red meat sauce that are popular in northern Michoacán), but they also install home altars for the Day of the Dead on November 1. During Thanksgiving, many families usually cook two turkeys, one with *mole* and the second with gravy because children bring gravy recipes home from socialization at school. Also, TV advertisements and the constant phone conversations about Black Friday with family members living in Mexico even led in November 2011 to the national adoption of a Black Friday in Mexico around the celebration of Mexico's Revolution.[78]

The celebration of funerals also suggests a process of gradual incorporation, as funerary associations are now promoting the purchase of spaces in Chicago's cemeteries as an alternative to corpse repatriation. While they do not discourage corpse repatriation to rural hometowns, leaders disseminate information about both options so that people can compare prices.[79] In a recent meeting of the Rincón de Dolores Club, members invited cemetery and funeral home sales representatives to talk about their special packages and discounts, and the majority seemed more interested in buying cemetery spaces in Chicago, arguing that if they wanted their children to visit their graves, it would be better to be buried in Chicago.

The adoption of identity symbols has also defined their collective identity as Michoacanos in Chicago through the binational sharing of a migratory butterfly. The monarch butterfly is one of the most salient symbols of Michoacano identity, and it is also the official state insect of Illinois.[80] Paradoxically, the image of the monarch butterfly has been reified to signify the beauty of migration, obscuring the very real negative consequences of human mobility. Each year, thousands of monarchs leave the cold temperatures in Canada and start their migration to warmer habitats, choosing Michoacán as one of the most important sanctuaries. In their long journey, they visit Chicago, feeding on native plants at community parks and family gardens while providing a deeply symbolic connection with migrant communities who welcome them to their new homes, providing a reminiscence of their rural life. To recognize the rich heritage of Michoacanos and the special significance of this insect in Illinois, FEDECMI has a collaboration agreement with Chicago's Peggy Notebaert Nature Museum to offer workshops to teach Michoacán families about conservation methods to preserve the population of monarchs. Michoacán HTAs have adopted the monarch butterfly as their preferred symbolic identity—in magazine covers, binational artists' exchanges, and murals in Pilsen's public parks—to share their heritage with all Chicago-ans. In those artistic renditions, the monarch butterfly is always juxtaposed with their new symbols of place attachment: Millennium Park, the Willis Tower, the Trump Building, Pilsen's murals, and Lake Michigan. Thus, HTAs' sense of place to signify their collective identity and place attachment has both an interpreta-tive perspective *on* the environment and an emotional reaction *to* their past and present inhabited environments.

But beyond the shared socialization of these symbols in the private sphere, the connections between the United States and Mexico also include binational gov-erning bureaucracies. For example, in April 2013 Governor Pat Quinn traveled to Mexico City to sign a sister lake agreement between Lake Pátzcuaro, Micho-acán, and Lake Michigan. During the official ceremony, Quinn mentioned that the state of Michoacán is the starting point for the migrating monarch butter-flies that travel from central Mexico all the way to Illinois, a symbol of the long-standing relationship between Illinois and Michoacán (Illinois Government News Network 2013).

The social practice of reminiscing is a frequent feature of family gatherings and social settings in HTAs. Due to the privileged position afforded to white Anglo-Saxon Protestant history and culture in U.S. public schools, children of Mexican migrants are unlikely to learn the culture and history of their parents' home states at schools. In any case, members want their children to learn about their particular villages and their home state, reimagining and reinventing tradi-tions. In the words of Rubén Chávez, a member of Francisco Villa Club: "In our annual Fourth of July picnic, the Wisconsin branch of the club is in charge of organizing the event in a public park. In 2005, they performed our *toritos de petate* and a theater play about the life of Pancho Villa because we want our kids to learn more about the hero our town is named after. Our kids don't know enough Mexican history and traditions. It is our duty to teach them."[81]

This public celebration of Michoacán traditions from a pre-Columbian and revolutionary past is sometimes juxtaposed with naturalization and voter reg-istration campaigns, as was the case during an annual picnic of La Purísima Club celebrated in Carpentersville's public park on the Fourth of July. In 2004, club members invited the Illinois Coalition for Immigrant and Refugee Rights to bring a booth with information on the naturalization process to encourage members who qualify to become citizens and invite youth to register to vote. However, these celebrations are not always welcome with open arms in all Chi-cago suburbs. In my observations, I noticed that annual hometown picnics that included *toritos de petate* or *banda* music were more likely to be received with interest and curiosity by passers-by in parks of northern suburbs, while people from western suburbs were more likely to react with hostility toward those gath-ered in public parks. In Carpentersville, a city well known for its restrictive ini-tiatives toward Latino immigrants located forty miles from Chicago, the annual picnic described above ended around 7 P.M. on a Sunday when police arrived to check on the party after a few neighbors complained that the *banda* music was too loud and they had to wake up early to go to work on Monday.[82]

Similar acts of hostility are experienced when HTAs organize fund-raiser events such as knockout soccer tournaments in which food is sold and live band music plays in between matches. At those events, it is common to see a large number of policemen observing the matches at close range. These are intimidation techniques that are not frequently seen during soccer tournaments organized by non-Latino soccer leagues in suburban areas. These acts of hostility contribute to the development of negative interracial relations and animosity as club members realize that racial discrimination toward Mexicans will not easily disappear even after becoming U.S. citizens. The excessive show of police is difficult to justify because club members usually obtain permission to use the parks for any large event. In fact, several Michoacano HTAs learned about park district bureaucracy the hard way, after canceling a couple of tournaments at the last minute because the volunteer in charge of securing the place failed to fill out a park reservation form.

The celebration of Mexican and U.S. holidays and traditions is the locus where dual national identities are reaffirmed and adopted among migrants and transferred to the second generation, creating a culturally hybrid integration process for American holidays and constructing distinctive hybrid identities, as many other immigrant groups did in the past. During the annual *posadas* celebrated at Casa Michoacán,[83] adults get up on stage between the Mexican and the U.S. flags and lead the singing of *villancicos* (popular Ibero-American carols) in Spanish, followed by a children's performance of Christmas carols in English. As Néstor García Canclini (1995) reminds us, the hybridization of culture is embedded in a constant process of de-territorialization and reterritorialization, crossing multiple borders and sometimes engendering violent conflicts: acts of aggression against recently arrived immigrants and discrimination at school and work that happens simultaneously on both sides of the border as returning migrants are not always easily incorporated into the Mexican public school system or offered jobs.

Despite negative experiences of social incorporation experienced in Mexico and the United States, collective identity created through topophilic attachments to birthplace fosters a legitimate and representative position to exercise long-distance civic engagement with communities of origin without obstructing the process of incorporation into U.S. society. Topophilic attachments toward new communities of residence develop and are demonstrated in HTA members' constant search for binational public recognition of their unique migrant identities that combine dual belongings to rural origins and new urban destinations. In this context, some HTA leaders found a calling and were successful; past experiences of discrimination did not hinder them. However, among those who experienced discrimination without finding appropriate outlets to address the problem and who attempted to change the situation, their leadership was frequently circumscribed mostly to charitable work for their hometown and did not diversify their social justice agendas, even among naturalized U.S. citizens.

THE ELUSIVE PARTICIPATION OF YOUTH

The successful incorporation of both Mexican and U.S. traditions in families who belong to HTAs produces important benefits to the second generation as youth closely witness the intense connections of parents with their home states. Although few decide to follow in their parents' footsteps as HTA leaders, they admire their parents for their generosity and altruism, becoming curious to learn more about Mexican social inequality, the root causes of migration, and development challenges in rural Michoacán. Since I became a professor at the University of Illinois at Chicago (UIC), I have been fascinated by the reaction of some of my students every time I offer an overview of Chicago-based HTAs in one of my courses. One day, during office hours, a senior student from a small town in Jalisco told me: "Professor, are HTAs the same thing as committees? [Yes, they are]. I ask because my dad is a member of one of those committees, and he says that he doesn't want to participate anymore because they are always bickering about the projects. Some members want to keep doing church renovations while others, like my father, would like to support different projects to bring progress to my hometown. My family used to participate more in the past when my sister won the Miss Jalisco pageant." A doctoral student in political science once shared that his dad was a former president of the Zacatecano federation of Illinois, and the niece of a former president of the first Michoacano hometown club approached me once after class to suggest that I meet her uncle, the founding member of the first Michoacano HTA in the city. While it is true that Mexican students are overrepresented in courses related to Latino topics at UIC and therefore these are isolated incidents, many students whose families have participated in these clubs at some point have integrated the existence of HTAs as part of their cultural repertoire while growing up in the city and the suburbs, and these experiences have positive consequences for the adaptation of native and foreign-born children of Mexican immigrants.

For example, hometown values of generosity and altruism are instilled early in the second generation. Yanitza Carmona is a third-generation U.S. citizen of Mexican descent and a senior in the honors college at UIC. She is the granddaughter of Manuel Correa, the founder of Taximaroa Club, the first HTA from Michoacán established in Chicago in the late 1960s. Yanitza's mother passed away when she was very young, and her grandparents raised her. She tells me that she was too little to remember when her grandfather was most active in his club, but she remembers that she once went to a fund-raiser dance. In college, she tried to become civically engaged as a tribute to her grandfather, who instilled in her the value of helping others. After taking a class on Chicana feminism and reading Gloria Anzaldúa's work, she decided to found the Nepantla Soccer Club for adolescent girls in her North Side neighborhood to provide after-school opportunities for Latina girls in an effort to prevent teen pregnancies. Yanitza became a mother at a young age and struggled to get a college education. Her civic engagement story is frequently repeated among those whose parents are involved in HTAs. While few decide to take leadership positions in HTAs to provide generational replacement, many become civically engaged in block clubs, educational projects, theater groups, sports clubs, and other activities with the support of FEDECMI's youth programs or through public schools in Chicago and the suburbs.

As this roadmap of the many ways in which binational civic engagements are performed in public and private spaces suggests, migrant participation in HTAs serves as an important vehicle for migrant integration into U.S. society, providing friendly spaces for exercising and reaffirming binational ethnic identities and national loyalties, including traditions, celebrations, religiosity, and cross-border ethnic solidarities, even amid practices of exclusion, social inequality, and racial discrimination experienced in host and receiving societies.[84]

Migrant generosity across borders has increased, produced, and perpetuated—sometimes unintentionally—complex systems of exchange and international economic policies. In this context, municipal and state governments have increased their attention to migrant communities in Chicago with the hopes of regulating the investments of collective remittances in communities of origin as a substitute for decades of public budget reductions to address the needs of the rural countryside. During their first encounters with HTAs, authorities were expecting to find a docile citizenry patiently waiting for the state to impose, once again, solutions to community problems unilaterally without input of those affected by public policies that had led them to their labor migrations in the first place. However, years of organizing in the United States, receiving the advice and support of many Latino and mainstream civil society institutions, slowly produced more egalitarian interactions between Chicago migrant organizations and their state authorities. Gradually, migrants demonstrated that they were capable of making claims to *two* nation-states, and requested increased resources to continue their advocacy on behalf of immigrant rights, despite difficulties in communicating their aspirations, messages, and proposals for migrant challenges to public sector officials in Chicago and Michoacán. Alongside this process of recuperation of social and political rights as Mexican citizens living in diaspora, migrants used their organizations to claim incorporation into Chicago's public spaces and demand recognition of their traditions, language, and social and human rights.

CHAPTER 4

❧

MIGRANT CLUBS
TO THE RESCUE

April 28, 2010, 6:30 P.M. Migrant club leaders take their seats in the conference room at the Mexican consulate in the West Loop neighborhood in Chicago. The event is scheduled to begin at 6:30 P.M., but organizers decide to wait a little longer to accommodate those stuck in traffic; they expect 120 leaders from Indiana, Michigan, and Wisconsin. The meeting has been organized by the Chicago office of the Mexican Secretariat of Social Development (SEDESOL) to offer an update on the Three-for-One Program and to encourage recently created clubs to submit new projects. Luis Mejía Guzmán, SEDESOL´s undersecretary of human and social development, is in town to accept the *Siervo de la Nación*, an annual prize that the Federation of Michoacán Clubs in Illinois (FEDECMI) offers to Michoacanos who have shown exceptional commitment to improve the lives of migrants, and to inaugurate the executive board for the Confederation of Mexican Federations (CONFEMEX). Mejía Guzmán expressed deep respect and admiration for the support of Mexico's rural development by hometown associations (HTAs), and opened his address with an intimate portrait of extreme poverty, which he found more shocking than the lack of sewage, roads, or potable water that most HTAs are eager to solve: "You don't know what it is like to see sixty-year-olds in Chiapas who look older than eighty because they have coal stoves inside their houses, whose lungs are completely charred as if they had been smoking. You have no idea what it is like to see kids losing their arms to those stoves. However, I do recognize that the Three-for-One is very important because it is just one more block in a broad spectrum of public projects for solving many of Mexico's development challenges."[1]

HTA leaders in the audience listen attentively, and during the question-and-answer session, some remind Mejía Guzmán that while they are not from Chiapas, they have been in contact with similar cases of extreme poverty in Guerrero, Puebla, and other states. Consequently, they are asking the government to help them provide basic needs, reduce bureaucratic red tape, offer earmarked funds to attract small migrant investors, and allocate full-time teachers to rural K–12 schools, and above all, they want SEDESOL to *let them decide* which projects should be funded with their charitable contributions.

For the past two decades, HTAs have demanded from their municipal, state, and, more recently, federal governments the right to help design and implement strategies to increase the potential of family and collective remittances to support development efforts. However, migrant HTAs' vision of community development does not always coincide with the priorities and ideas of governments and international finance institutions. HTAs believe that the charitable contributions they provide to solve pressing needs in their villages should be considered philanthropic endeavors by their governments. These matched remittances support basic social infrastructure and cultural preservation, and HTAs believe they should be complemented by long-term public policies to solve extreme poverty and generate well-paying jobs in rural communities. Every time migrant leaders get a chance to speak with government officials, foundations, and financial institutions, and at international conferences, they remind their audiences that one goal of their grassroots philanthropy is to generate opportunities in Mexico that would make migration only one of many options for Mexicans. This is what Mexican scholar Armando Bartra (2008) labels as the fundamental "right to stay home." In fact, HTAs are not naive and realize that their contributions alone will never stop migration unless governments take serious responsibility to offer solutions for structural inequalities in rural Mexico.

In a new global labor regime in which migrants are both praised for their remittances and criminalized for their labor gains—a status quo in the international division of labor—portraying migrants as major agents for development is a convenient ideological tool. In this way, sending states seek to convince organized migrant groups to engage with their countries of origin. As Nina Glick Schiller summarizes in her global economic power analysis, "On the one hand, the impact of the privatization of public services is somewhat deflected as migrant remittances pay for vital needs, such as health care, education, and infrastructure. On the other hand, remittance flows within a neoliberal context highlight locational disparities that are no longer addressed by state policies that would aim to even out regional disparities" (Glick Schiller 2009: 24).

According to politicians and international finance experts, if migrants' individual and collective remittances are channeled adequately to productive investments, they can create new jobs and offer opportunities that keep people at home. However, the political discourse has conveniently obscured the fact that remittances are complementary income that is mostly used in social reproduction without any significant amount for savings or job-generating projects. In addition, the enthusiasm of government authorities for stimulating migrant investments in sending communities is based on the assumption that migrants will return, so human mobility is viewed as a necessary but temporary development aid for sending countries (Portes 2007). However, migrants' permanent return to Mexico is very uncommon and consists mostly of people of retirement age, so the multiplier effects of those few who return permanently to invest in communities of origin are limited (Durand 2005; Espinosa 1998; Papail 2005). Moreover, family remittances tend to decline once the social networks that sustained these transactions evaporate. As families reunite in the new homeland, less money is sent back to the country of origin (Grieco 2004).

In this chapter, I analyze the last two decades of the discourse on migration and development, placing special emphasis on government authority and migrant views on the social, political, and economic significance of collective remittances in rural Michoacán. This chapter demonstrates that praising remittances became the preferred mantra of international finance institutions, and offered Mexican politicians and subnational governments a positive narrative to interpret the increasing cash flows sent by vulnerable workers living across the border in the United States. This discourse heralds the entrepreneurial capabilities of migrants as a solution to complex displacement processes. Consequently, direct and indirect beneficiaries of the profits generated by those flows (via consumer taxes, interest on Inter-American Development Bank [IADB] government loans, savings on public welfare, and international transaction fees) often hide the precarious labor conditions and frequent criminalization of remitters with and without legal status.

In response to the dominant discourse on migration and development, some migrant HTAs decided to challenge the rules of the game imposed from above and transfer knowledge acquired abroad, attempting to produce what Arturo Escobar (2008) calls "alternative modernities," albeit modest ones. However, it is important to stress that migrant HTAs do not embrace an ideological resistance to modernity and development. Rather, they demand to have access to it and collectively decide on best practices. In fact, the HTAs I profile here are not *against* development, but rather want to constructively engage rural communities with their own projects and models.[2]

In 2001, the IADB began to develop initiatives to stimulate productive investments with family remittances, such as promoting competition in the money transfers industry to lower costs and generate special loans for leveraging collective remittances in Mexico. Within this environment, migrant HTAs gradually increased their influence on the issue of remittances and development. Nevertheless, in spite of HTAs' efforts, the collective investment of Mexican family remittances is still negligible. By 2005, the investment of matching funds for collective remittances represented less than 0.01 percent of the national gross domestic product (GDP) and less than 0.05 percent of the total domestic investment in Mexico (Canales 2008).

There is no consensus on the volume of family remittances to Mexico. According to Banco de México, family remittances increased almost fourfold between

2000 and 2006, going from U.S. $7.5 billion to $23 billion. However, the Mexican immigrant population increased only moderately in the same period, from 8.5 million to 11 million, which has led to distrust of official figures.[3]

In any case, government officials have frequently praised family remittances, without offering evidence of their actual benefits in poverty reduction or contribution to the national GDP. In 2005, 6.3 percent of Mexican households (6.4 million people and 6.1 percent of the population) received remittances. According to estimates by demographer Alejandro Canales (2008), only 25 percent of individuals receiving remittances in Mexico have the possibility of significantly improving their income and attaining a solid path to upward social mobility.

While most new research on family remittances traditionally focuses on their impact on economic growth, poverty reduction, or fiscal effects (Campos-Vázquez and Sobarzo 2012), several new quantitative studies unveil the sociopolitical effects of remittances. For example, recent survey results reveal that higher volumes of Mexican migrants and remittances can decrease the levels of corruption at the subnational level (Tyburski 2012), diffuse democratic attitudes and encourage behaviors such as higher nonelectoral participation (Pérez-Armendáriz and Crow 2010), and increase political competition in municipal elections (Pfutze 2012, 2013).

Since most of this research relies on aggregated data of individual behavior as primary units of analysis, questions remain: What role have migrant organizations played in shaping the remittance and development discourse? What gains have binational migrant generosity produced to change the prevalent discourse? What are the challenges to establishing business cooperatives using collective remittances in rural villages in Michoacán? Starting in the late 1990s, Michoacano migrants began to de-emphasize migrant collective remittance generosity to finance community development projects as the most important issue on their agenda, placing a greater emphasis on the responsibility of nation-states to guarantee access to basic social infrastructure, education, job security, and full human and political rights for migrants. In their efforts to convince governments to pay attention to their demands, HTAs have gradually shifted their discourse from citizenship demands based on market membership ("I deserve rights because I send money") to demands based on participatory citizenship ("I deserve to participate in development planning because I am a concerned, civically engaged binational citizen").

REMITTANCES AND DEVELOPMENT: SYMPTOM AND SOLUTION

The dominant view in the political discussion on migration and development is based on the idea that the increasing flow of migrants' remittances can become an instrument, a lever, or a catalyst for development in the countries and communities of origin (Bate 2001; Iglesias 2000; Orozco 2003; Terry and Pedrodv

2006). Paradoxically, the underlying assumption of these proposals is that international migration as a whole is a problem that can be partially solved by the collective efforts of migrants via their organizations. After the first decade of renewed interest in leveraging remittances to promote national development in regions of labor expulsion, the World Bank commissioned global evaluations. The evaluations concluded that there is not strong evidence to warrant an excessive emphasis on public policies to redirect family remittances either collectively or individually. World Bank experts now recommend that migrant-sending states diversify their development policies, citing the paucity of evidence to support the development potential of family remittances (Fajnzylber and López 2007; Hall 2011).

Family remittances are at best, then, an indirect engine of regional economic development, although they can partially compensate for the lack of government assistance, especially in rural sending regions. Between 1990 and 2006, these transfers to Mexico totaled U.S. $163 billion.[4] In 1986, Mexico received U.S. $1.6 billion, and by 2011 family remittances had reached U.S. $22.8 billion, representing 2.1 percent of the GDP (Banco de México 2013; Instituto Nacional de Estadística y Geografía 2013). In spite of the fact that more than 90 percent of remittances are used as income and spent on social reproduction, the IADB's Multilateral Investment Fund (MIF) views remittances as a tool with great possibilities for development. The MIF holds that these flows, which typically benefit low-income households, can help spread "financial democracy" in Latin America and the Caribbean, expanding access to banking services, home ownership, and other asset-building initiatives in the region. However, this goal has yet to be fulfilled in Mexico, where 60 percent of family remittances are sent to small rural areas that lack financial infrastructure and access to credit or saving vehicles (Cruz Hernández 2007; IADB, MIF, and Bendixen 2006).[5] Due to the effects of income inequality in the hemisphere, migrants invest the largest portion of their meager incomes in social reproduction in the host societies. In the case of Mexican migrants earning less than $20,000 per year, a full 82 percent of their annual income is used to sustain themselves in the United States, while the rest is sent home to support family members with monthly stipends that average U.S. $300 per month (IADB, MIF, and Bendixen 2006).

Economic studies in high migrant-sending regions find that the largest beneficiaries of remittances are located in urban centers where people tend to make purchases. Therefore, critics of remittance-based development policies argue that it is highly unlikely that these investments can have a dramatic multiplier effect. They argue that because migrant-initiated small businesses in these regions have very low capacity to generate paid employment, their outreach is highly localized, and they follow a survival strategy where success is dependent on the overexploitation of nonpaid family employment. The few existing studies on the regional spillover effects of remittances conclude that there is no evidence that remittances generate development in the regions where these flows are concentrated (Canales and Montiel Armas 2004; Papail 2005; Suárez and Zapata Martelo 2007). One of the main obstacles to leveraging remittances is the low level of entrepreneurial activity among beneficiaries.[6] Similarly, some Mexican economists have pursued alternative measurements to generate strategic rather than standard cost-benefit assessments to evaluate the potential impact of remittances in the Mexican economy. In 2003, it was estimated that Mexican migrant labor in the United States contributed 8 percent to the U.S. GDP, while in the same period, the potential growth loss by the Mexican economy was calculated at 27.4 percent of GDP, suggesting that the host country reaps more profits than the sending one (Ruiz-Durán 2004: 5).

Several analysts have challenged the dominant discourse on migrant remittances established by the World Bank, the International Monetary Fund (IMF), and the IADB.[7] Critical scholars argue that the dominant strategy pursued by international financial organizations is based on the functionalist premise that migrant remittances are an indispensable source of foreign currency that provides macroeconomic stability and alleviates the social damage caused by poverty. These authors believe that most development studies do not really address the issue of international migration except as a secondary or external variable (Bartra 2008; Delgado Wise 2004; Delgado Wise and Márquez Covarrubias 2009; Fox 2006). Critics further question the neoliberal idea that a global social order necessarily needs immigrant-led civic organizations to supplement the state and the market in development (Burgess 2009; Faist 2008a, 2009). In sum, critical theorists are not convinced that current migration and development proposals are feasible if they fail to consider structural or institutional challenges in both sending and receiving countries.

Migration and Remittances in Michoacán

Following several decades of migration to the United States, we are now in a position to assess remittances to Michoacán as a supposed engine of development. In the period between 1990 and 2000, 370,000 Michoacanos left for the United States either temporarily or permanently. In 2003, the National Population Council estimated that one million Mexicans living in the United States were born in Michoacán, making this state the one with the second-largest diaspora, after Jalisco. The percentage of Michoacán migrants living abroad, compared to the total population born in the state, increased from 4 percent in 1970 to 12 percent in 1990 and 18 percent in 2003 (Zúñiga Herrera 2004).

After four decades of economic restructuring and the implementation of free market policies in the state's agriculture, social inequality has not been reduced. Michoacán has been unable to make steady progress in human development. Between 1992 and 2005, Michoacán's position in human development among all Mexican states fluctuated between twenty-seventh in 1995 and twenty-ninth in 1997 and 2000 (García García 2006). The volume of remittances has slowed emigration from the region in the past five years, but the region's long history of international migration has buffered it from the negative effects of the U.S. economic downturn due to dense social networks that offer solidarity to those temporarily unemployed. However, this has come at a high cost as dozens of generations of people have experienced family separation as the only option to modest social mobility.

The noneconomic impact of remittances appears to be more significant in Michoacán. For example, some researchers argue that family remittances have led to lower levels of corruption. Michoacán's corruption index decreased 55 percent between 2001 and 2007, as measured by Transparencia Mexicana's Índice Nacional de Corrupción y Buen Gobierno (INCBG), during a period in which the state was ranked as one of the highest remittance-receiving states. A similar effect has been measured for Guerrero, a state with high family remittances and a vast HTA network in Chicago and elsewhere across the United States (Tyburski 2012: 343).

In the past decade, HTAs have adopted multiple strategies to encourage authorities to provide a more equitable distribution of social investment funds in their villages. HTAs have used the federal Three-for-One matching fund program to increase needed basic infrastructure in rural marginalized villages, encouraging municipal governments to invest more public funds in traditionally underserved communities or in communities that are considered to be strongholds of opposition parties (Bada 2004). However, the ability of Michoacano migrants to influence municipal and state decision makers was limited, and required significant negotiation with government stakeholders.

Electoral Competition Increases Ties with Chicago's Diaspora

When President Carlos Salinas de Gortari was in office (1988–1994), proposals to improve economic prosperity and reduce the alarming increase in international migration rates mostly centered on free trade and liberalization as the best long-term solution (Flores-Macías 2008). In April 1991, President Salinas spoke at "The U.S. and Mexico: Threshold of a Trade Revolution," a forum organized by the University of Chicago. During breakfast with members of the Hispanic and Mexican American Chambers of Commerce, he spoke to Latino businessmen and asked for their support for his trade liberalization plans. "We go forward as brothers, not as partners," Salinas told them. During the forum, North American Free Trade Agreement (NAFTA) negotiators discussed the benefits of free trade with academics, U.S. and Mexican government officials, and prominent business leaders.[8] No migrant-led organization representatives were invited as speakers. In his address, the late history professor Friedrich Katz, probably in a last attempt to question the unstoppable NAFTA, remembered the Aztec repression against Indian groups who resisted the Aztecs' trade policies. NAFTA's application in 1994 gradually diminished the visibility of anti-NAFTA resistance organized by cross-border civil society groups.[9]

During Salinas's administration, there were scattered government efforts to link organized groups of migrants to collaborate in public infrastructure projects for communities of origin, especially in rural areas where basic services were lacking. Through the National Solidarity Program (PRONASOL),[10] some U.S.-based migrant groups had the opportunity to access public matching funds to build infrastructure in their villages. The Mexican government made these funds available in an attempt to defuse the growing discontent among those groups that had organized mock elections in Chicago and elsewhere in support of defeated presidential contender Cuauhtémoc Cárdenas Solórzano, who had obtained the largest number of votes but was nonetheless not recognized as the winner (see chapter 2). In Chicago, HTAs from Guerrero, Zacatecas, and Michoacán were among the first to obtain access to PRONASOL's International Solidarity funds between 1993 and 1997, the first period that SEDESOL combined resources with state governments to finance codevelopment projects (Monge Arévalo 2005; SEDESOL 2006).

According to official memorandums archived by Chicago's Mexican consulate, PRONASOL officials sponsored visits of state governors in the electoral year of 1994 to meet with their respective communities. However, PRONASOL did not provide sufficient funds, and thus consular officials requested donations from HTAs, Mexican businessmen, and state governments to cover logistics and the rental of meeting places. This signaled a new era of public-private partnerships for community development in the neoliberal agenda. For this outreach program, the federal government budgeted U.S. $12,000 to create groups, social clubs, and societies by region of origin to build social infrastructure in Mexican communities.

Despite the passage of the 1996 immigration reform laws, which tightened immigration controls and sanctions on migrant workers and increased deportations, migrant spending in remittance transfers to Mexico from the United States was simultaneously well received as a crucial way to promote business opportunities for remittance businesses that would then stimulate Illinois state revenues. Meanwhile, the Mexican government continued to withhold electoral rights for Mexican migrants living abroad, while encouraging them to sacrifice and send money to support development in the homeland.

In the 1990s, state governments with sizable emigrant populations living in Chicago, such as Guerrero and Michoacán, believed it was in their best interest to support organized migrant groups in an effort to counteract the influence of more threatening movements demanding democratic reform in Mexico. HTAs took advantage of this small political opening to attract more attention from their state governments and won political spaces for the opposition in a few municipalities. It is not a coincidence that the most visible and organized Chicago HTAs in the 1990s were from Jalisco, Guanajuato, Guerrero, and Michoacán—states where the Party of the Democratic Revolution (PRD) and the National Action Party (PAN), the two main opposition parties, won important victories in this and the following decade.

Víctor Manuel Tinoco Rubí, governor of Michoacán between 1996 and 2002, made his first official visit to Chicago in 1996. Following his meeting with constituents, Tinoco Rubí visited HTAs frequently, which led to continued discussions and eventual policy proposals to reduce emigration to the United States. For instance, in his annual reports, the governor began to include a migrant affairs section outlining policies to address the increased migration of Michoacanos. After the midterm election, the state congress created the first Commission for Migrant Affairs. During his visits, Governor Tinoco Rubí promised HTAs he would increase resources to address the needs of migrants. Most HTAs, however, viewed these promises as mostly empty rhetoric and believed that the governor used his closeness with migrants just to favor his party in elections.[11]

In the spring of 2000, in a leaked letter to FEDECMI members from consulate staff, the director of the Michoacán Migrant Affairs Office complained of the "poor performance" of several HTAs in midterm municipal elections, explaining that "unfortunately, the only club that passed the exam for having won the electoral contest was San Rafael in the municipality of Santa Ana Maya."[12] This was the last time the Revolutionary Institutional Party (PRI) prevailed in that municipality. The PAN won the municipal elections in 2001, deepening the PRI debacle in the state. Aspiring politicians and government officials had already noticed the increasing power of HTAs, and noted the political influence on families left behind.[13] Similar to Santa Ana Maya, in the late 1990s HTA leaders from the municipality of Hidalgo successfully negotiated with their PAN-governed municipality to cofinance social welfare projects, as real political competition slowly increased.

FEDECMI was unable to formalize a matching fund agreement with the state of Michoacán in 2000. After discussing the government's public pork-barrel tactics in dealing with the migrant community, HTA leaders thought that any promise made by a lame-duck governor was meaningless. Meanwhile, the PRI lost the presidential election to the PAN and Gonzalo Arroyo, FEDECMI's president, was invited to a private meeting that President Fox organized with the migrant community in Mexico City. At that meeting, Fox promised to improve relationships with migrants, which encouraged FEDECMI to raise its profile. That December, club presidents launched an aggressive media campaign in *La Voz de Michoacán*, a widely circulated newspaper based in Morelia. They wrote letters to the editor exposing a long list of unfulfilled promises to HTAs made by the governor. To prevent more political damage, Governor Tinoco Rubí agreed to meet with FEDECMI in Morelia in January 2001 to mend fences.[14]

During the spring, FEDECMI's club presidents decided to invite any political candidate for Michoacán's governorship to Chicago who would be willing to commit to public policy programs for migrants, in an attempt to reject being branded as patronage groups affiliated with the PRI. Some leaders feared a return to the political violence that had occurred in their state during the 1990s. PRI sympathizers also frequently viewed the PRD not as a victim but as perpetrator. Other skeptics did not want to provoke opponents for fear of reprisals to their families still living in Michoacán.

In September 2001, the PRI candidate Alfredo Anaya visited Chicago to rally support among migrants. HTA leaders kept to the script on demanding a formal matching fund for community development projects and public funds to purchase a building to open a Casa Michoacán in Chicago. Some HTAs that were PRI sympathizers even set up an unofficial campaign house in South Chicago and distributed calling cards to encourage phone calls to relatives and ask them to vote for the PRI. The PRD chose Lázaro Cárdenas Batel as its candidate for governor, a senator with prior experience in negotiating with the Mexican diaspora. During his term as congressman (1997–2000), he made several tours to the United States, meeting with civic leaders from the AFL-CIO, the South West Voter Registration Project, and the Center for Autonomous Social Action–General Brotherhood of Workers (CASA-HGT), among others.[15] In April 1998, he had submitted the first bill to regulate absentee ballots for Mexicans abroad to allow them to vote in presidential elections.

In October 2001, Cárdenas Batel held a meeting with migrants at the Zacatecano Federation headquarters in Chicago's Gage Park neighborhood. He was received by an enthusiastic group of approximately 300 migrants. Michoacano HTAs selected the venue to show that Zacatecano HTAs owned a building thanks to the initial seed money contributed by the government of Zacatecas, which was in the hands of the opposition since 1998. HTA presidents came well prepared, and enumerated a long list of requests they wanted Cárdenas Batel to agree to in order to mobilize support for his candidacy among their relatives. These demands were reiterated to PRI and PAN candidates as well.[16] Cárdenas Batel's campaign staff arrived early to distribute brochures addressing the PRD's migrant affairs platform, which prominently offered a new migrant affairs office that would provide administrative, legal, and advocacy services.

Cárdenas Batel won the election. During his term in office (2002–2008), he delivered seven of his eight campaign promises for migrants, including a large contribution to Casa Michoacán's down payment and a monthly stipend to pay for organizational expenses while FEDECMI consolidated its structure as a viable nonprofit. The PRD governorship did not use—at least not immediately—political party affiliation to block access to public infrastructure funds as the PRI had done with HTA leaders not loyal to the PRI in some municipalities during its many decades ruling the state (Bada 2001). Its only unfulfilled promise was perhaps one of the most significant for the migrant agenda: Governor Cárdenas Batel was unable to create an earmarked state fund to support small migrant investors interested in creating jobs in Michoacán.

In 2002, SEDESOL secretary Josefina Vázquez Mota met with HTAs in Chicago to promote the Three-for-One Program, after the new PAN administration decided to implement it at the federal level. HTA leaders took the opportunity to denounce the many irregularities they had detected in SEDESOL delegations in states where a Three-for-One Program was already operating. They complained about several federal, state, and municipal authorities who would frequently obstruct the construction of rodeo rings, scholarships for low-income students, hospitals, and church renovations with the argument that those projects were not productive. To show them how serious she was about meeting HTA expectations, Vázquez Mota removed some SEDESOL delegates in state offices, promised to revise the operating rules, and immediately accepted student scholarships as part of the Three-for-One package (Sada Solana 2006).[17]

In November 2002, Governor Cárdenas Batel attended the second Binational Forum of Michoacano Migrants Living Abroad in East Los Angeles, at the César Chávez Community College. At the forum, hosted by the recently created local Federation of Michoacano Clubs Lázaro Cárdenas del Río, the governor pledged U.S. $1 million in state funds, in addition to Three-for-One matching funds, to demonstrate his administration's willingness to cooperate with migrant federations. During a panel on economic development, federal, state, and municipal leaders discussed with HTA leaders basic policy guidelines for determining which projects to fund first. In some cases, HTAs defended their right to build rodeo rings, while state officials encouraged them to finance social infrastructure projects such as water wells. However, some HTAs countered that previously proposed social infrastructure projects had been turned down due to conflicting opinions about state responsibilities with regard to infrastructure. During this panel, I witnessed a heated discussion in which an HTA wanted to build a regional hospital, claiming the need to reduce travel time for patients. State officials responded that it was impossible to fund public hospitals because Three-for-One Program rules made no provisions for staffing. A proposal to build a high school in a nearby village met a similar fate, while state officials argued they could not commit to find teachers without the approval of the secretary of education. These conflicts represented fundamentally divergent views on the purposes of these funds and the role of local government. For HTAs, development meant addressing all social needs, while for state officials, it meant addressing needs that could be fulfilled mostly with bricks, asphalt, and pipes—that is, infrastructure that did not need personnel and focused on inexpensive, one-time investments.

Despite initial setbacks to developing mutually acceptable guidelines for funding infrastructure, the state of Michoacán played a pivotal role in developing migrant clubs as empowered transnational actors. This was achieved through an exchange of democratic power at the federal and state levels, and with financial and moral support offered by state governments, the consulate, and local Chicago non-profits. Other Mexican states subsequently became interested in maintaining eco-nomic attachments between emigrant populations and their home communities, and decided to support innovative state-society partnerships to reduce conflict and sustain migrant remittances to support infrastructure development.

However, during the 1990s, these isolated cases of democratic transitions at the subnational level did not trigger more broad-scale commitments to work with HTAs for community development. Likewise, the modest changes orchestrated by President Salinas de Gortari were not enough to encourage state governments to eradicate entrenched systems of patronage. Similarly, when Zacatecano HTAs signed matching fund programs in the late 1990s with state and federal authori-ties, this, too, did not produce a simultaneous national or local domino effect to expand public-private partnerships with migrant organizations in Southern California, where the majority of Zacatecano HTAs were concentrated, or in Chicago, where Zacatecanos had established robust organizations. Substantial and visible change in state-diaspora relations was particularly unlikely after 1998, when the PRD took power in Zacatecas, because few Zacatecano HTAs and feder-ations had the organizational maturity to scale up and out of their comfort zones in Southern California and Chicago. It was not until peaceful, democratic, and free elections came to the states of Jalisco (1995) Michoacán (2001), and Guer-rero (2005) that the quality of relations between state governments and migrants improved, and federal, state, and municipal funding for rural infrastructure became a reality for hundreds of rural villages with migrant organizations in the United States. This shift was propelled by the high percentage of migrants from those states living in Chicago and the increased visibility and influence of their budding organizations. Transition at the federal government was the final piece of the puzzle to convince state governments that it was profitable to construct respectful relationships with the migrant civil society.

REMITTANCE-EXTRACTING POLICIES TO FINANCE DEVELOPMENT

With improved relations between migrant civil society and the Mexican govern-ment, international finance experts took advantage of Mexico's new democratic transition as the perfect opportunity to devise new approaches to manage collec-tive and individual remittances. Almost immediately after Vicente Fox assumed power, HTAs instantly became the go-to organizations, sought out by foundations, remittance transfer companies, international finance organizations, the private sector, and subnational governments that came in search of strategic partnerships to leverage remittances for community development. Large companies such as Western Union, Satélites Mexicanos (SATMEX),[18] and the now defunct Constru-mex[19] quickly became interested in accessing the organizational networks of the

Mexican migrant community and were eager to support the work of HTAs with occasional sponsorships in exchange for publicity. Likewise, small and medium-size entrepreneurs saw an opportunity to increase their visibility among their audience during HTA banquets and became event sponsors.[20]

In May 2002, Presidents Fox and Bush signed an agreement to implement the Partnership for Prosperity, a bilateral plan to leverage private resources to promote economic growth in less-developed regions. The leaders envisioned this plan as one that would "foster an environment in which no Mexican feels compelled to leave his home for lack of jobs or opportunity" (Partnership for Prosperity Executive Group 2002: 2). However, the agreement was mostly a pledge with few commitments. Among the few proposals to create jobs in labor expulsions regions, the Inter-American Foundation would grant $2 million (to be matched by the private Mexican foundation Fundamex) to ninety communities in twenty-one Mexican states with the highest poverty rates and migration to the United States.

To tackle the capitalization of remittances into productive enterprises, one of the proposals promised to offer training to small businesses and HTAs in areas with significant Mexican migrant populations. The Multilateral Investment Fund of the IADB donated U.S. $1.1 million for a matching fund pilot program in Guanajuato, Zacatecas, Jalisco, Hidalgo, and Puebla. The local counterpart was expected to contribute the same amount, distributed among HTAs, state governments, and Nacional Financiera, a Mexican public banking institution (IADB-MIF n.d.). The program initially approved thirty projects in Zacatecas, Jalisco, and Hidalgo, but those quickly faced several challenges and were not successfully implemented. Executing agencies never required market assessments or business plans from potential investors, who also did not have sufficient experience doing business in Mexico. Moreover, there were no clear rules to guide the process, which eventually led to excessive bureaucracy and many participants losing interest and abandoning the program (Cruickshank Soria 2004). In the end, the pilot program only implemented five small business projects with these funds, two in Zacatecas and three in Jalisco (García Zamora 2006).

Paradoxically, one of the most visible responses to the population displacement caused by NAFTA was the concealed promotion of migration to the United States—the problem that NAFTA was supposed to address. Seen as a viable solution for Mexico's problems, from unemployment to rural development, the Mexican government actively promoted emigration. For example, in 2004 President Fox courted Mexican migrants while on a visit to Chicago, calling them "heroes" and praising their contributions to their country. In his view, migrants only needed to "learn" how to use the money more productively: "I know that the money you send to your families is used to eat but it is time for you to build some assets in savings accounts that generate some interest. We also have the Three-for-One Program so if you decide individually or collectively to transfer any amount to Mexico, or if you want to initiate a business, it doesn't matter, we will match three times the amount of your investment as a gift. This is not a loan, it is to encourage you to invest in your community."[21] Very few migrants answered his call to invest, but the government quickly adjusted the strategy and shifted the priority toward asking HTAs to continue their charitable donations for revitalizing battered municipal infrastructure through the Three-for-One Program. This can be viewed either as a disguised voluntary tax or as a remittance-extracting policy designed to obtain the largest possible remittance volume from vulnerable migrant workers. However, this voluntary taxation is not required from the Mexican middle class, and it asks vulnerable migrants to donate money to pay for public infrastructure in Mexico on top of their U.S. income taxes.

In 2006, the IADB commissioned an independent evaluation of the Three-for-One Program and offered a loan of $7 million to the Mexican government to add a fourth layer to the Three-for-One financial mix for three years.[22] With these funds, the IADB would finance social and productive infrastructure (63 percent), productive projects (19 percent), and institutional strengthening (18 percent) through a matching fund scheme. The program would follow most of the existing rules for the Three-for-One Program, but also added some special conditions. For example, the stay-at-home community would propose productive projects to the HTA, which would then choose from a menu of options (IADB 2006). This condition proved to be a challenge because there was little agreement between HTAs, and the stay-at-home community and SEDESOL could not find enough projects to meet the requirements. The IADB required SEDESOL to be in charge of providing technical assistance and training to parallel committees in the communities of origin that would be monitoring projects. However, SEDESOL struggled to monitor the completion of projects, let alone supervise the monitoring abilities of local parallel committees. After the initial frustration, SEDESOL convinced IADB to let it alter the rules to include some projects financed with this loan.[23] SEDESOL declared that it did not have the capacity to train HTAs participating in Three-for-One projects, citing a minimal operating budget. Still, IADB insisted that SEDESOL should train Three-for-One project participants to reduce corruption and increase participatory planning and project efficiency. However, neither HTA representatives nor local parallel committees were ever invited to meet with IADB officials to voice their opinions about operating rules. It is no surprise, therefore, that in 2009, the IADB Office of External Relations in Washington, D.C.,[24] sought to meet with HTAs after learning that the National Alliance of Latin American and Caribbean Communities (NALACC) was participating in protests against the "celebration" of the fifty years of the IADB in Latin America (Campaña Bid 50 2009) and had published a critical analysis of displacement caused by IADB-funded megaprojects.[25]

In Mexico, SEDESOL staff decided on the rules and regulations for the Three-for-One Program and rarely invited HTAs to participate. The ministry did not view the associations as valuable advisers in the creation of local development policies. The government's gap between rhetoric and practice raised false expectations about the potential of migrants as agents of development. As Natasha Iskander observes in her analysis of the evolution of the Three-for-One Program in Zacatecas, the state under Fox only saw what it wanted to see. Migrants were reduced to economic and political resources—into objects of policy—and were excluded from the process of policy design and from the generation of concepts on which the policy was built (Iskander 2010).

The state of Michoacán followed a similarly unsuccessful approach when it attempted to include migrant organizations in creating new development projects using collective remittances. The governor of Michoacán asked the State Ministry of Planning and Development to convene a series of meetings with migrants to discuss a new state development plan for the next thirty years. To that end, in November 2003 the government hired a group of consultants to organize a one-day public forum with HTA leaders at the University of Chicago.[26] During the meeting, these consultants shared their economic projections for the state, predicting that if the state economy did not grow in the next three decades, Michoacán would be expelling 45,000 migrants per year by the year 2030. They estimated that between 1995 and 2000, the state had been sending an annual average of 41,500 migrants to the United States.[27] They also predicted that the primary sector would only increase from 14.11 percent to 16.21 percent of economic activity by 2030, but this sector would be responsible for providing a livelihood to one-third of the population. Ultimately, these predictions were wrong. By 2005, the march toward the service sector in Michoacán was accomplished, occupying 56 percent of all employment, while the secondary and primary sectors experienced a considerable increase, participating with 23 and 21 percent of the economy, respectively. The informal economy and its concomitant job insecurity occupied 36 percent of total employment by 2007 (UNDP 2008).[28]

During the discussion at the forum, migrant leaders shared their opinions about the economic problems the state was facing and offered their recommendations to solve them. There were several unifying topics in their demands. Many mentioned problems in the countryside, including the lack of irrigation systems, low market prices for grains, unequal distribution of subsidies, and the lack of industrialization to add value to competitive agricultural products. Migrants demanded additional support for the primary sector, and were skeptical of increased exports and globalization as a strategy, arguing the state was too dependent on foreign investment and the domestic private sector was not strong enough to compete in international markets. Other migrant leaders recounted personal experiences with Korean textile factories that entered the state briefly without offering a living wage, thus making it very difficult to produce lasting transitions from peasant to wage worker.

In their evaluations of Michoacán's economic woes, migrants placed the responsibility of addressing development concerns with the government. They harked back to ideals of national protectionism and a strong Mexican welfare state. Even though many participants had been living in Chicago for twenty or thirty years under the relatively less protectionist U.S. economy, they clearly cited a preference for state protectionism. Several leaders argued that the state of Michoacán should curb the excessive privileges offered to foreign investors, and they wanted the government to offer more financial support to the Mexican private sector. When the topic switched to environmental protection, many also demanded more regulation of polluting enterprises and "for more environmental inspectors to make sure enterprises do not pollute water used for agriculture, the same way that the U.S. forces its companies to dispose pollutants in a proper way."[29] As a result of their constant communication with the homeland throughout their long residences in Chicago, HTA leaders showed an ability to understand the pros and cons of two different societies, romanticizing some aspects of the U.S. economy while showing nostalgia for the unfinished promises of the Mexican Revolution.

In the first round of oral interventions to voice their opinions to the consultants, José Díaz, a club president from Santa Ana Maya, issued a simple recommendation: "The government must help small entrepreneurs by giving them more money." Estela Adame, a college-educated club member from the city of Puruándiro now living in Indiana, added: "The government must create more jobs instead of thinking that development problems will be solved with remittances. Governments should find alternatives to stop migration to the U.S. and to Mexico's urban cities. Moreover, the migrant monument that was just built should be redesigned to represent migrants that have died trying to cross the border instead of just glorifying the crossing of borders."

When discussing agricultural development, most participants agreed that small farmers did not receive a fair price for their products, and lacked training to improve their harvest, and that improved access and management of water resources were badly needed in the state. All participants in the room explained that families still used remittances to buy seeds and work the fields regardless of market limitations, sometimes just to satisfy the elderly and to fight boredom.[30] They were convinced that migration was a response to disinvestment in the rural countryside. HTA leaders brainstormed collectively for solutions, and proposed changes to the agricultural model that would build more water-efficient and less-polluting greenhouses, instead of relying on traditional cash crops. Despite promises from consultants to send the results of all forums conducted in the United States, and to invite participants to share their recommendations with the government, HTA leaders never heard from them again.

Despite repeated visits to Michoacán by international finance organizations, expert consultants' elaborate analyses, and a new discourse to include migrants as partners in development policies, the state of Michoacán did not follow a radically different strategy from that of the federal government to include migrants in community development, beyond investing in some initially promising social cooperatives in the primary sector. However, migrant HTAs used their charitable donations to improve infrastructure and generate modest productive projects as their best weapon to show municipal and state governments that they were capable of participating in decision-making processes to solve the most urgent needs of their communities. This created a window of opportunity to make increased demands in areas that went beyond public-private partnerships for public infrastructure, such as education, access to rural credits, market regulation, state intervention to protect domestic markets, environmental regulation, labor rights, and the defense of human rights for all migrants in Mexican territory. For example, the initial proposal elaborated by a Chicago HTA from Michoacán to include scholarships for high school and college students as part of the Three-for-One Program got approval from SEDESOL and was later emulated in different states with large concentrations of HTAs in the United States.

Altruists Becoming Entrepreneurs

Throughout most of their existence, HTAs have been primarily interested in grassroots philanthropy to improve the quality of life in sending communities. However, few members have had the entrepreneurial skills or interest in creating permanent jobs in rural Mexico. The demographic profile of the membership includes several small business owners, but many do not have prior experience managing businesses in Mexico.

Since the late 1960s, HTAs have made frequent donations to their communities, including ambulances, fire trucks, medical equipment, school buses, and many other supplies salvaged from surplus storages in their workplaces or thanks to personal networks with local nongovernmental organizations (NGOs) sympathetic to the needs in developing regions.[31] The system of recycling refuse from developed to developing areas slowly transformed into fund-raising for small infrastructure projects in the 1990s and to larger projects with the Three-for-One Program. Over time, HTAs modified their fund-raising behaviors and exported some fund-raising models that are popular in the United States. For example, in a famous case that made headlines, Rosendo Sánchez, the president of Chehuayo Grande club, crossed the Cuitzeo Lake in a charity swim to raise MXP 60,000 to support the efforts of a local committee that had gathered MXP 37,000 to build a new church. Sánchez is a veteran of charity runs who has participated in the Chicago marathon to benefit the March of Dimes and other NGOs through sponsorships from his employer. Financing social infrastructure in sending regions was well received by community members and municipal governments; however, transforming philanthropy to job-generating productive projects became a daring proposal that was harder to accomplish than the 3.4 hour swim Sánchez completed in 2004.

Across Mexico, between 2002 and 2012 the Three-for-One Program implemented 18,573 projects; however, only 7.5 percent of them were categorized as productive (Gobierno Federal 2012). The rest of the budget was applied to infrastructure, and the most successful projects were construction or renovation of roads, sidewalks, gardens, and public squares. The percentage of municipalities benefiting from this program has ranged from 10 percent in 2002 to 20 percent in 2007 (Aparicio Castillo, Maldonado Trujillo, and Beltrán Pulido 2008). The federal match offered has been matched in equal amounts by state governments, municipalities, and migrant organizations, but has been limited and represents less than 1 percent of the total funds that the Mexican Congress allocates to SEDESOL. Despite the constant increase in its federal budget (from 114 million pesos in 2002 to 557 million in 2010), the Three-for-One Program's relative value remains negligible (Canales 2008). In response to the lack of job creation in sending regions, in the last decade the state's Secretariat for Migrant Affairs and SEDESOL officials encouraged migrants to engage in more productive projects, offering limited technical assistance and advice to implement them. In every instance where officials had to meet with migrant groups in Chicago, and in the workshops offered to municipal presidents since the establishment of this program, government officials constantly encouraged HTA members and municipal presidents to submit more job-generating productive projects to go along with infrastructure.

In Michoacán, the Three-for-One Program evolution has shown modest results. The total investment between 2002 and 2011 totaled U.S. $59 million, a small amount compared to the average annual family remittances received during the same period. Michoacán receives the highest amount of annual remittances both per capita (U.S. $650) and in absolute numbers. However, in 2006 the Three-for-One Program only assigned 2.5 percent of the federal investment and 10 percent of the projects to this state (Canales 2008). To date, the program has financed more than 1,100 projects, allowing migrants to learn more about the nuts and bolts of multiple state bureaucracies involved in the program administration and the allocation of public funds. Between 2002 and 2006, the program contributed with development projects to 97.5 percent of municipalities with high marginalization indexes at least once, mostly because prior to 2004, the program accepted proposals from any organized groups, not only from HTAs registered in the United States, and poor rural villages without HTAs took advantage of this matching fund opportunity to improve needed infrastructure. To get an idea about project distribution by category in the state between 2002 and 2008, see table 4.1.

In Michoacán, there are almost 12,000 villages in 113 municipalities; therefore, less than 10 percent have obtained a community development project using these funds because several localities with highly dynamic HTAs have received more than one project. One of the challenges of the Three-for-One Program is that it was conceived to serve marginalized localities and municipalities with high and

TABLE 4.1

THREE-FOR-ONE PROJECT DISTRIBUTION IN
THE STATE OF MICHOACÁN (2002–2008)

Type of Project	Number of Projects	Percentage
Social infrastructure	630	75
Productive projects	96	11
Beautification and churches	93	11
Educational projects	24	3
Total	843	100

Source: State of Michoacán's Secretariat for Migrant Affairs, 2009.

very high migration indexes. Yet as empirical evidence on the civic engagement patterns of migrants has confirmed, HTAs do not always represent the poorest villages. Consequently, as more HTAs mature in areas with low levels of marginalization, the program tends to allocate resources in areas with a high density of binational networks, but which are not necessarily the most in need of investments for new infrastructure (Aparicio and Meseguer 2012). In fact, after several years of negotiating with authorities to modify the target population for this program, the HTAs reached an agreement with SEDESOL to modify the operating rules to reflect more adequately the demand-driven nature of the Three-for-One Program. In 2009, instead of referring to poverty conditions and marginalization to define the target population as it had been described in the operating rules between 2002 and 2008, SEDESOL administrations agreed to change this definition stating that "the target population is constituted by the people living in sending communities and any other communities migrants decide to support" (Secretaría de Desarrollo Social 2012: 17).

With a program design that favors migrants' ability to submit proposals backed by HTAs, the Three-for-One Program allocates investments mostly in states where HTA networks are the largest. Therefore, in 2007, 59 percent of projects and 54 percent of the Three-for-One budget was allocated to three states: Zacatecas, Jalisco, and Michoacán (Aparicio Castillo, Maldonado Trujillo, and Beltrán Pulido 2008). Not surprisingly, despite cajoling from government officials who wanted to see an increase in the percentage of productive projects, between 2002 and 2008 only ninety-six productive projects (11.3 percent of the total) were financed with Three-for-One funds in Michoacán (Reynoso Acosta 2009).[32] Some of those projects failed, and others are struggling to keep afloat without technical assistance and with problems competing in the global market. Many HTA leaders learned that job-generating ventures without a business plan and technical assistance were difficult to maintain for more than five years, a common measure of potential stability for these microenterprises. There are not any serious evaluations of the failure rate of Three-for-One productive projects; however, HTA leaders estimate that more than 50 percent of projects financed through Three-for-One between 2002 and 2010 failed after a few years (Voces Mesoamericanas 2010). In 2010, only twenty-eight individual migrant-led projects (12 percent of the national total) were backed by SEDESOL in Michoacán using an interest-free loan model financed by the federal government and the IADB, and only nine job-generating projects (5 percent of the state total) proposed by groups of more than ten migrant investors affiliated with an HTA received 75 percent free cost-sharing through the Three-for-One Program (Secretaría de Desarrollo Social 2010b).

Despite many attempts to build sustainable projects, many Three-for-One job-generating projects failed to achieve long-term sustainability. For HTA members who became involved in those projects, the offer of free money to support their own "Mexican Dream" was too tempting to refuse. However, labor shortages in sending communities posed a significant obstacle to agricultural projects, and in the municipalities with high migration indexes, small landholders with greenhouse projects had a hard time finding day laborers willing to work for the prevailing wage of MXP 150 per day for agricultural labor in 2005. Many unemployed workers in those regions instead preferred to borrow some money or to save just enough to emigrate to the United States (Ávila 2007).

Poor planning and lack of knowledge about domestic and export markets also played a role in project failures. Projects established in highly marginalized areas failed fairly soon due to lack of basic infrastructure that facilitated sales in regional markets. Projects implemented in less marginalized areas had modest success, but mostly focused on teaching entrepreneurial skills and increased ties between migrant investors and stay-at-home community members. The most widely cited example of a promising social cooperative financed with Three-for-One funds, which triggered visits by IADB, HTA leaders from neighboring states, journalists, and even President Fox, was the case of Atacheo de Regalado and Ejido La Labor, two neighboring communities in the municipality of Zamora. Between 2000 and 2005, Atacheo de Regalado, a community of fewer than 2,000 people, experienced a deficit in population replacement, losing almost 300 inhabitants. Social development indicators show that the inhabitants of Atacheo de Regalado have only 3.7 years of schooling on average, 67 percent of the population does not have access to health care, and 50 percent of the workforce lives on under U.S. $10 per day, keeping Atacheo at some distance from extreme marginalization (INEGI 2006). Ejido La Labor is a tiny community of 149 inhabitants right next to Atacheo de Regalado. Due to their geographical proximity to the relatively prosperous agricultural corridor of El Bajío Zamorano, a social cooperative system in this region offered some promise for success.

During 2002 and 2003, in a migrant-state effort to offer some alternatives to slow down emigration using Three-for-One Program funds, Atacheo and La Labor received U.S. $556,923 to implement seven projects through a social cooperative with seventy-three migrant shareholders living in California after the local HTA financed several pavement projects, a community library, and the renovation of the church with the support and coordination of Marcos Linares, the local Catholic priest. The projects included greenhouses for chrysanthemums, red bell peppers, and tomatoes; a loudspeaker factory; and a goat and imported turkey farm. The flowers greenhouse started in 2002 with seven women employees, five of whom quit the daily job once they became shareholders. Salaries were U.S. $11 per day for a shift from 7 A.M. to 4 P.M., which was the prevailing wage for greenhouse work in Michoacán, considerably above the general minimum wage of U.S. $4 dollars for an eight-hour shift for the region. In June 2002, the first flower production was ready, and vendors took it to market. However, poor crop quality fetched below-market prices compared to flowers from greenhouses with quality-control systems. After subsequent setbacks, the flower shareholders shifted to tomato and bell pepper production, but also struggled to compete in the domestic and international markets. Most shareholders quickly grew frustrated by the slow progress and refused to travel regularly for meetings to monitor the production process. None of the projects had a board of directors, so they became easy victims of predators pretending to assist them (Molina Ramírez 2005). Alicia, one of the group leaders living in Atacheo, offers a convincing explanation of the flowers failure during a visit to the site in 2005:

> We didn't know anything about chrysanthemums, neither shareholders nor workers. The engineer we had to support us was a volunteer. He did not want to charge for his services but he seldom came to check the flowers. We did not seek support from the government and nobody advised us about strategies to produce with quality. It is hard to make ends meet here. The people you see here are the ones that are happy with having a little but the ones who leave are those with needs and they're not planning to return. I'm fine because I work for this project, manage it, have shares and besides, I am a beautician and cut hair every afternoon in my house. Plus, I am single without kids and some of my brothers live in California. I am here to care for my father and two younger brothers.[33]

The loudspeaker factory along with the goat and turkey husbandry projects did not fare any better. The factory received an impound order by 2005 as its speakers could not compete with cheap Chinese imports, and managers declared bankruptcy. The turkey chicks imported from Miami, Florida, to be raised in family farms needed an expensive federally inspected slaughterhouse in order to sell the meat to cold meat production factories because giant turkeys have a lower price in local markets than grain-fed ones due to different culinary culture tastes.[34]

Despite the many failures of these initial cooperatives, the state government was interested in proving the long-term sustainability of the social cooperative model and wanted to keep them afloat. The government provided rescue funds, but extra resources were diverted to cover urgent debts from bankrupt projects (Molina Ramírez 2005). The governor believed it was a good policy to offer some hope to social entrepreneurs who were willing to put up a good fight to compete in the global market. However, to make it work, he also believed that the state needed to link thousands of rural cooperatives in a united front to compete with large agribusiness, an endeavor that the state government was not ready to take on in a national climate that was more inclined to subsidize medium and large-scale agribusiness producers than small rural cooperatives.[35]

In 2005, to support the rural cooperative model, the government appointed Marcos Linares to lead the creation of a new Association of Social Enterprises (Asociación Michoacana de Promotores de Empresa Social, A.C.). This move provided an institutional home within the Migrant Affairs office and a monthly stipend of U.S. $5,000 to help with operating expenses. This became the civil society arm of a group of twenty-two greenhouse cooperatives trying to replicate the cooperative model in eighty municipalities in a state. The main objective was to export larger quantities of tomatoes, sweet yellow corn, beans, jalapeño peppers, and tomatillos to the U.S. market.[36] However, the learning curve proved to be too steep and frustrated many small migrant investors who had entrusted their modest production to the organization. For example, Chicago-based HTA investors complain that they have not received the agreed-upon payment for exported quality tomatoes, and that refrigerated trailer trucks sometimes mix produce that needs to be kept at different temperatures just to fill the container. Once the produce reaches the Mexico-U.S. border, it is often not accepted because it has been overheated, and farmers and investors have to bear the loss.[37]

Competing in the tomato export markets is particularly difficult for small producers. A few wholesalers control tomato imports from Mexico in San Antonio, Texas, and it is difficult to sell directly to supermarkets in the Midwest, which was the original plan of HTA investors (Calleja Pinedo 2009). After one decade of learning from failed experiences and frequent contacts with national organized producers, migrant HTA investors are now trying to compete in local and national tomato markets in Mexico, demanding that the state protect them against unfair competition from imports and acknowledging that having a carefully planned strategy is needed in order to compete successfully in a free market economy, which clearly did not happen in their first experiments. Michoacán is just an example of a larger trend among developing nations that are also experiencing unacceptable levels of damage to local economies as a result of unfettered free trade, and are now pursuing loopholes in trade regulations to implement protectionist trade barriers to prevent further erosion of local economies (Lowrey 2012).

However, small agricultural producers are not always on the list of priorities for protection (Mexican governments have been ideologically opposed, and NAFTA prohibits it), and other challenges also contribute to their lack of success. For example, a tomato greenhouse in the municipality of Santa Ana Maya financed by two Chicago-based migrants using Three-for-One funds went bankrupt in less than five years after investors failed to secure an affordable and efficient water supply. Before starting the project, municipal authorities promised to help to secure a federal permit for a well on their property. However, a neighboring municipality in Guanajuato complained, arguing that the well would affect its water supply for irrigation and urged the government to deny the permit. This led investors to close the greenhouse after a few years of losing money.

While partnerships between government, migrant civil society, and small investors failed to generate more jobs, similar challenges made financing sustainable projects difficult. For example, Western Union Foundation invested U.S. $1.25 million in a pilot project to increase the matching funds available in several Mexican states. The government of Michoacán signed an agreement with Western Union in 2006 to receive U.S. $250,000 for a 4X1 matching fund to be invested in productive projects.[38] However, after a two-year delay, only two projects were financed with these funds.

In the first evaluation of this program, authors recognized that some of the twenty-six projects financed with Western Union funds in a few Mexican states are experiencing modest success, and after a few years of operation are in the process of becoming financially sustainable. Others will likely fail due to the lack of promised funds pledged by the Three-for-One scheme, lack of technical assistance, and problems with commercialization in domestic and international markets, and above all because "few projects chose to include the community in the selection of the business venture, instead limiting those decision-making processes to associates invested in the business" (Orozco and Scaife Diaz 2011). Critics also warn that in some investments in greenhouse tomato production in Guerrero and Michoacán, the mass production techniques used by these businesses also risk flooding the local market and driving down prices for area farmers. Western Union did not renew the funds for this initiative and has preferred to focus on charitable donations to migrant shelters across Mexico and establish similar new pilot programs for African diaspora organizations in partnership with USAID (USAID 2011). This one-time pilot program suggests that Western Union offered these one-time funds to boost its media image after losing a class action lawsuit for failing to disclose the full fees to customers in their international remittance business, but was not really committed to support a long-term investment in community development at one of the company's most profitable business sites.[39]

Mexican businesses and private philanthropies remain absent in the Three-for-One scheme and have not donated money to diversify the funding of collective remittances projects in rural Mexico.[40] In contrast, some Latino philanthropies in the United States have supported HTA efforts to diversify funding sources, but results have been modest so far. For example, the IADB partnered with Hispanics in Philanthropy (HIP) to offer technical assistance to HTA projects by bringing private donors at the local level in Latin America to increase the bank's initial credit of U.S. $7 million. In the first three years, the initiative funded six projects in Mexico, Argentina, and the Dominican Republic. In Mexico, it obtained support from Western Union, Ford, Hewlett and Packard foundations, and the Chicago-based Daniel and Karen May Foundation to support two small projects: a cheese factory and a meat processing plant. In its evaluation, HIP summarized the success as an increase in organizational capacity among the groups it tried to help. HIP's report suggests that HTA groups did not have any previous experience in establishing microenterprises in Mexico and that private local donations were mostly used in self-serving charity projects. HIP had never directly implemented microenterprises and had to rely on part-time local consultants who were not entirely devoted to monitoring projects and could not offer round-the-clock technical assistance to solve problems. Eventually, many migrants who were initially involved as donors in the United States lost their jobs after the 2008 recession and returned to their communities without enough funds to invest (Hall 2011; Hispanics in Philanthropy 2011).

While evidence points to a long list of disappointments in the last decade of public-private partnerships for leveraging collective remittances, at least in Michoacán, not all organizations interested in providing alternatives to emigration failed. For example, the Club Indaparapeo of Berwyn, Illinois, proposed a successful approach to leverage collective remittances for development by seeking to improve educational outcomes. Between 1950 and 2000, Michoacán fell four positions in the national education ranking, with students severely underperforming in math and reading (UNDP 2008). Faced with this reality, the Club Indaparapeo was convinced that the best solution it could offer to improve people's position in the labor force was to fund their education. In Michoacán, thousands of students are forced to travel long distances to have access to education beyond grammar school. Access to high school education is only offered to 59 percent of students (UNDP 2008). The club's plan was to offer four-year competitive scholarships to help low-income students complete a college degree. SEDESOL viewed the proposal with skepticism because government officials considered that scholarships would deviate from the main program mission of providing social infrastructure or job-generating projects. After convincing SEDESOL of the merits of the proposal, the club registered as a nonprofit both in Berwyn and in Michoacán and established a committee to select the winners after a careful analysis of each application.

In the first year, the club offered twenty-five scholarships to students drawn by merit, need, and civic involvement from high school and college-age youth living in the municipality. Program participants were assigned a personal tutor and volunteered seven hours per week in their communities in their areas of their expertise. Parents were required to return a small sliding-scale percentage of the scholarship to help finance new students. The first cohort of twenty-five scholarship recipients finished college in 2010, and twenty-two of them got jobs in Mexico, a success rate of 88 percent.[41] Those who remained unemployed have migrated to the United States to find jobs. Project leaders in Indaparapeo and in the United States do not believe the program will stop migration; however, they want to offer an opportunity for new generations to stay with their families and finish higher education instead of leaving them behind to make ends meet.

The Club Indaparapeo plans to keep this program running for at least ten years. Luis Tovar, one of the club leaders who is also a business representative for Local 134 of Chicago's International Brotherhood of Electrical Workers, considers education as the only solution to bring progress to his hometown, and believes in offering alternatives that are more attractive for the youth than migrating. Nevertheless, the real challenge is how to generate jobs for college-educated people in a rural municipality of forty villages and towns ranging from 16 to 6,500 inhabitants. A sign of hope for the future of Indaparapeo emerged when two sisters who received scholarships declared to a *Christian Science Monitor* reporter that they were determined to finish college in Morelia before returning to Indaparapeo to open a preschool. However, an opinion of another engineering student at the Technological Institute of Morelia gives cause for concern: "A lot of my friends left for the US before finishing high school. . . . That's typical here, but it's not how I want to go. If I ever head to the US, it'll be for a PhD" (qtd. in Campbell 2006). If this young would-be engineer leaves to pursue a Ph.D. in the United States, the chance of return is further diminished, as Mexico cannot offer jobs to all Ph.D. graduates.[42]

Notwithstanding these obstacles, funding higher education for rural youth offers migrants the option to change the government discourse on what constitutes development. With these actions, migrants from Indaparapeo challenge traditional ideas of heroic benefactors searching for prestige and social recognition by funding only highly visible social infrastructure, such as water, electricity, rodeo rings, public squares, churches, and sports facilities.

Contending for Visibility and Inclusion in Development Policies

For many HTA members, participation in agriculture is a way to remain connected to their origins and families, and to renew peasant livelihoods while demanding access to a dignified quality of life. In the last two decades, programs advocated by international organizations to encourage migrant engagement have created an obsession with export agriculture and nostalgia markets to reconnect migrants with home country products without pausing to rethink alternatives to create new domestic markets that promote food sovereignty and local productivity chains—strategies that, according to modestly successful cooperatives of producers, appear to be viable alternatives for small rural producers (López Zepeda 2011; Suárez 2011).

After a decade of implementing programs to leverage remittances toward development purposes, these programs have advanced without much planning and without clear rules about how to transform philanthropic organizations without any prior experience in job-generating projects into successful social entrepreneurs. The examples offered in this chapter show the disconnect between cooperation ideals of international institutions, sending states, and migrant organizations for rural development. Following James Scott's (1998) critique of state-orchestrated schemes to improve the human condition, the good intentions of the Mexican government in bringing development and modernity to the countryside through migrant participation provides another example of the excessively standardized formulas devised by nation-states. These often result in disaster since they fail to consider the complexities of state-society relations, imposing a one-size-fits-all model on civil societies still unprepared to resist efficiently the temptation of attractive modernization projects presented as silver bullets to solve development challenges.

Stakeholders have to negotiate how to best use collective remittances. For their part, governments pursue a policy of essentially extracting extra tributes from expelled workers, while HTAs try to gain a seat at the table and obtain benefits for the groups they represent and for individual members. Only time will tell whether inequality between the dominant and the dominated will diminish in the long term if migrant civil society continues its quest to win more visible spaces of representation.

Migrant organizations do not advocate throwing the baby out with the bathwater. They imagine a future in which small farmers can successfully compete in fair trade markets, feed their families, and send their children to school. Migrant HTAs want to change the dominant paradigm in the migration and development nexus that has largely reduced their role to agents of labor and capital mobility. They demand to be included in decisions that affect the livelihoods of their families. According to their sense of justice and shared responsibility, HTA members believe that lifting rural Mexicans out of poverty is in everyone's best interest for the future of North America. To achieve that, they have increased their civic engagement, demanding that municipal, state, and federal governments listen to their agendas during political campaigns, and they have been able to monitor the delivery of those promises. Migrant HTAs demand that states fulfill their responsibility to guarantee a minimum livelihood to the majority of their population through stronger market regulations and more protections to vulnerable economic sectors such as agriculture.

In the future, a great challenge for migrant organizations will be to resist development interventions orchestrated by international organizations and states, and instead challenge efficiency models that do not take into account the cultural meaning and practices that are important for migrant systems of knowledge. This is a difficult task because a comparatively small number of migrants belong to HTAs, and many of these have been driven into development projects with poorly planned schemes frequently masquerading much more prominent obstacles such as unemployment, low-quality education, public insecurity, lack of market diversification, and chronic disinvestment in rural areas.

HTAs' seemingly small acts of resistance to state and federal policies and regulations (following Scott 1985) can be seen as wedges in the state decision-making apparatus for remittance-driven development. There is enough evidence to suggest that state structures are slowly being forced, albeit reluctantly, to invite migrants to the negotiating table as partners. HTAs represent many different migrant political perspectives. Some are in favor of food sovereignty and self-sufficiency in basic grains production, and demand that the Mexican state offer more subsidies to small producers. Others believe subsidies should be directed toward producers exporting nostalgia market cash crops to the United States. But the good news is that sustained dialogue is well under way. In any case, HTA members across the board seek a more serious engagement and commitment from their sending state and to be treated as equal partners among the stakeholders who will direct their country's future.

✤

CHAPTER 5

PARTICIPATORY PLANNING
ACROSS BORDERS

On a sultry summer morning in Chicago's Pilsen neighborhood in 2010, the conference room at Casa Michoacán is bustling. The governor of Michoacán is about to inaugurate the meeting of the Project Evaluation and Migrant Affairs Committee (COVAM),[1] and the media wants to capture the moment. This is the first time that this committee has met outside of Morelia, and migrant home-town association (HTA) representatives from Alaska, California, and Texas are seated across the table, anxious to begin the session. I notice several paintings adorning the walls, including a wall-size rendition of Frida Kahlo.

After the governor leaves the room, the chairman of the meeting begins the session with a warning: "I am very happy to be here but I hope that you won't ask me too many details about each project because all the files are in Morelia. This is the greatest challenge for bringing the COVAM to Chicago, we don't have all the documents to share with you." Five hours later, after long deliberations on the merits of each community development project passionately argued by municipal presidents, Secretariat of Social Development (SEDESOL) represen-tatives, migrant leaders, and Michoacán state officials, the session ends without major disagreements and with the firm conviction of migrant leaders that this would be the first session of many more to take place in receiving communities in the United States. It took HTA leaders five years of continuous advocacy to bring COVAM sessions closer to migrant donors, who believed project allocation was a mysterious process. Consequently, migrant organizations do not want this special occasion to be an exceptional case, but rather the inauguration of a new era of improved cooperation in state-society relations across borders.

Some of the municipal presidents attending COVAM are there after an official discussion of the trip's objectives at their city councils. In the past decade, it is increasingly common for local city councils of rural municipalities in Michoacán to discuss municipal president agendas and the potential benefits of official trips to the United States before agreeing to pay for them with public funds. At the turn of the twenty-first century, when the official visits of municipal presidents from Mexico to the United States became more frequent, a number of observers considered some of those trips "junket affairs."[2] Today, as Mexican municipalities experience high levels of emigration and migrant HTAs have increased their demands for social accountability from local authorities, municipal presidents from Zacatecas, Michoacán, Guerrero, Guanajuato, and other states must listen to their constituents living across borders and attempt to satisfy their demands. At least in the states of Michoacán and Chiapas and Mexico City's government, migrants are now potential voters who can change electoral outcomes in a closely contested local election.

In the spring of 2011, after meetings between Chicago-based HTAs and SEDESOL officials in Chicago, several HTAs submitted a proposal to SEDESOL to regulate COVAM meetings. HTA leaders from Guerrero, Jalisco, Zacatecas, Hidalgo, and Michoacán reviewed records of past COVAM meetings throughout the United States and noticed that the meetings did not have clear regulations to select and approve project proposals. The first meeting to discuss the adoption of new procedures for project selection was supposed to take place in a COVAM meeting for Michoacán projects in Las Vegas in the spring of 2011, at the headquarters of the Federation of United Michoacán Clubs of Nevada. However, one week prior to the event, SEDESOL canceled the meeting. The president of the Binational Michoacán Front immediately posted the cancellation letter to all Michoacán HTA federations in Google groups and asked leaders to demand an explanation.

Within hours, HTA leaders from California and Chicago exchanged opinions and ideas to mount a campaign to pressure federal and state officials and to send letters to the editors of local newspapers to resolve the situation. Two comments from HTA leaders from California capture the general reaction. Manlio declares: "It is a pity that once again, they are showing a lack of respect. . . . We need to take measures to make loud complaints against this action and take it to the federal level in SEDESOL and also let the governor know. It is not acceptable to play second fiddle with us." Rosalío, a California-based leader, wrote: "It is really a pity and an enormous lack of respect because many of us have already paid the hotel and scheduled those days to be away from our jobs and they are treating us as if we were their employees. They don't realize that we lose time and money attending those events."[3] The 2011 COVAM meeting was finally held in Chicago at the Mexican consulate, the official headquarters of SEDESOL in Chicago.

Practices of extraterritorial citizen participation in rural communities have increased in the last decade, generating new synergies between HTAs, municipal and state governments, and rural development organizations in towns and villages. The nearly two decades of negotiations among these actors to improve the well-being of migrant communities have been characterized by cooperation and conflict. Growing evidence of positive outcomes demonstrates that migrant civic and political engagement in newly created spaces for participatory governance in the sending countries is one of the best ways to tap into social participation to strengthen accountability, transparency, and coproduction of public goods at the municipal level, the core of Mexico's political structure (Ackerman 2003).

This chapter analyzes the role of Michoacán HTAs as agents of social accountability and participatory governance in the state of Michoacán. I show specific mechanisms that HTAs use to increase transparency and governance by promoting potentially efficient models of state-society cooperation for participatory planning, migrant rights advocacy, and electoral engagement across borders. The chapter describes practices of extraterritorial citizen participation in rural communities within municipalities and explores the possibilities for creating synergistic interactions between HTAs and other agents of public accountability and participatory governance within and outside the local state government.

Interpersonal trust across HTA networks has clearly increased their visibility and concerted actions, although the correlation between personal trust and higher civic engagement among Mexicans seems to differ depending on subnational political contexts (Cleary and Stokes 2006; Layton and Moreno 2010). In the state of Michoacán, studies of social capital help explain the lack of a robust civil society capable of demanding better services from the government and creating efficient alternative models to solve community problems beyond the local level. In 2005, Michoacán had more than 600 registered nonprofit organizations, including agricultural cooperatives, charities, and youth action groups; however, the levels of general interpersonal trust in the state are rather low except among the poor. Recent survey results indicate that high levels of collective action networks are mostly concentrated among the poor and usually activate to solve urgent community issues related to trash collection, electricity access, or water, as well as personal problems. This pattern presents challenges to find common synergies with organized migrant communities, which are less likely to form in localities with high levels of poverty (UNDP 2008).

Besides, Mexico's submunicipal rural governance regimes and their relations with civil society are seldom analyzed because they tend to be isolated from decision making and oversight in municipal governance. This chapter discusses the role of community-based organizing in state-migrant civil society participation to achieve community development and social accountability, and transform municipal planning for development. It focuses on HTA collaboration with local community organizations in social projects financed with the Three-for-One Program and local committees for community development.

The intervention of HTAs in state development plans illustrates the many hurdles that migrant leaders must overcome to regain their voices as full citizens while living thousands of miles away from their hometowns. It also demonstrates that the relationship between the state government and the Michoacán migrant community has shifted from pompous discourses that praised their economic contributions to the state via individual family remittances, to the inclusion of migrant leaders in policy decisions affecting the everyday lives of migrants and their family members on both sides of the border. Still, there is great inequality between the resources that state actors have compared to those of the civil society. For example, state actors control the rules of the game in many invited spaces of participation, determining forms of state-society interaction, restricting exchanges, and failing to implement recommendations made by migrant and local groups interested in development issues. When the state apparatus exerts excessive control over the invited spaces of state-society interaction, there are higher risks that state-society interfaces can lead to corporativist and clientelistic practices (Cunill 1999).

Michoacán state governments have shown an interest in retaining the loyalties of migrants abroad to attract collective remittance projects. This has opened small windows of opportunity for HTAs to effectively increase their levels of participation in governance and social accountability by demanding to be included in government decision-making processes related to migrant rights and community development. In response to the increased visibility of migrant organizations, state governments have created new institutions and designed cooperation models to promote development in sending regions. These new state-migrant civil society collaborations present a unique opportunity to create civic engagement models that are not only based on "market membership" due to their economic contributions but also include migrant citizen engagement in community development agendas beyond collective remittance investments.[4] The Three-for-One Program, in particular, has proved very useful in fostering the creation of new migrant organizations across the United States. This is an unintended consequence of a program whose main objective is to improve the well-being of Mexican rural communities through infrastructure projects, access to better community services, and new employment opportunities.

PARTICIPATORY PLANNING ACROSS BORDERS IN CHICAGOACÁN

Mexican migrant organizations play a critical role as negotiators in channeling collective remittances for rural development through the Three-for-One Program—the first nationwide matching funds program. Moreover, they have successfully advocated to regain electoral rights in local and national elections and to demand innovative laws aimed at protecting migrant political, cultural, and economic rights.

Despite the increased visibility of activities organized by the Mexican migrant civil society in Mexico and in the United States, research on Mexican civil society and its impact on democratization and political parties has largely ignored the influence of Mexican migrant organizations in the United States (Olvera 2003, 2010a).

HTAs are the latest addition to the list of democratic innovations to increase citizen participation in government decision making from below. Participatory appraisal for community development decisions is a fresh breath of air in a country with a long history of a centralized federalist system with low account-ability mechanisms and high levels of corruption.[5] The state of Michoacán offers a great case study to observe the new dynamics of participatory planning across borders because it has implemented a relatively successful model for addressing the demands of the migrant community living in the United States and has been nationally praised for its outreach programs and collaborations with hundreds of HTAs and federations (Bada 2007).

In the last two decades, Mexican municipalities have slowly been consoli-dating their abilities to manage resources thanks to an increase in their policy-making authority. However, the new governing opportunities have also brought new responsibilities and challenges for delivering resources and services to towns and villages (Fox 2007; Fox and Bada 2008; Grindle 2007). The so-called New Mexican Federalism has brought opportunities for democratic innovations in participatory appraisal, although some critics question if there is any real con-nection between participatory appraisal and decision making and believe this process is little more than a large-scale consultation on the part of public author-ities with little results (Cooke and Kothari 2001; Smith 2009).

While the experience in the state of Michoacán does not offer its citizens the same opportunities found in, for example, the participatory budgeting expe-riences of Porto Alegre in Brazil or the small-scale social audit mechanisms implemented at some municipalities in Guatemala and El Salvador (Olvera 2003; Reames and Lynott n.d.; Smith 2009), the state has implemented several mechanisms to engage citizens from highly marginalized areas with community development at the village government level. For instance, in the last decade, Michoacán implemented an innovative scheme to increase citizen participation in decision making for community development in the fourth level of govern-ment through the establishment of local Community Development Committees (CODECOs) in thousands of rural villages, similar to the Municipal Develop-ment Planning Councils that were inaugurated in 1981 to increase citizen partici-pation in municipal development across the country with few results.[6]

Since January 2002, the Party of the Democratic Revolution (PRD) has governed Michoacán twice, and the state's municipalities have experienced increased electoral competition.[7] In 2011, the president's National Action Party (PAN) only controlled 34 percent of the municipalities in the state (Instituto Electoral de Michoacán 2011). Competition has forced municipalities to improve relations with constituents. The state has also facilitated new mechanisms to increase direct citizen participation in development planning and the inclusion of migrant voices in federal and state programs addressing migrant needs.

In the 1980s, migrants created the vast majority of Michoacán HTAs inter-ested in community development in communities of origin. By the turn of the century, many municipal presidents became interested in encouraging the creation of new migrant groups that could organize fund-raisers in the United

States to finance infrastructure projects through the Three-for-One Program. As a result of the renewed voice and power exercised by migrant organizations in rural development, more migrant organizations have been formed "by invitation" from the state. The creation of new invited spaces for binational community organizing to participate in rural development decision making offered a unique opportunity for HTAs to get closer to municipal governments and channel new demands for improvements in education, health, and access to municipal services.

The interest of municipal presidents and state officials to address migrant needs is frequently anchored in personal experience. The vast majority of municipal staff have family members living in the United States. In a survey conducted by El Colegio de Michoacán of all municipal presidents in the state of Michoacán in the term 2002–2004, researchers found that 35 percent of municipal presidents had been migrants at some point in their lives, and seven were U.S. citizens (Cárdenas Batel 2004). In 2004, during midterm elections in the state of Michoacán, several migrant candidates ran for seats in the state legislature, and in the 2005–2007 state congress there were at least seven migrant legislators who obtained their seats after returning to Michoacán to run for office. Between 2001 and 2004, the state government supported the inclusion of migrant candidates in the midterm state elections, and as a result of the advocacy done by migrant legislators, the state government began to address migrant needs by extending its services to citizens living beyond its geographical borders in several domains, including health, basic education, cultural programming, and job training, especially in California and Illinois.

Social Accountability in the Three-for-One Program

One of the Three-for-One Program's most important accomplishments has been its success in attracting organized groups of migrants and offering the opportunity to participate directly and oversee local development projects. For instance, the state of Michoacán offers a Three-for-One transparency session once a year with the state Secretariat for Migrant Affairs (SMA) and SEDESOL. In this public session, HTAs are offered the opportunity to ask questions and discuss the progress of their projects with several state government representatives and learn about all the social programs offered by SEDESOL for the stay-at-home community. State representatives provide HTAs with an advance report of all projects financed with collective remittances. Throughout the year, the SMA organizes periodic workshops to disseminate the matching funds program to new clubs in California, Nevada, Texas, and Illinois, and to municipal councils in Michoacán. Since 2005, many municipalities with high numbers of Three-for-One projects have created the position of Three-for-One coordinator as a new addition to their public works staff, and there are centers for migrant affairs in all municipalities that offer services to the migrant community to advance in the decentralization of government services and prevent unnecessary trips from remote villages to the SMA in Morelia.

Beyond the annual transparency sessions, the SMA's Transversal Programs Directorate has served as an important migrant advocate across state government offices that are more reluctant to address migrant requests for improving social services and infrastructure in communities of origin. In Michoacán, the establishment of the Three-for-One Program in the state coincided with the first opposition government, and the new partnerships between migrant organizations and state offices led to new transborder state-society cooperation models to improve participatory governance. The SMA has acted as an allied policy maker, assisting with project approval and technical assistance related to Three-for-One projects and providing protection for donor funds and advocacy for HTAs among hostile or indifferent state and federal officials.

The most important tool that HTAs have for improving the allocation of funds for underserved communities is the opportunity to effectively raise their voices at the state level and, with less success, at the federal level.[8] The HTAs have in many cases attained direct access to state authorities in the capital city of Morelia and have used this power to denounce uncooperative municipal authorities. They have organized statewide workshops with municipal presidents to disseminate the success of projects carried out with collective remittances and convince these presidents to participate in the program. In addition, HTAs frequently inform state authorities about unfulfilled municipal government promises related to underperforming public schools and the lack of basic infrastructure, including water, electricity, and paved roads. In response, the state government has tried to increase awareness among the municipal presidents on the dire conditions that many remote communities face. As a result, in the state of Michoacán 73 percent of projects financed with collective remittances between 2002 and 2005 were implemented outside of town centers (Burgess 2005; Fox and Bada 2008).

The HTAs have had less success as watchdogs to prevent government corruption in project implementation, due to their lack of capacity and resources to follow up projects effectively and a poor understanding of their role in public accountability. To work effectively and trigger cogovernance mechanisms, a process of public accountability should involve constant interactions and exchanges between citizens and governments (Mulgan 2003). In a survey of Three-for-One Program beneficiaries, researchers found that 43 percent of project participants interviewed understand their right to access to information related to projects financed with federal funds, but only 4 percent have ever submitted a formal complaint to appropriate authorities to solve corruption cases in this program (Secretaría de la Función Pública 2006).

For many HTAs, requesting public information from the federal authorities is complicated due to cumbersome bureaucratic procedures, and in their past experience complaints have rarely if ever been translated into sanctions. However, some migrants have been able to uncover acts of public corruption thanks to cooperation with academics. For instance, in the municipality of Tanhuato, a Chicago-based HTA leader worked with a graduate student doing fieldwork on this issue to request documentation of twenty-eight Three-for-One projects implemented between 2002 and 2007. After a careful review of project invoices, they found that 85 percent of all projects lacked transparency. Among many irregularities, they discovered that only 52 percent of invoices were valid. The rest were either invalid or had never been approved by SEDESOL (Córdova 2010). These findings have not resulted in any sanctions against the municipal presidents involved, but it is a first step toward greater transparency in the program. The lack of sanctions against municipal authorities involved in mismanagement of program funds means there is no effective deterrence mechanism for other municipalities across the state. In the state of Zacatecas, HTAs from Chicago have also been instrumental in uncovering corruption in this program, but the few successful sanctions imposed to those found guilty mostly stay on paper, buried. As a result, responsible authorities have not been effectively punished (González Hernández 2011).

Budget deficits in the state are another challenge for those demanding accountability in the implementation of Three-for-One funds, as the state shifts its budget allocation to other priorities when shortfalls occur. For instance, in 2011 the state did not fulfill its obligations with approved projects and refused to deliver the money that it convened with SEDESOL for the Three-for-One Program. In February 2012, three months after the elections that brought the PRI back to the governorship, Federation of Michoacán Clubs in Illinois (FEDECMI) leaders organized a meeting in Chicago with new state legislators from the PAN and the PRD (now in the opposition) to ask them to intervene to release those funds, but the legislators' first reaction was to request that FEDECMI show them a written agreement to demonstrate that the state government had actually promised to finance those projects. It seems that federal bylaws and COVAM resolutions were not enough proof to the freshmen legislators.

The most important empowering tool HTAs have to increase participation in project selection is voting at COVAM to assure that selected projects are at least feasible, in the absence of clear criteria to decide the merits of each proposal. The committee has representatives of the three levels of government involved in the financing, plus the HTAs. Each committee member has the right to vote in project selection. Despite their increased presence and participation in the program's evaluation committee, HTAs have not always been successful in convincing municipal authorities to carry out all the development projects that are needed in remote communities. Rejection rates are high; demand for Three-for-One projects has more than doubled in the first decade of operation, without a significant expansion of its public budget. One of the main problems that migrant organizations face in getting their proposed projects approved is their lack of training in project evaluation and verification of full compliance with operating rules. As a result, during COVAM meetings, HTA representatives have had the most success when seeking approval of projects that have been scrutinized in advance by known migrant organizations and are going to be implemented under the supervision of HTAs with a respectable track record, or with the direct involvement of organized groups in the community of origin.

HTAs in Michoacán have one problem they have not been able to solve since the establishment of the program in 2002: differences in criteria for defining budget priorities in project selection. For SEDESOL, project selection must give priority to communities with the highest marginalization indexes, as stated in program rules. For HTAs, the priority should be given to project proposals that meet basic bureaucratic requirements and have been submitted by an existing migrant organization, regardless of geographical location. For them, projects should be implemented in places where migrant organizations—at times in consultation with stay-at-home community members—have jointly decided on the most important project needed in a community.

Migrant organization leaders firmly believe that the government should be responsible for solving basic infrastructure problems in the most impoverished communities without forcing migrant organizations to invest in those projects. For SEDESOL, the Three-for-One Program was conceived to bring new development projects to the poorest rural areas with the help of migrant organizations. Government officials initially expected to find a perfect correlation between migrant organizations and high marginalization. In practice, HTAs are less likely to exist in highly marginalized villages and towns, as those tend to have newer migration trajectories and less maturity among migrant networks. Therefore, it is not unusual to listen to SEDESOL officials complain to HTAs that the majority of Three-for-One projects are established in municipalities with relatively low levels of marginalization. In an official speech comparing SEDESOL programs for priority regions without basic services and the Three-for-One Program in Chicago's Mexican consulate, a SEDESOL delegate stated:

> Those municipalities benefited with Three-for-One projects are not necessarily the poorest in the state because in the poorest villages and municipalities there is simply no migration. Poverty is so extreme in those regions that people can't migrate anywhere. However, there are certain municipalities that have benefited from migration, and twenty years after, these municipalities have lots of water wells, many schools, etc. This year we have 60 million pesos to allocate but we have received requests for 160 million, which multiplies the demand 2.5 times and it is difficult to fund that many projects.[9]

In practice, COVAM frequently approves projects that are not going to be implemented by existing migrant organizations because municipalities have devised clever mechanisms to decrease the costs of financing basic infrastructure with the Three-for-One Program in areas with low levels of marginalization. For instance, it is common for municipal governments to convince a small group of migrants to sign a project request to comply with program rules when the municipality has plans to pay 50 percent of the project or when a local stay-at-home community group has committed to pay 25 percent of the project.[10]

When Chicago-based HTAs decided to form an ad hoc committee in 2011 to write a proposal to regulate project selection, they had a clear idea about the most common practices that needed eradication. Many members had participated in COVAM and had evaluated projects. In this process, they began to detect suspicious collaborations between municipalities and ghost migrant organizations, thus effectively transforming their participation from passive donors to active participants and watchdogs in public policy decisions. After a decade of learning best practices to improve advocacy in transborder cooperation with municipal, state, and federal levels of government, Chicago-based HTAs from various states exchanged information on the most common corrupt practices used by municipal presidents and state representatives and were ready to demand more transparency and social accountability.[11]

Rejection Rates and Electoral Bias in Funds Distribution

In the Three-for-One Program, rejection rates illustrate the constant bargaining between government and civil society. For instance, between 2002 and 2004, the Three-for-One Program rejected 192 projects and approved 252 in the state of Michoacán. The political maneuvering that takes place to obtain project approval offers a glimpse of competing interests involving migrant organizations when they negotiate with authorities. Although "clientelism" has recently lost its descriptive power as a catchall phrase encompassing a myriad of practices—from vote-buying to pork-barrel politics—in this case, clientelistic practices refer to direct exchanges in which actors maximize their interest to obtain goods or services in conditions of equality or inequality (Hilgers 2011). The constant pressure applied by HTA leaders to expose suspicious arrangements between municipal and state authorities has encouraged more transparency, albeit unintentionally.

Bureaucratic challenges and bad timing are among the most cited reasons for project rejection. In these cases, a project gets rejected because paperwork is incomplete or because it was submitted too late in the fiscal year when the program had no more funds left. Also, municipal presidents tend to be more interested in financing "easily visible" public infrastructure projects as an indirect vote-buying mechanism to protect incumbent parties in municipal elections. For example, sewage projects are not always successful because they are not easily visible. In addition, migrants need to convince municipal governments to sign the project application as a first requirement to submit a proposal. This practice grants a de facto veto power to municipal presidents and is one of the most difficult barriers due to competing understandings of development priorities. In addition, if the proposal letter does not have a migrant committee backed by an HTA federation, its chances of approval are diminished because it will not be a priority for HTA federation representatives in COVAM meetings.[12] At FEDECMI, all dues-paying members get personalized attention to channel their projects to the appropriate authorities. FEDECMI leaders have one voting representative at COVAM, and they have extended networks and have cultivated relationships with SEDESOL officials and municipal authorities.

Due to the separation of church and state and the many federal regulations that prevent using public funds for church-related projects, some rejected projects involve church renovations. Of the 192 rejected projects in the 2002–2004 period, 11 percent were related to church renovation, 3 percent to rodeo rings, and 20 percent to productive projects (SEDESOL 2005). The most common reason to reject profit-generating ventures is the small number of investors involved. Municipal presidents commonly argue that it is difficult to justify the use of public funds to benefit a small group of community members.[13]

Productive projects or any project not oriented to basic infrastructure are likely to be rejected if proposed for a municipality with a high marginalization index. SEDESOL rules are clear on preferring "white flag" projects such as sewage, electricity, and water instead of ornamentation or income-generating ventures in those areas. Regardless of federal rules, HTAs in the United States have pressed to have more freedom in deciding what type of projects should be financed in highly marginalized areas, arguing that the spirit of the program is to invite migrants to jointly decide on community development priorities. HTA members argue that the government should be responsible for basic infrastructure and that they should be allowed to finance productive projects in any community they want.

Suspicions of electoral bias are also common sources of rejection. Some municipal officials believe Three-for-One projects have the risk of tipping the scale in favor of the PRD and PAN during electoral campaigns. Some municipal presidents believe that the state government appointed a dedicated staff for the Three-for-One Program at the SMA to serve as advocate and favor the PRD, the ruling party until 2011.[14] Also, allegations of PAN partisan bias have been backed by quantitative analysis on the program at the national level performed by independent evaluators. Political scientists find evidence of partisan bias in the program between 2002 and 2006, concluding that "states and municipalities ruled by the PAN are significantly more likely to participate in the program, and electoral support for the PAN is associated with more funds or projects awarded" (Aparicio and Mesenguer 2008).

In the case of Michoacán, the numbers of the first three years of the program offer subtle evidence that the most benefited party in the state was indeed the PAN. Between 2002 and 2004, PAN only controlled 7 percent of the state, yet PAN municipalities were allocated a remarkable 16.5 percent of the total. The rejection rate received by each political party reveals more details about this process. The PAN got the highest rejection rate, with fifty-four rejections and only forty-two approvals. However, PAN managed to submit ninety-six projects in only nine municipalities controlled by this party.[15] It would be necessary to conduct in-depth studies of the projects submitted by PAN, but my interviews with non-PAN municipal presidents indicated a belief that the disproportionate allocation of Three-for-One funds to PAN municipalities is related to their close relationship with the federal government, thus offering better and faster access to information related to federally sponsored programs.

In the local print media, allegations of clientelistic practices benefiting the PRD and PAN in the Three-for-One Program summarize the constant ebbs and flows since the program began. In June 2010, the municipal president of Tacámbaro, a PRI municipality, published the following statement in *Cambio de Michoacán*—a local newspaper—after participating in a summer COVAM meeting for project selection in Chicago:

> There is an electoral and clientelistic bias in the federal and state social programs; especially in the Three-for-One Program. . . . Twelve PAN municipalities obtained projects with an investment of 9.4 million pesos, but according to the percentage of municipalities controlled by this party (11.5 percent), the program should have assigned only 5.1 million pesos to those municipalities. In PRD municipalities, the Three-for-One projects approved totaled 15.4 million pesos, but according to the municipalities governed by that party (34.1 percent), they should have received 15.9 million pesos. Finally, the PRI municipalities were allocated projects for 18.8 million pesos but according to the percentage of municipalities governed by our party (48.7 percent), the program should have delivered 21.9 million pesos [to us]. (Torres Delgado 2010)[16]

Civic Engagement with Municipal Planning for Development

Besides the allocation of state funds to previously underserved communities, another positive aspect of the Three-for-One Program is that it has improved the relationship between geographically isolated communities and town centers. Historically, the communities lying outside municipal seats or towns have tended to be neglected regarding public infrastructure and basic services. This is in part because these communities are poorly represented in the municipal government. In Michoacán, submunicipal authorities in small villages do not have direct representation in the town council. These authorities are democratically elected every three years, but sometimes they work at a very low salary or no salary at all, thus making it difficult to devote full time to this appointment. As a result, these representatives cannot make frequent visits to the town center, sometimes because it is far away and they lack transportation or because they do not get reimbursements for official trips. Submunicipal authorities seldom attend the meetings of the municipal planning committee (COPLADEMUN), mainly because not all town councils have one or if they do, the committee does not hold regular meetings. This system of representation presents many obstacles to the interests of small communities served.

To measure the effectiveness of HTAs in promoting equity among municipalities, it is useful to observe the geographical location of the projects. In many parts of rural Mexico, it is common to find small villages without running water, electricity, or roads connecting them to the town center, located in municipalities with very low marginalization indexes. The allocation of new projects in the most disadvantaged communities has helped to reduce inequalities between town centers with low and very low marginalization indexes and isolated villages within the same municipality. Although collective remittance investment in Michoacán municipalities remains small when compared with municipal budgets, there has been a steady increase in the number and significance of projects. These investments now represent 5 to 10 percent of the total public budgets in some municipalities, while in others the amounts do not surpass 1 percent, especially in urban municipalities with sizable populations and higher access to state and federal funds.[17]

In general, during the last decade the HTAs have done a great job in reaching out to municipal authorities in town centers. HTA leaders have direct access to the state SMA, which makes it is easier to get an appointment with the municipal president. Depending on community location, it is not very difficult for migrant leaders to take a flight to Morelia or Guadalajara, drive to their town council, and communicate the needs of their isolated communities faster or more effectively than the appointed submunicipal authorities. Therefore, these leaders are frequently playing the role of "assistant mayors" because they can mobilize more resources and have better access—geographic, monetary, and political—to town centers.

Migrant relationships with their municipal authorities are frequently cultivated when municipal presidents visit migrants in the United States. Sometimes, lodging or transportation expenses for official trips are partially paid with HTA funds, or municipal authorities stay at migrants' houses with the hope that a closer relationship will boost their possibilities of attracting the municipal president's attention for faster approval of community development projects.

Besides, in municipalities with organized migrants, HTA leaders learned to notice the unfair systems that some municipal presidents use to distribute public funds to finance infrastructure and have devised clever mechanisms to channel funds to their hometowns. After years of constant haggling with municipal authorities to convince them to match funds for their projects, leaders became good at reading annual municipal reports and began to observe distribution patterns in the allocation of infrastructure. They observed that only villages with trustees and aldermen advocating on their behalf in municipal government got any infrastructure paid for by the municipality. In theory, council members represent the interests of the entire municipality, but in small villages, trustees and aldermen have the pressure to address the demands of constituencies from their hometowns. In response, migrant leaders frequently intervene on behalf of their villages that do not have any representation in the municipal council, demanding presidents to pay for 50 percent of new infrastructure in exchange for their signature to submit a project for their hometowns through the Three-for-One Program in cases when they do not plan to organize fund-raising to contribute to new infrastructure. In the calculation of HTA leaders, the municipal authorities are highly likely to say yes because they only have to pay half of the cost. If institutionalization of the Three-for-One Program by the state was meant to adopt a permanent extractivist policy toward organized migrants, the HTAs have found subtle but effective ways to bring the state responsibility back with development with the means at their disposal.

While their participation as power brokers to obtain federal, state, and municipal support to finance basic infrastructure in geographically isolated communities might be seen as a modest victory, this system works well when HTAs make a commitment to perform watchdog functions in all the projects that they help to get approved to prevent embezzlement, corruption, and fund diversion. Without direct participation and involvement of HTAs in projects where migrant remittance money is not at stake, the municipality is less likely to keep HTAs informed if funds do not arrive on time or if the project is never finished, which are common complaints. However, these new partnerships generated between migrants and municipalities to improve the services offered to migrants interested in participating in development empowered citizens and altered the channels of intermediation. This outcome has been previously observed in similar cases of participatory empowerment by local civic associations in other Mexican states (Selee 2011).

The increased participation of HTAs in municipal development has also helped to offer direct services to the migrant community within the municipalities. The SMA is located in Morelia, and it is difficult for rural community members to travel to the capital for migrant-related services such as birth certificate translations, advice on children's reincorporation into schools for returned migrants, how to organize the absent community for development projects, and inquiries about U.S. Social Security Administration checks and direct-deposit options. To cover this need, HTAs requested that the SMA install satellite offices in municipal town centers to decentralize services. To date, the SMA has established cooperation agreements to offer direct migrant-related services in all municipalities across the state, thus alleviating the burden of long-distance travel to receive these services.

Also, as a consequence of increased attention to the state migratory phenomenon, in the last decade some municipalities have started to include a specific chapter on the relationship between migration and development in their municipal development plans. In an analysis of municipal development plans between 2002 and 2005 conducted of eleven municipalities in the state, I found that all of these plans include a section addressing the migratory phenomenon, its root causes, and the consequences for municipal development (see table 5.1).

TABLE 5.1

MIGRATION DIAGNOSTICS OF ELEVEN MUNICIPAL DEVELOPMENT PLANS, 2002–2005

Main areas	Causes of international migration	Consequences for municipality	Proposed solutions
Education	Public education system does not retain young people	Young people drop out of school to find jobs in the U.S.	Increase quality and quantity of public schools
	Lack of rural high schools	Lack of relevant skills makes it harder to find good-paying jobs in local communities	Create more publicly funded scholarships
	Low-quality public education	School closures due to decreased student enrollment	Create programs for retaining vulnerable age groups
			Invite migrant organizations to consult on youth migration
Culture	Many families left behind have a strong desire to live in the U.S.	Migration as imitation transferred from parents to children	Foster a sense of identity through celebration of local festivities
	Increased number of single-parent households, fragmented families, and grandparents as heads of family	Absence of parents triggers disobedience and illicit activities	Sponsor family-oriented cultural activities such as music festivals
	Rejection of indigenous past	Increase of gangs, vandalism, drug addiction, alcoholism, and vagrancy	Create municipal offices specializing in women's rights
	Loss of local culture and traditions	Loss of identity and importation of foreign dress codes	
	Women need to take care of children and family members	Living in "El Norte" brings the best social status	
		Women are abandoned by husbands living abroad	
		Increased domestic violence and discrimination against women	

(continued)

Main areas	Causes of international migration	Consequences for municipality	Proposed solutions
Economic development	General unemployment	Population displacement to larger cities and the U.S.	Create more employment in agricultural sector through productive projects
	Low competitiveness in agricultural sector, especially corn, beans, and other staples	Negative population growth and demographic stagnation that will cause the disappearance of several communities in the short-term	Involve migrant organizations in investment projects
	Lack of private investments to finance secondary sector	Appearance of ghost towns and places with mostly elderly people	Increase civic participation in community development projects
	Large percentages of rural families live under two minimum salaries	Lack of civic participation in community development	Create specialized municipal offices to offer legal advice and social services to the migrant population
	Steady decline of agricultural sector and cattle farming	Labor shortages force employers to import workers from elsewhere	Invite the private sector to invest in agricultural and industrial projects
	Lack of jobs paying a living wage	Decrease in remittances captured as entire families establish permanently in the U.S.	Request more financial support from state and federal government to develop primary and secondary sectors
	Very low levels of labor force participation of all working-age groups	Decreased dynamism of commercial sector	

Source: Analysis of eleven municipal development plans of Michoacán.

All municipalities now also have websites with an interactive menu for migrants, where they can post messages and requests to municipal authorities.

For instance, the municipality of Panindícuaro has a one-page description of the local migratory phenomenon, and the municipality of Chavinda has several pages devoted to this topic. In the case of Panindícuaro, the new interest in addressing problems brought by massive migration in the municipal development plan is related to the direct experiences of some HTA members who had the opportunity to serve as municipal elected officials after their permanent return to their hometowns. One of the strategies that the 2002–2004 municipal development plan mentions is to strengthen relationships among the municipality, HTAs, and businessmen from Panindícuaro living in the United States. They include plans to invite them to invest or promote new investments in the municipality.

Chavinda has a very extensive chapter on migration in its development plan. Migration to the United States from this municipality goes back more than a century (Alarcón 2003), and its development plan notes with concern that this municipality now has to import workers from other states to meet its agricultural needs, due to the lack of local workers willing to work in the fields of the Bajío Zamorano region.

In Panindícuaro, the 2005–2007 municipal president was a former migrant who used to be the representative of a successful parallel committee in the small community of Urequio. During one visit, members of this parallel committee showed me records going back a decade detailing the exact amounts that both the migrant and stay-at-home community donated (both in money and in voluntary communal work called *faenas*) for the construction of a well and a health clinic under the Three-for-One Program.

This Venice-based HTA also maintains a permanent mutual-aid fund to pay for corpse repatriation of village members. During one of my visits to the village in 2004, the town had recently experienced the death of a young soldier in Fallujah, and although the U.S. Army was paying for funeral expenses, the HTA decided to give mutual-fund money to the mother anyway. The funeral was taken as an opportunity to conduct a census of the villagers settled in Venice. According to the club representative, approximately 300 villagers from Urequio attended the funeral. During my last visit to the municipality of Panindícuaro in December 2006, the war in Iraq was included as part of the daily landscape. Conversations of family members serving in Iraq were frequent, and "Support Our Troops" yellow ribbons attached to local cabs driving the streets across the municipality served as visible signs of the close contact villagers had with this war.

Transforming Municipal Decision Making for Community Development

In the first two years of operation, the Three-for-One Program accepted projects submitted by any organized civil society group. However, migrant organizations quickly realized that available funds were limited and lobbied to have the operating rules changed. Since 2004, the Three-for-One Program only accepts proposals submitted by migrant HTAs established in the United States and Canada. As a result, projects have been implemented in communities with large, dense, and mature migrant networks capable of establishing migrant organizations with the financial capacity to initiate community development projects, which creates conflicts with SEDESOL's objectives to eradicate poverty by concentrating projects in the poorest communities. Another conflict is that many migrant organizations prefer to finance beautification projects in their communities of origin regardless of marginalization levels.

According to the new rules, the Three-for-One Program only receives and approves requests from organized migrants; however, HTAs claim that some approved projects are granted to organized groups without verifying the direct involvement of migrants, an allegation that coincides with reports from Zacatecas (García de Alba Tinajero, Jáuregui Casanueva, and Núñez Sañudo 2006). These situations commonly happen in the most marginalized areas, where finding organized migrant groups can be difficult.[18]

Despite the many challenges faced by existing stay-at-home parallel committees, these committees have the potential to demand greater accountability and improve their roles as watchdogs of public fund expenditures. These committees are often elected in a community assembly or are chosen by HTA leaders to represent them. Their main function is to supervise construction, negotiate with government officials, and make sure projects are built on time and with transparency. The formal constitution of parallel committees to help in project supervision has increased since the program started. In 2006, a national survey conducted of ninety-one projects found that 87 percent of the projects had a formally constituted parallel committee (Secretaría de la Función Pública 2006).

Unfortunately, these committees have been found to be lacking in capacity to fulfill their duties due to poor training and low literacy levels.[19] In Michoacán, barely 10 percent of these committees are working properly, and very few have effective bargaining power with municipal authorities and HTA leaders.[20] Issues such as the lack of a clearly stated division of labor between local committees and U.S.-based HTAs hinder their effective performance.

From my observations in several communities in ten municipalities, the low involvement of the parallel committees often results when the HTA involved does not make consensual decisions with local citizens about projects with the highest priority. HTAs ask some community members to send them project proposals, but local citizens do not always have the last word about which projects will be approved, making it difficult for the members of parallel committees to feel invested in the project and to play a more active supervisory role. In communities where there is a correspondence between collective remittance projects financed with Three-for-One funds and infrastructure projects financed by local CODECOs, it is more likely to find high levels of cross-border cooperation and empowered participatory cogovernance spaces. This cooperation encourages more transparency within town councils and state and federal government structures.

One independent evaluation of the program found that 63 percent of HTA members declare that decision making is handled basically by the HTA in the United States, and 16 percent said that project selection is decided by municipal authorities. The report also shows that during the long face-to-face interview process, "a surprising number of migrants" revealed that they offer resources to municipal authorities and allow them to decide the most important priorities. In return, the municipalities offer several choices, and the club decides which projects will receive their support. This nationwide data comes from a modest sample of fifty HTA members in Los Angeles and Chicago, but it offers a window to explore the details of the decision-making process to distinguish pork-barrel-style bargaining from more authoritarian or coercive clientelism (Servicios Profesionales para el Desarrollo Económico 2005).

Previous studies of the Three-for-One Program acknowledged that the change in the program from a matching fund designed for any citizen group to an exclusive program for organized migrants is the result of the advocacy led by Zacatecano HTAs in 2004 (Burgess 2005; Iskander 2010; Smith and Bakker 2008). While it is true that HTAs played an important role in restricting Three-for-One funds to organized migrant groups, in practice, this restriction meant that local organized groups are now encouraged to find migrant organizations in the United States or ask their relatives to form an HTA in order to submit a project on their behalf, thus strengthening synergies between the stay-at-home community and migrants, and encouraging parallel committees to become more involved in the supervision of projects and in fund-raising efforts to contribute funds to projects.

During visits to dozens of projects financed through the Three-for-One Program, municipal presidents and community members living in Michoacán explained how the stay-at-home community contributed to many of the infrastructure projects, either with small monetary sums that were commonly raised selling food during town festivities or with *faenas*. Recognizing the participation of both segments of the transnational community is an important step to advance in the building of trust for the continuation of these participatory practices without producing unnecessary social conflicts, especially in communities that have seen their social fabric affected by the massive expulsion of some of their most talented members.

This cooperation mechanism helps the most impoverished communities to get projects approved in this federal program even in cases without established HTAs in Michoacán. Yet the official discourse commonly criticizes migrant investment decisions when they do not coincide with the state's priorities. In reality, the state wants partners to provide basic services in rural and marginalized communities and chooses migrants to pay this "voluntary tax." Interestingly, the nonmigrant middle class is not required to pay for basic infrastructure above and beyond their tax share. For example, in 2005 the newly appointed SEDESOL representative for the matching fund program in Morelia shared his perspective on the difficulties in convincing HTAs to fund basic infrastructure:

> It is no secret that the highest proportion of migrants living in the United States comes from the Bajío and the North but few of the municipalities in the Bajío are marginalized. Therefore, 60 percent of the matching fund program usually goes to municipalities with high migration indexes but not necessarily those with high marginalization. We have only been able to allocate 40 percent of the budget to thirty-five municipalities with the highest marginalization indexes. These communities don't have water or sewage but migrants want to fix the public square, build a church or a rodeo ring. We try to encourage them to fund projects that focus on immediate and basic needs but we can't oblige them. The program has decided to respect their will so if they decide to finance a rodeo ring instead of sewage, we allow them to submit the project to the validation committee. We let the validation committee decide the projects with the highest merits to support with public funds.[21]

In Michoacán communities that have at least a couple of Three-for-One projects, it is increasingly common to find new approved projects without collective remittance funds from organized migrant groups. Instead, local community members have organized ad hoc project committees to collect funds for community projects and have asked municipal authorities and/or their network of migrant friends for support in getting approval from a registered HTA in the United States. Quite often, an HTA will agree to support a project without funding it immediately and will promise to match the investment of the local ad hoc project committee to finance future projects. Since there are no written contracts regulating these types of intercommunity loans, these are good-faith arrangements in which no sanctions will be imposed in case the HTA fails to gather the funds to pay back the investments made by local community groups. In practice, these cases create synergistic interactions when HTAs and local groups decide to join forces and accept unofficial rule modifications to increase municipal investment funds for community development.

Community Development Committees
and HTAs: Are Synergies Possible?

Many civil society groups in rural municipalities are requesting Three-for-One projects because there are not enough public funds available to finance basic infrastructure. If a local group without social networks with HTAs in the United States finds the opportunity to obtain a Three-for-One matching fund for a basic infrastructure project, it often tries its luck at the municipal offices anyway. During the first PRD administration in Michoacán, the state Ministry for Social Development (SEDESO) established a social coresponsibility program to finance socially oriented projects submitted by local civil society groups in 2004. However, the maximum amount authorized per request is U.S. $13,000. In contrast, the maximum amount authorized by the Three-for-One Program is U.S. $65,000, including the contributions of all three levels of government.[22] The unequal access to public resources sometimes creates resentment among some local civil society groups that are unable to organize fund-raisers to match government subsidies due to salary disparities between Michoacán and Chicago.

In 2009, the state Ministry of Social Policy (SEPSOL)[23] had a registry of 271 civil society organizations, and 55 percent of those are concentrated in the capital city. In that year, civil society organizations in the state of Michoacán experienced a 47 percent decrease compared to official numbers registered four years earlier (Secretaría de Desarrollo Social 2005b; Secretaría de Política Social 2010). The appearance and disappearance of civil society organizations from official government rosters, at least in the case of Michoacán, is related to an excessive dependence that many of these organizations have on government funds that do not last more than a few years. Few civil society organizations established outside Morelia are successful in diversifying their funding sources to guarantee long-term viability.

In spite of difficulties to access government funds to strengthen their capacity and visibility, in 2010, 106 civil society organizations received U.S. $618,000 from the state government to implement new social projects. In contrast, the state invested U.S. $2.4 million in the Three-for-One Program in the 2009 fiscal year. Due to lack of funds, sixty-two projects submitted by civic groups were rejected that year, and only one project submitted by a local affiliate of a U.S.-based HTA received state funds (Secretaría de Desarrollo Social 2010a). Although civil society groups requesting SEPSOL subsidies do not usually invest these funds in public infrastructure, the comparison offers an idea of the power of organized migrants when lobbying for infrastructure funds at the state congress.

In a similar spirit as HTAs, the local CODECOs are interested in revitalizing community development from below and involving the migrant community. Between 2003 and 2005, there were 803 CODECOs established in eighty-four municipalities (Secretaría de Desarrollo Social 2005a). By the end of the first PRD government, 1,900 CODECOs had been established, although their numbers decreased with the new administration (see figure 5.1). This new organizing mechanism for participatory planning to share community development decisions and demand more funds allocated to remote villages has had a hard time convincing municipal presidents of its efficacy. Many believe that the new scheme is duplicating the responsibilities and authority given to submunicipal authorities in local villages, who report directly to the municipal government. In my interviews with municipal presidents and municipal staff, this program has

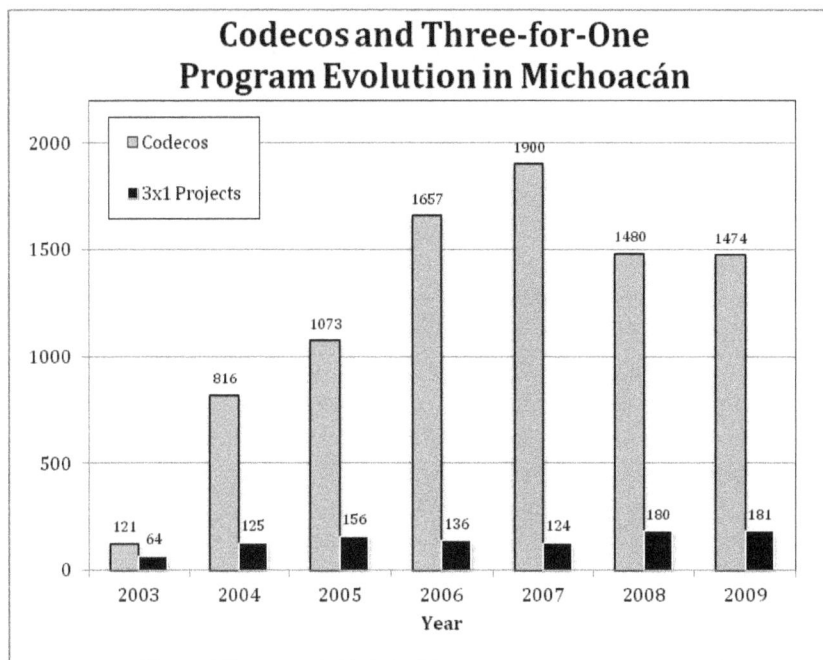

Figure 5.1 CODECOs and Three-for-One Program evolution in Michoacán. Source: Michoacán's *Informes de Gobierno* 2004–2010.

also been accused of clientelism mainly because municipal and regional coordinators of CODECOs are appointed directly by SEPSOL and thus are considered employees of the state government. The tension is even more acute in municipalities governed by the opposition. Since SEPSOL staff overseeing CODECOs usually get an office inside the municipal building, wear a uniform with the state logo, and work under direct supervision of state offices, some municipal presidents not used to cooperation among different political affiliations believe their authority is being undermined when dealing with submunicipal authorities on issues related to community development plans.

In practice, CODECOs have organized independently from submunicipal authorities, and state offices have been careful to negotiate written agreements with the municipalities for the installation of CODECOs. CODECOs have to negotiate project funds with municipal and state authorities, so unless there is an agreement between the state and the municipality, the CODECO cannot obtain approvals for new projects. It is still too early to predict the viability of the new model, but the initial meeting to form the committee is always convened by submunicipal authorities. While some HTAs form spontaneously in the United States and others are established by invitation of municipal presidents, all local

CODECOs are established by invitation from submunicipal authorities, and many subsequently transform into autonomous spaces.

Michoacán is not the only state where the fourth level of the state has been granted some decision-making authority. Since 2001, the state of Tlaxcala has the figure of village delegates (*regidores de pueblo*). These are elected and have a vote in the municipal council (Olmedo 1999). In Michoacán, submunicipal authorities can be formally elected, chosen by the mayor, or elected by plebiscite (Fox 2007). However, submunicipal authorities do not have a seat at the municipal council. The 2008–2011 state development plan conceives of CODECOs as important figures in the development planning process from below. According to the development plan, CODECOs should decide on investment priorities for their communities and negotiate and arrange appropriate mechanisms to execute their plans. They are responsible for designing and evaluating community development projects at the village, municipal, and regional levels in close consultation with regional planning councils and municipal development planning committees. In the future, CODECOs are expected to establish regional networks and integrate local or regional councils recognized in the state planning system. The state congress is also discussing new legislation to include the figure of participatory budgets to increase the decision-making power of CODECOs, but the proposal is still being debated in the state legislature.

Since 2003, CODECOs have been trying to decrease paternalism and build citizen participation in marginalized communities in the areas of social infrastructure, alternative medicine, culture, community relations, and participatory planning. While CODECOs are present in 11 percent of the most marginalized areas of the state, they receive less funding than Three-for-One projects to finance a larger number of smaller projects (see table 5.2). The funding differential between CODECOs and Three-for-One projects underscores the priority given to the empowerment of organized migrant actors by state and federal governments compared to the empowerment tools offered to local citizens. The comparison suggests that the government uses a market membership model to encourage migrant civic engagement and maximize the revenue obtained from family remittances. In a country where income tax collection is low, collective remittances invested in Three-for-One projects function as a profitable, nontaxation scheme for citizens who are more likely to make fiscal contributions through value-added tax (VAT) instead of income tax due to their foreign employment.

In theory, CODECOs have the potential to collaborate with HTAs that seek to maximize the resources and services that can be obtained from the government for new community projects. Considering that this participatory planning mechanism at the village level was implemented one year after the Three-for-One Program, I quickly became interested in the cooperation between CODECOs and the local committees monitoring Three-for-One projects. In my fist visit

TABLE 5.2

SELECTED COMPARISONS OF CODECO DEVELOPMENT PROJECTS
AND THREE-FOR-ONE DEVELOPMENT PROJECTS

Fiscal Year 2009	CODECO Development Projects	Three-for-One Development Projects
Number of projects	1,335	181
State coverage in localities	11.2%	1.5%
Federal investment	None	45.9
State investment*	22.4	28.5
Municipal investment*	20.5	33.7
Beneficiaries/migrant investment*	22.5	40.4
Total investment*	65.4	148.3
Three-for-One and CODECO in same villages	52	52

Source: SEPSOL and SEDESOL databases.

*In millions of Mexican pesos

to SEDESO in 2004, I became puzzled when one of the senior advisers for the creation of CODECOs explained that he was not aware of the implementation mechanisms of the Three-for-One Program and did not know that Three-for-One projects usually had a local committee in charge of supervising the work.

Considering that HTAs pursue community development projects only in their hometowns, CODECOs would be the most natural ally of a local Three-for-One committee to leverage a larger pool of public funds to finance social infrastructure in hundreds of rural localities that have not received enough funding for social infrastructure from municipal town centers. After observing the implementation processes of dozens of Three-for-One projects between 2002 and 2007, I noticed that HTAs would frequently ask the stay-at-home community to contribute money or labor to help them pay for their share for many of those projects. At the national level, a survey conducted by the Ministry of the Public Function found that 59 percent of stay-at-home community members contributed some money to approved Three-for-One projects (Secretaría de la Función Pública 2006).[24] Therefore, when I started asking Chicago-based HTAs about the effectiveness of CODECOs in their villages, I was not surprised to hear that several members were quite familiar with these committees. Some migrant leaders had actually participated in the implementation of CODECO projects during brief stays at their villages and knew current and former CODECO leaders.

In hundreds of rural and marginalized communities of Michoacán, citizens are faced with two possibilities to finance new infrastructure: enlist the help of HTAs and establish a local committee for oversight, or participate in a CODECO. The two forms of civic engagement are quite similar. CODECOs are established through an open community assembly convened by submunicipal authorities, and HTAs are usually formed by migrants from the same village living in the United States.

Trying to reach a consensus between the development priorities of the stay-at-home community and the migrant organizations is a task with no easy solution. For instance, in 2006 the Inter-American Development Bank (IADB) evaluated the Three-for-One Program. After detecting some problems, the bank proposed alternative solutions to improve project quality and offered a loan to the Mexican government for sponsoring specific Three-for-One projects between 2006 and 2009 (see chapter 4). With the earmarked budget, the IADB would finance projects through a matching fund scheme using most of the existing rules for the Three-for-One Program, but adding an extra requirement: the stay-at-home community would propose productive projects to the migrant organizations in the United States, and the HTAs would decide which ones they were interested in funding (IADB 2006). This condition became a real challenge because Mexican migrant HTAs in the United States had fought with the Mexican government precisely to make sure that the projects would be first proposed by them and not by the stay-at-home community. When SEDESOL officials tried to find project proposals to be included in the new financial mix, they became frustrated because there were not enough projects meeting IADB requirements. Since the loan had already been approved, SEDESOL had to change the regulations for distributing the IADB funds in order to allocate the money to projects in several states.[25] The experience demonstrates that the Mexican government has not understood migrant organizations' ideas of participatory planning despite repeated attempts to reinvent the rules of the game.[26]

SEPSOL officials in charge of community development initiatives claim that CODECOs have been successfully implemented in more than 1,000 rural communities between 2003 and 2010. These committees offer technical assistance, organizational capacity building, and economic resources ranging from U.S. $1,000 to $75,000, including in-kind donations and voluntary labor to build basic infrastructure or community-oriented productive projects. There is still little relationship between CODECOs and HTAs, but in 2009 fifty-two different communities had simultaneous access to new development projects implemented with CODECOs and Three-for-One projects.[27] In 2006, the state CODECO coordinators had only recorded three cases of cooperation between Three-for-One local committees and CODECOs, and in 2005 I stumbled upon one case in which a CODECO decided to loan initial seed money from the state development office to an HTA in Chicago to help pay its share in a church renovation project approved with Three-for-One funds in the town of Tupátaro.

Better coordination to decide labor distribution between HTAs and parallel committees is needed because project maintenance is never included in Three-for-One projects. For example, in Tupátaro, an HTA with members in Chicago, Waukegan, and Mundelein built a soccer field with an official investment, according to SEDESOL records, of U.S. $72,000, a price tag that is hard to believe after visiting the mostly abandoned soccer field. After completion of the project, grass grew out of control, and the fences became rusty. The HTA owed money to private lenders because the HTA did not have the money ready when it was needed and had to borrow from commercial lenders, a frequent situation as construction only starts after all parties have deposited their share of the cost. During my visit to the project in 2005, I asked a member of the local committee why the place looked so abandoned, and he explained:

> When we started the project, there were many young people interested in playing soccer in the community. However, once the field was finished, they all left for the United States. We need to make more tykes to use the field because the seventeen members of the soccer team left. Ninety percent of the boys in Tupátaro leave to work in the U.S. Four or five boys are now working for the U.S. marines and three are serving in Iraq. Here, there are not even 300 people left. We now have a new group of young people interested in forming a music band because there is a very successful band in Chicago with people from the town and the boys here are interested in getting some training before trying their luck in the U.S. We will ask the HTA to help us get a new Three-for-One to buy instruments for the band.[28]

In spite of challenges, positive signs are emerging. During a visit to twelve communities in seven municipalities where CODECOs and Three-for-One projects had been successfully implemented to build new infrastructure in June 2010, I met with CODECO coordinators and HTA parallel committee leaders to study the evolution in the levels of cooperation between the two committees implementing the projects. I expected to find high levels of isolation between CODECOs and parallel committees, but to my surprise, I found that in seven communities, the members of the local CODECO were also coordinating the implementation of Three-for-One projects at the local level. In the rest of the localities, CODECOs and the parallel committees were working independently, and different groups within the community were overseeing the projects. From interviews with CODECOs and parallel HTA committees in seven communities with overlapping functions, I found the following cooperation trends:

1. Communities with high levels of collaboration between HTAs and CODECOs tend to be very small (less than 1,000 inhabitants), which increases possibilities for intimate transborder connections.
2. These communities have a high degree of reported social cohesion and a long history of community participation to solve problems, with

community participation prior to the existence of the Three-for-One Program or CODECOs.

3. All municipal presidents have directly intervened in the formation of committees, suggesting candidates during the selection of the Three-for-One parallel committee members in close consultation with HTAs in the United States.

4. Projects financed in communities where CODECOs and Three-for-One committees collaborate are successfully finished and closely monitored.

5. CODECOs and Three-for-One committees are directly engaged in project oversight (for example, local committee members independently select providers or contractors, close financial supervision detects and solves budget inconsistencies promptly, and savings are used to extend project goals).

These are modestly inspiring signs of synergistic empowering spaces between migrant-led organizations and locally based committees and innovative mechanisms to increase participatory democracy in rural localities. However, the frequent suspicions aired in local media and among participants that the CODECOs and the Three-for-One Program are used by the state and federal government for electoral purposes makes it difficult to extend these programs to more localities. For instance, CODECO participants frequently mention that every three years CODECOs need to be reorganized after municipal elections, and when incumbent parties lose it is highly unlikely for CODECOs to survive the political transition.[29]

Compared to CODECOs, Three-for-One projects have not been able to cover a large number of communities in a state with almost 12,000 villages (see table 5.2). Lack of funds for increasing federal investment in the Three-for-One Program is frequently cited as one of the reasons explaining the modest presence of the program in the state. Strong migrant organizations are not established overnight, and a lack of faith in municipal and state governments to listen to their demands works as a deterrent for many new organizations interested in development in their communities of origin. Nevertheless, CODECOs have been able to maximize resources at the municipal and state levels, producing a larger number of smaller-scale social infrastructure projects with fewer financial resources. As CODECOs increase their capacity to advocate for more municipal resources, it is likely that they will become interested in extending partnerships with HTAs in the United States to maximize the resources and coordinate priorities for local development in remote villages.

Transnational theories focusing on grassroots organizations are an emerging field (Faist 2008b; Pries 2008). There is still the need to find appropriate theoretical frameworks to understand the impact of transborder organizing on public accountability and participatory governance in developing democracies. Existing theories on social movements have been able to explain the impacts of community-based organizations (CBOs) and nongovernmental organizations (NGOs) on social accountability and cogovernance in capitalist systems and emerging democracies (Fox 2007; Olvera 2010a); however, Mexican HTAs and federations defy inclusion in classical theoretical frameworks because they are neither CBOs nor NGOs working in a single territorial space. HTAs represent a new breed of organizations anchored to multiple translocal/transborder organizing territories at the grassroots level. Researchers interested in building new theoretical frameworks to understand the complexities of civic engagement in transborder migrant organizations need to find more appropriate theories for mapping recent developments in the connections among HTAs, governments, and locally grounded civil society organizations.

After a decade of observing interactions among HTAs in Chicago, local HTAs committees in communities of origin, CODECOs, and municipal and state agencies responsible for social development, I find that HTAs have made clear inroads for increasing the accountability mechanisms vis-à-vis the state authorities at the municipal and state levels. However, the HTAs need to improve their capacities for playing a more salient role as effective social auditors in their communities of origin. They need to have a better understanding of the nuts and bolts of the Mexican system in order to detect mismanagement and incompetence, and to be able to challenge corrupt authorities more effectively. Without a precise knowledge of how bureaucracies work, HTAs cannot constitute an effective social control group with possibilities of challenging municipal and state authorities through their binationally organized civic and political participation. They also need to be more attuned to the social organization of the stay-at-home community to increase collaboration among all social community agents that are genuinely interested in participating in community development from below.

Some level of caution needs to tame any excessive optimism, due to great resource disparities among organized groups in deliberative democracies. While organized migrants and stay-at-home groups still have limited and unequal access to resources to increase civic engagement, state bureaucracies can easily mar the few gains obtained in participatory democracy when they disregard recommendations of organized groups or implement innovative policy reforms on paper without a genuine interest in executing them in practice.

CHAPTER 6

❧

EXPANDING AGENDAS AND BUILDING TRANSNATIONAL COALITIONS

In 2011, more than a decade after the creation of the Federation of Michoacán Clubs in Illinois (FEDECMI), Casa Michoacán bustles with activity, reflecting its motto: "Opening Borders, Uniting Communities." In February, it hosted a meeting with Linda Machuca, one of the first Ecuadoran migrants to win a seat in Ecuador's congress representing migrants living in North America. Machuca was visiting Chicago to inform constituencies about recent constitutional amendments to recognize Ecuadorian citizenship as universal and respect the rights of all foreigners living in Ecuador. In April, Virginia Martinez, the legislative attorney for the Mexican American Legal Defense and Educational Fund (MALDEF), and a bipartisan commission of state representatives offered a course on legislative redistricting and how the new maps might affect Latino representation. Later that month, FEDECMI held a community briefing with fellow member organizations of the Illinois Coalition for Immigrant and Refugee Rights (ICIRR) to discuss a trip to Springfield to advocate for the Illinois DREAM act[1] and protest against the introduction of new anti-immigration bills. In June, they received the archbishop of Morelia, who came to inaugurate the Presencia Michoacana in the Midwest with a community mass at El Cerrito del Tepeyac in Des Plaines, and asked him to encourage parishioners to be more engaged with immigrant legalization campaigns.[2] In July, Casa Michoacán invited Electoral Federal Institute (IFE) officials from Mexico City to discuss the status of absentee ballots and staff from Michoacán's Electoral Institute (IEM) to brainstorm on improving outreach to register Michoacanos living abroad to vote in gubernatorial elections.

Multiple Identities, Multinational Engagements

As the above sample of the civic and cultural activities of hometown associations (HTAs) demonstrates, migrant engagement through Chicago's HTAs connects local, national, transborder, and global scales. Migrant activities display multiple membership affiliations with a human rights framework that expresses several group identities: Michoacanos, Mexican citizens, Latino voters, Catholics, U.S. citizens, and Latin Americans.

HTAs are not the only migrant organizations that are based on multiple and often overlapping collective identities. Other organizations that make up migrant civil society, such as independent worker centers or migrant-led religious congregations, function in a similar way. This fosters larger support networks but poses challenges for building coalitions and alliances with immigrants of other nationalities or second-generation Latino groups. While it is true that shared collective identities can reach consensus more easily on certain organizing strategies, they can also block others that conflict with their organizational goals and vision (Bada and Mendoza 2012; Barvosa-Carter 2001; Fox and Gois 2010). Although globalization has created multifarious social attachments that span borders, there are still many obstacles preventing the participation of larger immigrant groups in successful local and cross-border initiatives such as block clubs, Chicago Alternative Policing Strategy partnerships, local school councils, HTAs, or transnational organization coalitions. Much of their success, or lack thereof, depends on the commitment of several institutions including governments, bureaucracies, and the nonprofit sector.

In this chapter, I examine the organizational challenges, sociopolitical agendas, and scaling operations of HTAs, placing special emphasis on the evolution and expansion of their networks to build a fledgling migrant civil society across borders. In a difficult environment to attract the attention and increase the civic engagement of disadvantaged minority groups, the most important gain for this new cohort of Mexican binational migrant activists working in HTAs and other migrant-led membership organizations is their capacity for self-representation. The point of departure here is that many adult Mexican migrants are initiated into civic life in their country of origin or through projects oriented toward their country of origin. These projects are a form of migrant civic binationality that is playing a growing role as their organizations scale up and out in different geographical and thematic arenas.

For many groups of Mexican migrants, civic engagement begins directly in their new Chicago neighborhoods and later is oriented toward their country of origin, or is simultaneously oriented to both countries. Decisions to become civically engaged depend on the contexts found during departure and upon arrival. Factors that encourage involvement include the presence of strong labor organizations in the workplace, access to educational opportunities, engagement with culturally active churches, more schooling prior to migration, marital status, and

English-language proficiency, among other factors (Bada et al. 2010; Fox and Bada 2011).

Some critics of dual civic engagements argue that bilingualism, multicultural-ism, and some transnational practices of Latino immigrants pose a threat to the United States' Anglo-Protestant culture, national sovereignty, undivided national loyalty, and electoral system. In fact, until recently, several academics assumed that the question of whether to be involved in the United States or Mexico in the twenty-first century was mutually exclusive, and migrants, especially those who acquire U.S. citizenship, should be forced to choose one national arena for political and civic engagement.[3] There is still a debate over whether civic binationality—based on migrant participation in sustained practices of civic engagement in their countries of origin and their new communities—can or should replace the traditional concept of assimilation. Nonetheless, in practice many Mexican migrants are becoming full members of both U.S. and Mexican civil societies at the same time, engaging in practices of civic binationality that have a great deal to teach us about new forms of Latino immigrant integration into the United States and will likely transform the character of this nation when Latinos reach one-third of the total U.S. population by 2050.[4]

The massive demonstrations in the spring of 2006, when millions of foreign-born Latinos and their supporters peacefully rallied in cities across the United States to be included in society as human beings with rights, revealed a transition in these forms of self-organization from a closed-circuit focus on communities of origin to a rights-based approach to activism in their new communities. HTAs' practices of civic binationality had been largely invisible outside the migrant community since they primarily focused on their communities of origin, rather than on their communities of residence. Recent policy studies of Mexican HTAs describe their relative isolation from mainstream U.S. institutions as one of their most pressing challenges (Somerville, Durana, and Terrazas 2008). However, over the past decade, HTAs have increased their involvement in civic life in the United States and have become important actors among the many previously low-profile forms of organization that "came out" in the spring 2006 marches. The three states that experienced the largest turnouts in the marches by far—California, Texas, and Illinois—are also the three states that together account for a full 69 percent of registered Mexican HTAs in the United States and Canada. Among the 160 U.S. cities that held at least one march or protest during the immigrant rights movement of 2006, HTAs had at least one organization in 31 of those cities. By 2007—just one year after the historic marches—Mexican HTAs were present in 65 of the 160 cities where 2006 demonstrations took place, sig-naling more than a 100 percent increase between 2006 and 2007 (Duquette-Rury and Bada forthcoming).

The rate of immigrant participation in civic organizations reported through survey research might be considered low for the future consolidation of a vibrant transnational migrant civil society, but if we consider the sharp decline in civic participation structured around membership-based organizations in the United States in general—from labor unions to social clubs and political organizations—and the low participation of Mexican citizens in Mexico's formal civil society, then the rate of participation in HTAs is an inspiring sign (Putnam 1996, 2000). Moreover, participation in HTAs seems to encourage rather than discourage participation in U.S. civic society. A 2003 survey of 1,512 foreign-born and U.S. Latinos in the Chicago metropolitan area found that 7 percent of foreign-born Latinos belong to HTAs and 70 percent of HTA members belong to at least four additional Chicago-based community organizations. The survey also found that foreign-born Latinos are much more likely to belong to a community or civic organization than are the U.S. born; 53 percent of the first group belong to one or more community or civic organization compared to only 37 percent of the latter (Ready, Knight, and Chun 2006).

The concentration of HTAs' civic action in Chicago, Los Angeles, and Dallas reflects more than just a large Mexican-born population. By 2006, Chicago and Los Angeles HTAs and their federations were actively and broadly engaged with city governments, state legislatures, local trade unions, and mainstream Latino civic organizations. So why do these cities seem to encourage more Latino immigrant engagement? It is not a coincidence that migrant-led HTAs, federations, and their recent networks and alliances with Latino immigrant organizations flourish in urban centers. But why is it that the Mexican HTA model has flourished more in Chicago and Los Angeles and less in Charlotte, Las Vegas, or San Francisco? Why is it that cities hard-hit by the economic crisis and experiencing processes of decay do not exhibit the same degree of transnational organizing as more dynamic urban centers with worldwide reputations as desirable places to live?[5]

Part of the reason lies in the context of reception in places of destination and the political will of sending state governments to recognize and support fledgling civil society structures in global cities rather than in rural or less metropolitan destinations. It also has to do with the organizational maturity and presence of previous cohorts of Latino immigrants and their descendants and the support offered by faith-based organizations, ethnic media, and labor organizations. For example, Latino immigrant organizations in San Jose, California, are less visible than their counterparts in San Francisco due to a number of factors that characterize the cities themselves, including lower access to resources and training programs, and fewer established networks with city officials (Bloemraad and Gleeson 2012).

The attitude of city government officials toward immigrant presence also affects the civic participation of migrants and their organizations. Since the 1990s, Chicago entered a postindustrial economic stage era that urban planners call the Third City period (Bennett 2010). This period involved a rescaling process that prevented Chicago from suffering the fate of decaying cities in the urban Midwest and was partly possible thanks to a pliable immigrant labor force (De Genova 2005). Mayor Richard M. Daley (1989–2011) based the prosperity of the city on attracting jobs and employers to the growing service sector, emphasizing the revitalization of downtown areas and recognizing multilingualism and cultural diversity as important tourist assets.[6] City government officials also sought decentralization and privatization of public education, and public-private partnerships for new infrastructure development. Parallel to what happened in rural Michoacán, neoliberal projects in Chicago included reduction in state services and benefits, much lower public investment in neighborhoods, and the diversion of public monies to develop private service–oriented industries. In an environment of public-private partnerships, migrant-led organizations were embraced by different local nonprofits as a partner organization that shared similar human rights and social justice agendas. In time, city government officials began to pay attention and included HTAs as part of the Chicago civic landscape, albeit with limited clout compared to older Latino civil society organizations with better name recognition.

While it is true that Mexican immigrants tend to have lower indicators of human development compared to the U.S.-born second generation, the status of Latinos in Chicago and Illinois has progressed slowly, with minimal gains in education or economic parity in the last two decades. In recent years, organizations with a binational agenda and those mostly focused on solving Latinos' problems in the United States have found more common ground in spite of their challenges to create strong coalitions and alliances to advocate for shared agendas. Because of its strong local development, Latino activism in Chicago has always preserved a relative degree of autonomy from the three largest Latino national organizations: the League of United Latin American Citizens (LULAC), the National Council of La Raza, and MALDEF. It is in this context that contemporary HTAs are trying to carve a niche that simultaneously advocates for resources from Mexican and U.S. governments to provide needed services to minorities in the city while maintaining a solid membership base and autonomy for advancing a nonpartisan agenda to reduce economic disparities and political disenfranchisement among Latin American immigrant communities across borders.

As Nancy Fraser reminds us, it is difficult to conceive of transnational public spheres because they include actors in "communicative arenas in which the interlocutors are not fellow [legitimate] members of a political community, with equal rights to participate in political life. And it is hard to associate the notion of efficacious communicative power with discursive spaces that do not correlate with sovereign states" (2009: 77). Besides, the notion of citizenship rights and practices among migrants is further complicated by the two faces and divided meanings of citizenship. Within a political community, citizenship embodies inclusion and universalism. But to outsiders—that is, noncitizens such as not-yet-naturalized migrants—citizenship means formal exclusion from participation in political life. Yet in the United States, as in other liberal democracies, migrants with and without legal status are not entirely outside of civic institutions, practices, and experiences, such as attending neighborhood or school meetings, participating in after-school programs, or organizing to build needed parks for their children.[7] In summary, the citizenship practices embodied by HTAs bridge two nation-states in which they claim rights by virtue of residence, citizenship, or both, constantly fighting for inclusion and demonstrating that citizenship practices are much more than the electoral power of those who have access to political rights.

As seen in previous chapters, Chicago HTAs are transplanted adaptations of robust rural village organizing systems, and not necessarily the result of an increased exposure to American democratic and philanthropic values during the adaptation process. According to the principles of participatory democracy, people should have access to opportunities to participate in decisions that directly affect them and their families, regardless of their citizenship status (Fung 2004). Civic engagement through HTAs offers migrants a collective social education in which they learn to trust and to work and act collectively for common ends. In this process, HTAs cling to their cherished collectivity and create ethnic-based social spaces as a form of resistance to the excessive individualistic culture found in their new host society. With their empowered participation with municipal, state, and federal authorities across multiple geographical sites, HTA members connect public policy with civic engagement at points where particular problems arise, offering innovative solutions to establish fledgling transnational systems of empowered participatory governance using cross-border public-private partnerships as those observed in chapter 5.

CLAIMING RIGHTS TO URBAN SPACE AND VISIBILITY IN THE CITY

In the 1990s, scholarship on migrant organizations was scarce because the main focus of the literature on immigrant behavior was on studying individual actors and responses to the nation-state, frequently using Albert Hirschman's (1970) choice framework of loyalty, voice, or exit. This position centered on migrants' loyalties to nation-states and supports what social anthropologists Nina Glick Schiller and Ayşe Çağlar (2011) characterize as a linear understanding of the migration process in which transnational connectivity is seen as a flaw in migrant incorporation. This reading fails to include the multiple forms of incorporation in non-state-centered relationships in new communities and ignores the function and density of migrant organizations' transnational connections. Using a broader framework to reinterpret Hirschman's model and apply it to human mobility, more recent analysis demonstrates that migrants and their organizations are capable of exercising multiple forms of voice and loyalty after exit, and these voices can be extended to cross-border civic engagement networks. These

networks depend on the urban contexts of reception to succeed as scale makers and to branch out from traditional ethnic comfort zones (Bada et al. 2010;
Fox 2007; Fox and Bada 2008; Pierre-Louis 2006; Smith and Bakker 2008; Smith
2006; Stephen 2007). In the face of weak governmental responses to incorporate newcomers as members of neighborhoods and cities, receptivity to migrants
relies on civil society resources, including volunteers, people willing to share past
experience in solving community programs, leadership networks, and the ability
of civically engaged communities to identify and solve community problems.
Consequently, civically engaged communities are more likely to mobilize and
rally support toward immigrant incorporation (Deufel 2006).

Institutional studies of immigrant community politics have stressed the rel-
evance of political contexts and structures for explaining the relations among
immigrant civic engagement, grassroots mobilization, and electoral participation and representation (Cordero-Guzmán 2005; Landolt and Goldring 2009;
Portes, Escobar, and Walton Radford 2006). In addition, Patricia Landolt (2008:
54) suggests that the immigrant capacity to mobilize resources and defend political action is dependent upon the "institutional opportunity structure" at the
local level. Indeed, the historical persistence of immigrant associations seems to
be connected to differences in the context of reception that could have encouraged (or discouraged) the vitality and survival of these associations over time
(Hirabayashi 1986; López Ángel 2004; Moya 2005). In other words, "place" matters to determine the visibility and empowerment of migrant-led associations.

Informal practices—such as singing with a mariachi band at a family gathering, preparing tamales, or listening to Spanish-language radio—often fall outside
traditional nonprofit and commercial arts experiences, but occupy a significant
place in the social infrastructure of Mexican migrant communities. These practices help to build individual and collective identity, bond Mexican nationals
within Chicago and between Chicago and Mexico, and bridge Mexican immigrants with other U.S.-born groups. Key individuals and organizations facilitate
this bonding and bridging, from social and cultural organizations that arise from
or target the recent Mexican immigrant population, to schools and churches that
sponsor arts education with a Mexican emphasis, to individuals who are unusu-
ally active or well connected.

In Chicago, the presence of HTAs as important agents of immigrant incorporation into the social fabric responds to a long history of immigrant participation
in the city's civic life from unions to political parties and ethnic churches. For
Latinos, the constant replenishment of culture and tradition through new arrivals and the increased visibility of a small but progressive cadre of 1.5-generation
community advocates[8] help HTAs flourish in the city and establish a binational
agenda, including home and host governments as targets of their demands to
improve the quality of life of all Mexicans. The HTAs seek to influence two governments, acting as liaisons to stimulate conversations of a shared binational

responsibility in the massive displacement of millions of Mexicans. This conversation is uncomfortable among those who wish to limit the conversation to *either* incorporation (assimilation style) *or* immigrant flows. For HTAs, both topics are equally central to their mission.

The relative absence of harsh nativist or anti-immigrant public displays against Mexican migrants in the vast majority of Chicago's neighborhoods is due to Chicago's strategy to market itself as a city of diversity. Using Chicago's public image as a less anti-immigrant city than some of its neighbors, Mexican HTAs have demanded that their distinctive cultures be included in mainstream festivals sponsored by the city government at the iconic Navy Pier. Chicago's HTAs insist that Mexican culture be represented beyond the clichés of mariachis playing alongside women dancing the popular Son de la Negra; they want P'urépecha and other indigenous traditions represented with their own music and traditions, as indigenous migrant organizations from Oaxaca have done in the past decade in California (Escala Rabadán 2008; Ybarra-Frausto 2006).[9] These contemporary social movements to reaffirm the contributions of Mexican immigrants to United States' diversity can be seen as a response of minorities to the growing inequalities and disempowerment that have accompanied the implementation of neoliberal agendas through the disappearance of public funds to support cultural representations of disadvantaged groups living in working-class neighborhoods.

These movements also challenge the widespread conviction among city residents—native and migrant alike—that citizens lack the capacity to participate in the decisions and institutions that shape their daily life and future. Using multiple forms of discourse, cultural displays, and identity claims, these forms of social action can be understood as claims to a "right to the city" (Lefebvre 2006). According to Purcell (2003), the right to the city has two main dimensions, the right of city residents to participate in decision-making processes that affect the quality of city life, and their right to appropriate and use urban space, thus transforming inhabitance in a privileged status granting citizens and noncitizens alike a right to participate in public policy making. While these radical conceptions of participation beyond formal citizenship constraints are encouraging to improve participatory democratic governance, it is important to recognize that these dual dimensions can also result in simultaneously empowering and disempowering transnational experiences when differences in socioeconomic power give city residents with higher economic power unequal access and voice in public and private decision-making processes regardless of citizenship. A good case in point is the gentrification processes that U.S. expatriates have created in Sayulita, Nayarit, and San Miguel Allende, Guanajuato, appropriating urban spaces, increasing real estate prices, and rendering property ownership virtually inaccessible to the local native-born population (Smith and Guarnizo 2009).

In the case of Michoacano organizations, the consolidation of their transnational civic engagement has more to do with the quality of their cultivated social capital in the last two decades than with its density.[10] The types of social connections that HTAs have been able to nurture across borders are one of the most convincing explanations for how activities have expanded in particular U.S. cities (Smith and Bakker 2008; Smith 2006; Stephen 2007). As the following examples of local civic engagement illustrate, HTAs and federations act as intermediaries among Latino-led organizations, mainstream nonprofits, grassroots initiatives, local government agencies, and political parties, translating vital information to increase members' incorporation into social and civic life in different geographical scales.

In November 2005 on Chicago's South Side, the Balleño family shares a Saturday night dinner with a group of family, friends, and club members who usually gather once a month to enjoy their favorite food from Michoacán. Salvador Balleño is the founding member of Club La Purísima and a devout churchgoer, after converting to Protestantism and joining the Christian and Missionary Alliance, a small Latino congregation formed with Puerto Ricans, Guatemalans, Colombians, and Mexicans in Humboldt Park in 1977. Over dessert, he explains how his participation in church activities opened several opportunities for civic engagement.

When he moved with his family to the South Side in the 1990s, he met a white neighbor, a bilingual pastor from his same denomination, who invited him to join a block club in his new multiracial neighborhood. In conversations with the pastor, Salvador learned that the club was not working well due to lack of members' motivation. Salvador volunteered to help, using the skills he had previously applied when he knocked door-to-door trying to convince his fellow *paisanos* to donate money to build a well for his hometown:

> My strategy to build unity in the block club was to tell people that it was our right to live in a safe neighborhood and I asked them for five minutes of their time. I invited Carlos, Joaquín, and other Mexican neighbors to join me. We asked our neighbors if they would like the children of the block to know each other and to collect a phone tree for emergencies. Our first victory was to organize a block party. Since then, every year we ask permission to close the street, and grills come out and neighbors cook together. Soon, our block club was organizing garbage pick-up brigades and agreed on reasonable curfews for our children to discourage drug dealers from visiting our neighborhood. I was elected as president of the club, after the pastor finished his term. Our club decides who should attend the Chicago Alternative Police System (CAPS)[11] meetings at the police precinct to discuss safety issues and we also send representatives to town hall meetings with our alderman to be informed about his agenda to improve our neighborhood.[12]

Mexican HTAs in Chicago frequently encourage members to participate in neighborhood initiatives such as community gardens, Bible study groups, Christian Base Community groups, CAPS meetings, block clubs, local school councils, and many other opportunities to foster incorporation into their new communities.

Through their active participation with their umbrella federations, HTAs distribute culturally relevant and useful information to all their constituents in Spanish and English.[13] A good example of their local and transnational outreach efforts is found at the bilingual annual magazine that FEDECMI has published for the past twelve years with free distribution to community members.[14] In the 2011 issue, HTA members find a list of the infrastructure projects they financed, a summary of legal permanent resident rights, requisites to naturalize, and updates on the Secure Communities Program.[15] Members also find useful voter registration information to participate in U.S. elections, Michoacán elections, and Mexican presidential elections. Finally, readers learn about services offered by the Illinois Office of New Americans and by Casa Michoacán, including providing birth certificates, workforce development courses, and adult education programs such as cancer prevention, parent engagement in early childhood education, and distance learning college opportunities financed by Michoacán's Colegio de Bachilleres and the Universidad Michoacana de San Nicolás de Hidalgo. With more than forty articles to read, they have enough material to keep them connected with their transnational communities until the next issue appears.

Slowly, FEDECMI has come to play a prominent role in the Pilsen neighborhood, making alliances and collaborating with local organizations serving the needs of Latino immigrant communities even amid fiscal austerity. In 2011, FEDECMI collaborated with Chicago's Field Museum, Pilsen Environmental Rights and Resource Organization (PERRO), and El Hogar del Niño[16] to find some green space for children attending El Hogar's early childhood education programs. After long negotiations with the owner of a vacant parking lot close to El Hogar, FEDECMI secured the space on loan from the owner to build the Mary Zepeda Native Garden. With the help of volunteers, they cleaned the space and requested the Field Museum and the U.S. Forest Service to help them design a park to attract monarch butterflies to the parking lot to contribute with conservation efforts because the Midwest has struggled to keep healthy levels of milkweed plants to prevent the extinction of monarch butterflies.[17] Local neighborhood artists and dozens of HTAs, El Hogar, and PERRO volunteers collaborated to create a large mural that since the spring of 2012 adorns the park space along with dozens of milkweed plants that will host and feed the monarch butterflies on their way to Michoacán, offering a valuable lesson in the possibilities of environmental preservation in urban spaces for Pilsen residents, and a reminder of the migratory routes that bind both human and butterfly populations to distant and sometimes treacherous lands.

Mexican migrant civic and political visibility highly depends on having a visible organizational presence in city life that reaches beyond their explicitly intended audience. Immigrant groups organized around specific interests or causes, or around a shared background or social exclusion, improve their odds of being seen, heard, and recognized by public and private local institutions

(Bloemraad and Gleeson 2012). Formal organizations have better access to resources compared to informal/grassroots ones, and consequently the latter are less likely to engage in highly visible activities such as political advocacy to pursue public policy reforms to benefit the communities they serve, invest in larger facilities to build more autonomous public spaces, or engage in capacity building for their members to multiply their outreach.[18]

In the past decade, Mexican HTAs in Chicago have used their increased visibility to mobilize for a new legalization program for undocumented migrants. In September 2000, under the leadership of ICIRR and with the participation of the now extinct Association of Community Organizations for Reform Now (ACORN), the Service Employees International Union (SEIU), Centro Sin Fronteras, and other Chicago-based immigrant rights organizations, approximately 10,000 people rallied in downtown Chicago to demand legalization for the undocumented. The highly spirited protest was considered the largest held in Chicago since the Harold Washington era. After the September 11 attacks, however, immigration became connected to the issue of national security, and proponents of legalization needed a new context for regaining public visibility. In Chicago, that opportunity was provided by attacks by the Minutemen and the Sensenbrenner bill of 2005, which occurred when many HTAs and other Mexican political groups were preparing to register voters for the following year's Mexican presidential elections. Regardless of their legal status or country of origin, many immigrants living in the United States perceived the measure as a unifying force, demanding dignity, respect, and a reaffirmation of their rightful place as productive, law-abiding members of U.S. society.

In the spring of 2006 immigrant rights mobilizations, Mexican HTAs became directly involved, acting as organizers. Michoacanos opened up their privileged location close to downtown, and Casa Michoacán became one of the most important planning hubs for march organizers, providing an opportunity for HTAs to scale out and increase their local networks with public and private organizations advocating for immigrant rights. In recognition of the vital role played by Casa Michoacán as a civic engagement site for Latino immigrants, Second District state representative Edward Acevedo (D-Chicago) supported FEDECMI's request to obtain a U.S. $100,000 State Capital Grant in 2012 to allow Casa Michoacán to have an entrance and bathroom accessible to people with disabilities and to improve the heating, cooling, and electrical systems.[19] After eight years of operations, Casa Michoacán is now a visible membership-based nonprofit that simultaneously engages with the civil societies of Mexico and the United States.

Scaling Up and Out

Several studies on civic engagement point to existing inequalities as an obstacle to higher levels of public visibility for HTAs. Among the most important are the disparities in access to public and private resources, the lack of visibility to mainstream civil society and public officials in the countries in which they participate, and the capacity to create sustained networks, coalitions, and alliances, as well as their capacity to influence public policy decisions (Bloemraad and Gleeson 2012; Ramakrishnan and Bloemraad 2008; Ramakrishnan and Viramontes 2010; Sites and Vonderlack Navarro 2012).

An important factor that explains the increased civic engagement of migrant-led organizations is the support of government actors in both home and host countries. Political institutions matter in the thickening of civil society, although the outcome depends on the maturity of the networks when opportunities arise. For HTAs, the initial support received by the Program of Attention for Mexican Communities Abroad (PACME) in the 1990s created a fledgling civil society across the United States that struggled to gain autonomy from government authorities. The HTA federation model was frequently imposed on migrant-led organizations by Mexican consuls after the initial success of the Zacatecano federation in Southern California, supposedly as a way to leverage bargaining power with state and municipal governments. However, while some organizations adopted the state-led model without many changes, others decided to use this window of opportunity and slowly gained autonomy to expand their spheres of action outside their partnerships with consulates.

In Chicago, the size and diversity of the Mexican immigrant population allowed the emergence of distinct topophilic identities that played out well as a basis for initial organizing in the 1990s. Topophilic identities allowed HTAs and federations to preserve the cultural distinctiveness of their migrant experience while strengthening ties with different government scales in Mexico. However, after their initial success with the Three-for-One Program, HTAs embarked on an ambitious new project: to move beyond the philanthropic model and include binational political rights in their agendas. The frequent consultations among federations on strategies to implement the matching fund program in their home states led to discussions about the many challenges Mexican migrants face in the United States.

In 2002, HTAs' participation in decision making on issues of integrating Mexican immigrants into U.S. society increased when several migrant leaders organized a task force to decide Chicago's representation to the advisory board of the Institute for Mexicans Abroad (IME), a governmental organization created in 2002 by the Ministry of Foreign Affairs (SRE) to strengthen relations with the Mexican diaspora. Chicago became the only city in the United States in which Mexican leaders reached an agreement with consular officials to organize a citizen-led popular suffrage to elect seven council members to represent the city's metropolitan area. The HTAs, along with many other Mexican organizations and the Mexican consulate, established an ad hoc committee to organize this election in Pilsen's Benito Juárez High School. In this first electoral exercise,

814 votes were cast (Bada 2010). IME's advisory board members serve for three years, and since the first election, the elections in Chicago have become more organized with higher turnouts; voting booths scattered throughout suburbs with high Mexican populations such as Melrose Park, Aurora, and Waukegan; and more candidates registering for the competition, including young candidates representing the 1.5 generation. This first council of more than 100 members across the United States was responsible for leading the final push toward passing legislation to grant absentee ballots for Mexicans living abroad to vote for the first time in presidential elections in 2006 and for advocating to establish a formal agreement between the U.S. Department of Labor and the Mexican consulates to jointly disseminate and enforce immigrant worker rights in Chicago, Los Angeles, Houston, and many other urban centers across the United States (Gleeson 2012).

In order to transform HTAs' initial bonding social capital into network bridging opportunities, by 2003, several Mexican federation leaders in Chicago decided to form a larger coalition and created the Confederation of Mexican Federations (CONFEMEX), an umbrella organization representing nine federations of Mexican migrants.[20] In Chicago, CONFEMEX quickly expanded its networks and joined the ICIRR, enabling them to obtain funds from the New Americans Initiative to encourage legal permanent residents (LPRs)[21] to become U.S. citizens. In addition, CONFEMEX began to participate in interracial and multi-issue social justice campaigns. For example, it collaborated with the African American community through the Chicago Latino Chapter of the Rainbow/Push Coalition on immigration policy, employment, and human rights issues. In 2003, CONFEMEX sent representatives to the buses of the Immigrant Workers Freedom Ride Coalition organized in Los Angeles by the AFL-CIO and hundreds of multiracial faith- and community-based organizations inspired by the 1961 Freedom Ride traveling in the South to fight against racial discrimination.[22] These relationships enriched their networks and encouraged them to engage with international social movements focused on immigrant rights. In 2005, CONFEMEX members reached out to like-minded Guatemalan and Salvadoran organizations to compare different models for creating sustainable organizations with spheres of action in the United States and in countries of origin.[23]

During 2004 and 2005, Chicago-based migrant HTAs benefited from a training program supported by Enlaces América, a now defunct program initiative of the Heartland Alliance for Human Needs and Human Rights with the mission of empowering binational organizations to design social justice agendas, including migrant rights in both sending and host societies. Enlaces América replaced the Mexico-U.S. Advocates Network, a previous similar initiative housed at Heartland Alliance, and the name change was in part a reflection of a new leadership after the board hired Oscar Chacón, a Salvadoran American, as Enlaces's first executive director. With a grant offered by the Ford Foundation, Enlaces implemented a capacity-building workshop series for HTA members to increase HTAs' binational advocacy skills to encourage the creation of local, regional, and national networks that culminated with a collectively written theatrical performance, aptly titled *El Nacimiento de la Unidad* [The Birth of Unity], premiered at the National Museum of Mexican Arts in Pilsen.

The capacity-building training offered by Enlaces América allowed HTAs and federations to get acquainted with non-Mexican immigrant leaders in Chicago and beyond. While Mexicans were well aware of the important role they had to play in the discussion of immigrant rights, they had been working in isolation. Therefore, several migrant leaders decided to expand their networks and explore the possibility of creating an organization that could represent their regional transnational agendas. The first step for the formation of a national alliance happened in 2004, when a group of thirty migrant-led organizations convened a Latino immigrant summit in Washington, D.C., to discuss President George W. Bush's proposal for immigration reform. This proposal was pivotal to stimulate a debate among many grassroots organizations interested in having a direct voice in the fate of Latin American immigrants across the country and exercising their capacity of self-representation. As a result of increased ties with different organizations, the National Alliance of Latin American and Caribbean Communities (NALACC) emerged as a small coalition of thirty organizations that now includes more than seventy member organizations with headquarters in Casa Michoacán. NALACC's cross-border advocacy engagement with home country policies distinguishes it from other immigrant-led organizations, and its migrant-led character differentiates it from older and more established U.S. Latino organizations that are more likely to have close ties with elected officials mainly interested in cultivating voting constituencies (Fox and Gois 2010).

To encourage participation in international forums discussing immigrant rights, in 2005 several NALACC members, including Chicago-based HTAs, attended the First World Social Forum on Migration in Porto Alegre, Brazil.[24] Held a few days before the Fifth World Social Forum that took place in the same city, 600 participants from thirty-five countries discussed the notion of universal citizenship and how migrants might use it to stand up for their rights. For HTA members, it was the first time many of them had the opportunity to meet with migrants from different countries and realized the importance of transnational agendas to become more effective in advocating immigrant rights.

In November 2005, Chicago became the center of attention for any organization concerned with innovative solutions for immigrant integration amid federal inaction when the governor of Illinois announced the creation of the Illinois New Americans Immigration Policy Initiative. The executive order was the result of a public-private partnership led by the ICIRR with the assistance of the Migration Policy Institute and the National Immigration Forum and sponsored by the MacArthur Foundation and the Carnegie Corporation of New York. In the packed grand ballroom of the Navy Pier, the executive director of Casa Michoacán led the event as the master of ceremonies. This moment marked an important shift in HTAs' civic engagement priorities toward simultaneous civic binationality. Since then, even as state government budgets to finance greater migrant incorporation into Illinois keep dwindling, migrant HTAs have taken advantage of the discourse in the public sphere that boasts of Chicago as a welcoming city in a welcoming state, to demand greater inclusion for immigrant rights as an important public priority for the state of Illinois.

In 2007, NALACC and CONFEMEX took advantage of the political opportunities afforded by the Illinois New American Initiative, their postmarches visibility, and their accumulated social capital with the state of Michoacán to convene the first Latin American Community Migrant Summit, held in Morelia. Illinois Democratic congressman Luis Gutiérrez served as the meeting's keynote speaker. The event brought together more than 1,000 individuals and representatives of Canadian, European, and U.S. grassroots organizations to promote the development of healthy communities in both countries of origin and destination and obtained financial support from the Chicago-based MacArthur Foundation. The summit sought to develop innovative proposals to address the root causes of emigration and challenges faced by migrants and their families in both sending and receiving countries. Participants discussed the need to increase immigrants' civic engagement by taking into account the political experiences and cultural frames in countries of origin. After the discussions, participants issued a list of recommendations to reinvigorate a broad human rights agenda, including the need to raise awareness on anti-immigrant legislation being proposed and applied in many U.S. cities, and the importance of acquiring the right to vote in the host country so that migrants can have a voice to challenge the policies that discriminate and violate their rights (Gzesh, Venet, and Santillo 2007).

The Latin American Community Migrant Summit paved the way to increase self-representation among international organizations and institutions dealing with human mobility. Since 2007, NALACC and Mexican HTAs have participated in the annual Civil Society Days of the United Nations' Global Forum on Migration and Development (GFMD)[25] and were invited to integrate the organizing task force when the GFMD took place in Puerto Vallarta, Mexico, in 2010. They have also participated in the People's Global Action on Migration, Development, and Human Rights (PGA),[26] an independent forum organized by a diverse transnational network of social justice organizations that is held simultaneously with the GFMD to provide an alternative platform to fight for demands that are usually neglected by GFMD participating governments, such as discussions of political rights or human rights abuses.[27] As the new representatives of U.S. civil society fighting for humane immigration legislation across the Americas, NALACC and HTAs have developed a legislative agenda as well. Upon returning from the GFMD in Puerto Vallarta, NALACC organized a meeting in Chicago with some Illinois representatives in the U.S. Congress to request an opportunity to meet with members of the House and Senate committees on foreign policy for Latin America to present their views on immigration reform for the hemisphere on Capitol Hill and to urge them to take a look at the recommendations issued by the GFMD's Civil Society Days forums and rally support for the their implementation by the U.S. government.

As a consequence of the increased visibility of migrant civil society in international circles, migrant organizations have extended their networks with national Latino organizations whose agendas include advocacy on behalf of Latino immigrant rights and social justice in Latin America. For example, in 2012, under the leadership of the Chicago-based Latino Policy Forum, ICIRR, FEDECMI, and NALACC, the National Latino Congreso (NLC) took place in Chicago for the first time after six years of being held in the Southwest. Launched in 2006, the NLC is an informal shared space of nonbinding deliberations involving leaders from MALDEF, LULAC, the Hispanic Federation, the Labor Council for Latin Americans Advancement (LCLAA), the William C. Velazquez Institute (WCVI), the Southwest Voter Registration and Education Project (SVREP), and NALACC. Neither a coalition nor an alliance, the NLC encourages collective analysis and creative strategies to respond to the many challenges faced by Latino communities to determine priorities for the next few years. In 2012, NLC agreed on the need to prioritize alliance-building at the local, state, federal, and international levels, looking for allies in key social constituencies such as women's rights groups, LGBTQ communities, African American organizations, organized labor, youth organizations, and communities of faith, among others (Chacón 2012). Among the keynote speakers, representatives of Lambda Legal, the largest civil rights organization of the LGBTQ community; the Mexican Movimiento por la Paz con Justicia y Dignidad; and the National Organization for Women (NOW) spoke about strategies to build successful coalitions with different constituencies to advance progressive legislation to benefit group members. Most Chicago HTAs and federations—including Guerrerenses, Jalicienses, Zacatecanos, and Michoacanos—submitted panel proposals and resolutions to NLC's plenary sessions.

Increasing visibility requires resources, and Latino migrant-led organizations with transnational advocacy agendas frequently need to make important decisions about balancing provision of direct services with advocacy work to confront a climate of punitive anti-immigrant legislation, given their limited time and funding resources. Frequently, the easiest path for many organizations serving vulnerable communities is to submit proposals for public funds to provide necessary services, but often times this path leads them to cut back on organizing and advocacy strategies to influence public policy decisions that affect their constituents. Therefore, for HTAs and migrant-led coalitions such as NALACC, it is crucial to inform member organizations of the value of having independent, membership-based grassroots organizations committed to fund their work with varied strategies including membership dues, fund-raising campaigns, foundation grants, corporate donors, U.S. government funds, and home country public and private financing.

While Latino-led immigrant-serving organizations including HTAs consider immigrant legislation reform and legalization of undocumented immigrants one of their most important priorities, the fact remains that civil society organizations with anti-immigrant agendas are frequently better funded or enjoy the support of well-organized nativist organizations (Pear 2007). Latino-led nonprofit organizations in Chicago face enormous challenges to have access to public and private funds, human resources, and facilities, and these problems are exacerbated among younger organizations with limited track records that rely on volunteers and small paid staffs such as HTAs and federations. For example, in a survey of sixty-six Latino-led and Latino-serving nonprofits in the Chicago metropolitan area, researchers found that the majority (60 percent) of these nonprofits were created in the past twenty years (1998 or later), a minority (7.5 percent) have annual budgets between U.S. $1 million and $2 million, and only 11 percent offer immigration-related services such as citizenship application assistance, immigrant worker rights dissemination, or immigration reform advocacy activities (Levin and McKean 2009).[28]

In Chicago and elsewhere, access to resources for immigrant-serving organizations tends to privilege organizations with proven track records offering direct service provisions and those representing large coalitions. To give an idea of the resource inequality among nonprofits, compare the annual budgets for selected Chicago nonprofits serving Latino immigrants for 2009. During that year, FEDECMI's yearly total expenditures were less than U.S. $350,000 and NALACC spent less than $700,000 for all its programming. In comparison, the ICIRR, an organization formed in 1991, spent more than $7 million in statewide programs, while Heartland Alliance for Human Needs and Human Rights, one of the oldest mainstream immigrant-serving institutions in the city, spent more than $10 million. Mujeres Latinas en Acción, a well-established migrant-led Latina organization established in Chicago in 1972 to provide services to low-income women regardless of immigration status, spent close to $4 million in programs that included domestic violence prevention, workforce development training, and breast cancer prevention, among others.[29] Service provision is one of the most effective paths to increase organizational resources, frequently at the expense of advocating for influencing public policy decision making that could produce long-lasting positive effects in the lives of immigrants.

For now, Michoacán HTAs continue to seek financial support from public and private sources of funding in two countries to deliver services and programming to Mexican migrants on both sides of the border. However, they are not interested in becoming a provider offering services for which the governments are responsible. In their role of advocates to increase the quality of life of migrant communities, they strive to increase capacity-building in member organizations but do not let governments off the hook; they continue to push for more public services for migrants across borders. They want the Mexican government to guarantee minimum standards of well-being, and they demand the same from local, state, and federal governments in the United States.

Are HTAs and federations assimilating into mainstream U.S. philanthropy, in the traditional pattern of immigrant organizational integration? Or are they creating a new form of civic engagement by working on the various levels of community services, advocacy, and grassroots social and political organization? It is still difficult to predict if FEDECMI's membership-based model will succeed in bringing a permanently sustained transnational approach to organizing Latino immigrants while building bridges and sharing agendas with native-born Latinos. However, from my observations of its first decade of operation, FEDECMI has a clear vision of building a strong, dues-paying membership organization that will enable it to have a degree of autonomy from local governments and to diversify spheres of action.

The organization also avoids having to respond to the directives of a single funder—a common challenge to advance independent advocacy agendas that represent members' interests. For example, in his analysis of the failure of national Latino organizations to defend the interests and basic civil rights of Latinos in the United States, Rodolfo Acuña (2012) recognizes that excessive reliance on a few funders has made major national Latino organizations too dependent on approved strategies dictated by donors. He sadly observes how no major national educational organization supported the Save Ethnic Studies movement in Arizona, and he puts part of the blame on mainstream leftist organizations that only seek after their own interests and issues.

Despite the enormous challenges to gaining access to resources, migrant civil society is slowly thickening, gaining autonomy through a long process of transnational social capital accumulation. The breadth and density of connections and coalitions built (informal and formal) between HTAs and other Latin American immigrant-serving organizations in Chicago, the United States, Latin America, and other countries with high migrant populations are remarkable after the spring 2006 mobilizations opened a window for scaling up and out from their traditional comfort zones with the different tiers of the Mexican government.

EXPANDING CITIZENSHIP PRACTICES ACROSS BORDERS

The concept of citizenship has historically been employed to exclude those who do not qualify as members of a geographically circumscribed polity, but constant human mobility has pushed nation-states to reconsider those qualifications. Today, the exercise of citizenship signifies membership in a national community and is an empowering tool to expand democratic governance in a globalized world. Paradoxically, many migrant sending countries in the South are redefining citizenship by expanding its territorial scale to incorporate their nationals abroad into new transterritorial and global national communities, while receiving nations in the North increasingly restrict access to citizenship to recent immigrants and curtail basic labor rights of migrant workers. The nation-states' reasons for following such different agendas depend on their geopolitical context. In the South, nation-states want to empower their citizens to become naturalized citizens in the host societies to reduce the pressures of having to defend their rights while retaining their loyalties as frequent visitors and senders of remittances. In the North, nation-states refuse to recognize their dependence on cheap labor and ignore the exploitation of vulnerable workers to maintain low wages without sacrificing productivity. This labor force strategy creates severe obstacles to the wider civic engagement of migrants (Guarnizo 2012).

In the United States, citizenship rights are restricted to those who can claim *jus soli* or *jus sanguinis*, or who declare loyalty to the nation-state via naturalization after years of holding legal status as permanent residents. Permanent residence status has been very difficult to obtain since the legal amnesty offered to most undocumented immigrants in 1986. From this bleak perspective, it would be relatively easy to conclude that global capitalism establishes illegality and marginality to maintain a vulnerable workforce, and that in this context, there are few avenues for Mexican migrants without access to full political rights to participate in civic engagement activities in sending and receiving communities (De Genova 2005). However, for many Mexican migrants living in the United States, lack of formal citizenship has not prevented the creation of civic organizations that use multiple migrant identities to build social networks and improve the quality of life in more than one geographical space, combining local, rural, urban, translocal, national, regional, and transnational geopolitical memberships.

Binational migrant civic engagement offers a social education experience to act collectively for common ends without the constraints of formal political participation that requires citizenship status to vote in the United States and freedom of mobility to vote in Mexican elections. By connecting with institutions that facilitate incorporation and improve the well-being and social infrastructure in sending and receiving communities, migrants solidify their trust of those who belong to their networks and increase solidarity ties through their sharing of common culture, traditions, and belief systems regardless of legal status. Mexican HTAs now strongly encourage U.S. naturalization among those who qualify, a stark difference with some of their early twentieth-century predecessors who were more likely to restrict membership to those who retained exclusive loyalty to Mexico (see chapter 2). HTA members and leaders believe that the best way to increase binational political and civic engagement is through committed citizens who have political rights in the two countries to which they contribute socially and politically.

Mexican HTAs have transformed the traditional civic participation that is expected from citizens with full political rights. For example, Mexican migrants living in the United States had been largely disenfranchised in Mexican electoral democracy since they did not have access to absentee voting rights until quite recently. However, political disenfranchisement was never a deterrent for engaging in other types of civic participation, such as improving the well-being of their compatriots through infrastructure and beautification projects in their hometowns and villages and, more recently, their civic involvement in the defense of human and labor rights of migrant workers in the United States.

In Chicago, Mexican HTAs have mobilized their social capital and organizational resources to increase naturalizations and voter registration in the aftermath of the 2006 immigrant rights protests against the Sensenbrenner bill, a highly anti-immigrant legislation attempting to criminalize undocumented immigrants. Since 2006, HTAs' members have participated in large marches and demonstrations on behalf of immigrant rights, carrying the important message that civic participation is not only exercised through the voting booths. In these marches, one of the most popular slogans read: "Today we march, tomorrow we vote." The national immigrant demonstrations in the spring of 2006 spurred campaigns to encourage LPRs to acquire U.S. citizenship and participate in U.S. elections while also making sure that legal status was not an impediment to volunteer for immigrant rights advocacy organizations.

By 2010, due in part to HTAs' encouragement and the efforts of hundreds of immigrant rights organizations in the state of Illinois, 65 percent of the Mexican immigrants who came to Illinois before 1980 were naturalized U.S. citizens compared to 61 percent of the same cohort in the state of California, 53 percent in New York, and 58 percent in Texas.[30] The positive outcome of increased naturalizations offers new avenues for understanding variation among naturalization rates depending on the contexts of reception. It also requires rethinking the importance of dual nationality and the potential benefits of voting in more than one country as innovative mechanisms to increase political engagement in U.S. elections among naturalized Latino immigrants.

One issue that united Mexican migrants with different political affiliations in the last decade was the demand for the right to vote absentee in Mexican presidential elections.[31] While this victory was largely won through a coordinated national effort that included Mexican HTAs and other Mexican organizations, they enjoyed the support of prominent leaders of the Latino community. For example, in a passionate speech offered at the Washington, D.C.–based Woodrow Wilson Center for International Scholars during an event on Mexican migrant civic engagement in late 2005, Ann Marie Tallman, then MALDEF's president and general counsel and a third-generation Mexican American, offered her unequivocal support to Mexicans' right to vote in Mexican elections:

> Before we start talking about Mexican nationals and their voting in Mexican elections I think it is important to recognize that any expatriate, anyone living in other countries, Iranian Citizens, Iraqi citizens, any individuals not living

in their country of origin, that are living in a foreign land, they all must
have the ability to vote in their home country elections. There is not a lot of
debate or discussion about allegiance when you are talking about voting by
foreigners in other countries because there is not a geographical proximity,
but you do get that debate when you are talking about Mexican nationals and
I think that any citizen deserves equitable application of electoral democracy
and I often see racist ethno attacks against Mexican nationals living in this
country because of the proximity of Mexico to the United States. I think that
we have to recognize that countries allow their expatriates to vote and this
country is a democracy that encourages voting and it encourages that all
people have the opportunity to exercise their right to be heard so I think it
is important to be mindful of those principles and to be mindful that often
times the debate around allegiances becomes very different when you are talking about a community that is more geographically close to the United States
than when you are talking about other communities.[32]

In 2005, Mexican migrant organizations understood that it was important
to orchestrate an immediate response to the Sensenbrenner bill despite their
busy workload with the Mexican election. After some unsuccessful attempts to
encourage the Mexican Federal Electoral Institute to move quickly with the distribution of absentee ballots, the HTAs soon realized that their efforts to increase
voter registration for Mexican elections were going to bring scant success due
to the highly restrictive rules. Therefore, the HTAs decided to use the momen-
tum created from the voter registration drive to fight against the Sensenbrenner
bill.[33] Their simultaneous engagement with issues of political representation in
both Mexico and Chicago supports the conclusions of James A. McCann, Wayne
Cornelius, and David Leal (2009) that there is a positive and highly significant
correlation between migrant engagement in the public affairs of Mexico and of
the United States. In the 2006 Mexican presidential election, educational and
income levels were important predictors of migrant citizens' decisions to register
to vote. However, the density of migrant organizations in urban areas also contributed to a higher engagement with Mexico's electoral campaigns. According
to an analysis of registration patterns across the United States, two additional
variables increased the electoral participation rates among Mexican migrants living abroad: the presence of Spanish-language media and ethnically oriented civic
organizations. In those urban areas where these two variables were significant,
the registration rate increased in 30 percent (Leal, Lee, and McCann 2012).

While civic binationality and engagement with U.S. politics have certainly
expanded among Chicago-based migrant organizations, the diversity of HTA
networks makes it difficult to speak about a unified agenda for the migrant civil
society. Association members belong to different political groups and follow different advocacy strategies. Since many HTAs strive to preserve their organizational autonomy within the structure of federations, tensions frequently arise

when deciding the best strategies for nonpartisan political advocacy efforts on behalf of immigrant communities. While many HTA members lean toward the Democratic Party, there are a considerable number of Republican and Independent voters as well. Often undecided between the presidential candidates and discouraged by the lack of action on immigration reform, HTAs should not be counted as unconditional loyalists to any particular political party. In fact, in a truly nonpartisan spirit, these organizations are increasingly reaching across the aisle and offering openings for both parties to make gains. It is still too early to tell whether the 2012 presidential election results, in which a vast majority of Latino voters favored the Democratic candidate, might change this dynamic.

Many HTA leaders hold pragmatic rather than partisan views of politics, since they realize that the urgent needs of their members should prevail over party loyalties when long-term family separation is at stake. Due to backlogs in processing family reunification, many families endure separation for decades. To bring family members from Mexico for short visits to Chicago, some HTAs have advocated temporary solutions to family reunification.

The Illinois-based Abuelita (Grandmother) Visa Program is an excellent case to show the tensions that arise when HTAs make demands to any elected official who might offer a quick fix to ease the pain of family separation regardless of that politician's views on comprehensive immigration reform. In 2009, a couple of Waukegan-based independent HTAs invited Mark Kirk (R-Ill.) to visit Michoacán and Mexico State to thank him for the sponsorship his district had offered to many of their charitable projects and for the creation of a temporary visa program to reunite grandmothers with their grandchildren in Waukegan, Aurora, and Chicago. Although Kirk does not support a legalization program for undocumented immigrants or the DREAM Act, his office supported the binational work of HTAs when he was U.S. Congress representative for the Tenth District and agreed to sponsor a discretionary thirty-day nonrenewable visa program for Mexican grandmothers with families in Illinois in an isolated effort to alleviate the immigration problems of a small sector of his less-affluent constituents. Since 2005, thirty-three trips with approximately forty grandparents each have been accomplished, and Kirk visited two rural towns in Michoacán and México State to meet with the families of his constituents and municipal presidency staff in 2009.[34]

To some FEDECMI leaders, it was inappropriate to invite a congressman who had voted against the DREAM Act to Michoacán. They convinced the secretary of migrant affairs in the state to decline an invitation from the U.S. Embassy to meet with former congressman Kirk during his visit in an effort to lower the political profile of the visit. When I asked a member of an HTA who decided to participate in the visa program sponsored by Kirk his opinion about FEDECMI's lack of support for the visa program, he said: "Accepting the visa program for my grandmother does not oblige me to vote for the Republican Party. I have never voted for the Republicans and never will. However, the public profile of this program has become a minor nuisance for our organization because some Republican candidates now call me in search for endorsements from my club and as a courtesy I invite them to our fund-raisers to show them our projects and meet our members."[35] In this leader's view, he was simply accepting a special government service that a network of HTAs in Waukegan had obtained to benefit HTA family members.

If federal inaction to solve the situation of undocumented families continues, naturalized Mexican immigrants will continue exercising their U.S. citizenship rights and voting power to support programs to reunite families. This could encourage limited programs from politicians who do not support broad legislative change to offer long-lasting solutions but are eager to please constituents to attract Latino votes. Vanessa Guridy, a University of Illinois at Chicago graduate student who has interviewed several Abuelita Visa Program beneficiaries and county government officials familiar with the rules of this discretionary visa program, believes that "some of those who use the program are so removed—or feel removed—from the formal political process, that they don't always know much about the differences between political parties. Instead, beneficiaries see that one group is doing something concrete to help them reconnect with their families. Their focus is much more on the direct benefit they are receiving rather than the political implications attached to that aid. In any case, as an unintended consequence, HTA membership has expanded due to the interest in benefiting from this visa program."[36]

Contesting Hegemonies, Fighting for Inclusion: Migrant Civil Society in the Twenty-First Century

Practices of civil binationality can be addressed from many sociopolitical fields. This book has concentrated on the subnational analysis, paying close attention to the transfer of migrant social integration and human rights responsibilities from federal to state governments in two national spaces. Considering the difficulties in addressing migrant social and cultural needs on both sides of the border, federal Mexican and U.S. governments have not solved immediate problems, leaving subnational scales to step up to find solutions. In Mexico, state governments have increasingly created new offices to address the needs of their migrant populations living in metropolitan cities, while in the United States, cities, counties, and states try to regulate immigration in the absence of federal immigration reform (Varsanyi 2010). In these new contexts, transnational migrant organizations have become forceful advocates in local, subnational, and binational spheres. They are challenging pressures from diverse hemispheric political systems and cultures that attempt to oblige them to define their engagements in terms of mutually exclusive nation-states (Fox and Gois 2010). Within HTAs, healthy levels of distrust toward government institutions have served as an effective mechanism to improve public-private partnerships. As Karen S. Cook, Russell Hardon, and Margaret Levi suggest, "when distrust stimulates the development of improved institutions, it may facilitate cooperation, not hinder it" (2005: 2).

HTAs provide empirical evidence that contemporary citizenship has become pluridimensional, multiscalar, and fluid. Its forms often result from interactions with different organizations and state policies in more than one nation-state, with practices embedded in an unequal global economy dominated by a dual discourse centered on liberal democracy and free market fundamentalism. In the words of Luis Guarnizo, one of the pioneer scholars in the study of Latin American migrant transnational practices:

> Citizenship has been reconfigured as a multiscalar (as opposed to singularly scaled) and fluid (as opposed to "established") mechanism of governance resulting from dynamic and multifarious grassroots practices and state responses to hypermobile global society. Overlapping scales of excluding, controlling, and ruling dialectically intersect with new ways of belonging, participating, and resisting. These dialectic relations are often expressed by the exercise of subnational citizenship rights (including mobility) by people who have been nominally barred from having any formal rights. (2012: 28)

At the start of the twenty-first century, the largest and most visible HTAs in Chicago usually avoid exclusive reliance on the public-private collaborations favored by neoliberal policies and steer away from the all-too-common rhetoric of valuing Mexican migrants *only* as hard-working, enterprising, and self-reliant individuals. HTA leaders argue that they develop public-private projects due to selfless philanthropy and solidarity in the absence of sufficient resources to address the special needs of communities in need of bilingual and culturally sensitive programs.[37] HTAs' public discourse and activities encourage both Mexican and U.S. publics to value Mexican migrants as human beings who transmit culture, language, values of family harmony, and diverse ethno-national identities to their children. While it is true that HTAs frequently remind U.S. and Mexican governments of their contributions as taxpayers to the former and remittance senders to the latter, they equally demand access to full political and civil rights for all Latino immigrants claiming membership in more than one nation-state.

In this globalized context, HTAs defy the traditional conception of legal citizenship, defined as a formal institution used by states to regulate and govern those included or excluded from membership to a community of shared law, whose members do not necessarily belong to clearly delineated territorialized communities attached to *only one* nation-state. Through their binational collective action agendas, HTA members demonstrate that everyday practices of social citizenship can be exercised in spite of legal exclusion. In Mexico, HTA members participate in municipal, state, and federal public policy design although very few exercise their electoral rights due to the overwhelming obstacles of absentee voting regulations. In the United States, they participate in public policy design in their local, state, and federal governments regardless of legal status, sending text messages to congressional representatives, attending rallies and marches, attending public hearings on redistricting laws, and engaging with schools, churches, and public safety campaigns.

Mexican and U.S. government authorities who embrace and support HTA programs and missions do so because it facilitates the implementation of their neoliberal agendas, including the severe decline of public responsibilities and the increased privatization of critical social services. In Mexico, HTAs defray the costs of vital social infrastructure for rural areas, while in the United States, HTAs provide undocumented migrants, LPRs, and naturalized U.S. citizens with critical tools to succeed outside of their ethnic niches and help fill the gaps in insufficient public services.

From the evidence presented in this book, some could be tempted to conclude that HTAs' partnerships with subnational Mexican and U.S. governments does not give them a strong independent voice, since it puts them in league with the very authorities they are contesting. However, in the minds of HTA leaders, it is best to cooperate closely with authorities in equitable relationships as it gives them the opportunity to act as watchdogs. In reality, these processes of urban rescaling, empowered accountable autonomy, and the institutionalization of transnational connections between grassroots and states highlight the multiple and seemingly contradictory alliances that migrants decide to make in processes of organizational rescaling.

The Mexican nation-state has rescaled its outreach to immigrants with differential outcomes depending on the degree of maturity of established organizations. For example, subnational policies addressing migrant affairs have differed across Mexican states, producing stronger organizations among populations of states with more structured public policies toward migrants and weaker organizations in states with less structured ones. In the United States, a similar phenomenon occurs as states decide to design their own public policies to address immigrant issues in response to inaction from the federal government. In this new context, in cities with robust migrant-led organizations, synergistic public-private processes to improve the quality of migrant life lead to more welcoming environments for newcomers. In Chicago, historical Latino organizations, transnational migrant organizations, and multiethnic immigrant coalitions collaborate with state authorities to create friendlier immigrant legislation, or at least more tolerant environments with modest results. These miniature cracks in the highly restrictive federal immigration control system are the product of constant negotiations among key players from civil society, municipal, and state level authorities to alleviate the obstacles in the daily lives of migrant workers in Chicago, the suburbs, and the rest of the state.

But how inclusive and participatory is migrant civil society? Following Nancy Fraser's conceptualization of the public-sphere's legitimacy, to satisfy the *inclusiveness condition* (who participates), discussion must be open to all with a stake in the outcome, and *participatory parity* (how one participates) is achieved when "all interlocutors must, in principle, enjoy roughly equal chances to state their views, place issues on the agenda, question the tacit and explicit assumptions of others, switch levels as needed, and generally receive a fair hearing" (2009: 93). Following Fraser's rules of engagement to determine the legitimacy of transnational action in the public sphere, the transformative role of migrant organizations cannot be measured as uniformly contributing to struggles for social justice due to its unequal distribution and outreach in global spaces. Yet these organizations hold great potential, and it is necessary that civil societies in Mexico, the United States, and many Latin American countries with vast populations living abroad acknowledge their work and support grassroots transnational coalitions with shared social justice agendas. In Mexico and Latin America, there are only a few migrant-led organizations with visible transnational and/or binational agendas and many more local groups whose voices and demands remain silent because they do not have the resources to participate in the global arena.

In the future, migrant civil society will continue its expansion only if migrant populations are included as subjects with rights and obligations in all governance structures in which they interact. Civil societies require a sense of belonging to shared principles of conviviality that go beyond national spaces. For any given problem, the relevant public should match the reach of the governance structure that regulates social interactions. Where such structures transgress the borders of states, the corresponding public spheres must be transnational (Fraser 2009). While Mexican HTAs' civic and political strategies to defend their human, social, and economic rights as migrants living in the United States are still in the initial stages and it is too early to predict their future direction, the development of new strategies for participation suggests not only their willingness to intervene both in the United States and in Mexico but, most of all, the emergence of a migrant civil society working simultaneously in Mexico and the United States. One of the most important challenges for these binational organizations will be the definition of a feasible binational agenda and the discovery of best strategies to build successful alliances, networks, and coalitions with similar organizations in the American continent and beyond. But what about the future of HTAs' organizational dynamics? One important question that will be worth exploring is the internal transformation of HTAs' collectivist organizational structure. Will the transformation of HTAs to conform to norms of the organized civil society tilt them toward less collectivism and more individualism? Let's hope that their original values of generosity and reciprocal exchanges will prevail even amid external forces pushing them toward individual organizational identities, measurable goals, rigid program evaluations, and many other consequences of their newly gained organizational visibility across borders.

NOTES

PREFACE

1. To learn more about the Tepeyac Association of New York, see Gálvez 2011.

2. For a cross-national comparison of the role of digital diasporas in transnational civic engagement, see Brinkerhoff 2009.

3. Pilsen is a neighborhood in Chicago's Lower West Side. Prior to the 1950s, German, Irish, and Bohemian immigrants settled in this area, mostly along Eighteenth Street. Due to liberal immigration laws that supported family reunification and the forced removal of Mexicans from the Near West Side to expand the University of Illinois at Chicago, Mexican migrants became predominant in Pilsen in the 1950s and 1960s. Today, Pilsen is still considered a predominantly Mexican ethnic neighborhood. See Gellman 2005.

CHAPTER 1 — MIGRANT GENEROSITY AND TRANSNATIONAL CIVIC ENGAGEMENT

1. The name is real. From this point on, all names are real unless otherwise indicated. In a few instances, I use only first names to protect the identities of those who either are or have at one time been undocumented in the United States and to protect family privacy. In this book, the names of a few individuals and locations as well as incidental details have been disguised when necessary to ensure confidentiality.

2. A *posada* is a traditional Catholic celebration that is popular in Mexico and other parts of Latin America. Since 1987, the Chicago Catholic Archdiocese organizes an annual *posada* that is celebrated in downtown Chicago with a pilgrimage on Michigan Avenue followed by piñatas, tamales, and *champurrado*, a chocolate-flavored hot corn drink (Redacción 2010). Mexican HTAs frequently make in-kind donations to this celebration. To learn more about *posadas* in the context of transnational civic engagement, see Hondagneu-Sotelo, Gaudinez, and Lara 2007.

3. President Fox faced midterm elections in the summer of 2003, and, according to his then foreign minister, Jorge Castañeda, "Fox was unable to resist the temptation to use his anti-Bush opposition in the [UN] Security Council for domestic electoral purposes (to no avail, by the way: Fox's party received a drubbing in the July 2003 vote)" (2007: 102). Independently of the electoral result in Mexico's midterm elections, the plan for immigration reform had already been derailed after September 11, 2001, when antiterrorism efforts

occupied the entire U.S. foreign affairs agenda after the attack on the Twin Towers in New York City.

4. By April 2003, there were 6,994 Mexican-born migrants in the U.S. armed forces: 2,776 in the army, 907 in the air force, 1,102 in the marine corps, and 2,318 in the navy (Krauze 2004). In July 2004, a naturalized U.S. citizen born in Guanajuato died in Iraq and returned to his homeland to fulfill his family's wishes to be buried in his hometown. During the funeral, a group of Mexican soldiers burst into the ceremony to prevent the U.S. Marines from firing volley shots as a salute in the military funeral. The Mexican army and local politicians argued that the presence of a foreign army bearing arms was a violation of Mexico's sovereignty. Jorge Santibáñez Romellón, then president of El Colegio de La Frontera Norte in Tijuana, in a two-part editorial on the issue explained that the attitude of Mexicans was equally divided depending on where they lived: Mexicans living in the United States were in favor of the U.S. military funeral taking place on Mexican soil while Mexicans living in Mexico were adamantly against it (Santibáñez Romellón 2004a, 2004b).

5. The new demography in the Chicago metro area is characterized by the significant presence of Mexican migrants, who represent 47.5 percent of the total population of Latinos of Mexican descent (a mix of legal permanent residents, citizens, and those who are undocumented), and an increased population of rural migrants from small towns living in the same neighborhoods and suburbs (American Community Survey 2010).

6. Of the Mexican travelers to Illinois, 35.4 percent engaged in business or professional activities; 22.7 percent visited on holidays; 25.1 percent were visiting relatives or friends; and 15.2 percent attended conventions or conferences (State of Ilinois Trade Mission 2013).

7. For a qualitative and quantitative overview of the literature on the role of political parties, community organizations, labor unions, Spanish-language media, and other U.S. civic institutions, including Mexican HTAs, and particularly their role in encouraging immigrant civic and political participation, see Pallares and Flores González 2010; Ramakrishnan and Bloemraad 2008; Voss and Bloemraad 2011; Wong 2006.

8. For a theoretical discussion and overview of Mexican emigrant incorporation policy before and after the 1980s, see Sherman 1999. Since the mid-1970s, state-diaspora relations had been characterized by a Mexican government attitude that Mexican scholar Manuel García y Griego famously defined as a "policy of no policy" in a 1985 academic conference in Mexico City (García y Griego 1988).

9. See Tijerina 1992.

10. For a historical analysis of Mexican state strategies to change foreign policy toward the incorporation of Mexican migrants, see, among others, Délano 2011; Fitzgerald 2009; Sherman 1999.

11. For notable exceptions focusing on the cases of Oaxaca, Guanajuato, and Zacatecas, see Fox and Rivera-Salgado 2004a; Smith and Bakker 2008; Stephen 2007.

12. For a discussion of the many challenges to capture the world of informal migrant organizations using official IRS databases of 501 (c) 3 organizations, see Bloemraad and Gleeson 2012.

13. Still today, Mexican HTAs remain concentrated in a few states: 60 percent of Mexican HTAs registered at Mexican consulates across the United States represent just five states: Guanajuato, Guerrero, Jalisco, Michoacán, and Zacatecas. See Fox and Bada 2011.

14. For reviews of the literature on transnational communities, see, among others, Fletcher and Margold 2003; Guarnizo, Portes, and Haller 2003; Levitt 2001; Portes, Escobar, and Walton Radford 2007; Waldinger and Fitzgerald 2004.

15. For a comprehensive conceptual discussion of the sectors that conform the emerging migrant civil society in Mexico and the United States, see Fox and Bada 2011.

16. On the organization of P'urhépecha indigenous migrants from Michoacán, see Leco Tomás 2009.

17. The Three-for-One Program is a federal poverty alleviation program established in 2002 by the federal Secretariat of Social Development (SEDESOL) in which contributions from Mexican HTAs abroad are matched by federal, state, and local governments in equal amounts. One of its main objectives is to multiply the government financial support offered to infrastructure projects financed with collective remittances. For every peso donated by an HTA for any approved project, each level of government (federal, state, and municipal) invests an equal amount. For more on the history of the program, see Iskander 2010.

18. For a general overview of neoliberal reforms and privatization in Mexico during this period, see MacLeod 2004. For a detailed analysis of the relationship between agricultural modernization in rural areas and increased migration to the United States, see, among others, Bartra 2004; Delgado Wise 2004.

19. For an overview of the meaning of *faenas* in the construction of political and social subjects in rural Michoacán, see Zendejas Romero 2003. For a comparison of the erosion of *faenas* in municipalities with high indexes of migration in the state of Puebla, see Smith 2006.

20. In 2010, the state of Michoacán received U.S. $2.6 billion in federal expenditures and revenue sharing. In 2009, the state received U.S. $2.4 billion. For a comprehensive evolution of federal expenditures and revenue sharing at the national level, see Tépach Marcial 2011.

21. Political scientists have recently taken this approach using mostly survey research methods analyzing attitudes and behaviors. See, among others, Burgess 2010; Danielson 2011; Duquette 2011; Fernández 2005; Germano 2010; Goodman and Hiskey 2008.

22. For a good exception, see the analysis of transnational citizenship practices of migrant leaders, including their rural development ideologies, in Smith and Bakker 2008. For a conceptual overview on indigenous migrant civil society organizations, see Fox and Rivera-Salgado 2004b. To learn more about historical and contemporary Mexican immigration policies, including the relationship of migration and development in policy design using a state-centered perspective, see, among others, Délano 2011; Fitzgerald 2009; Iskander 2010.

23. See Voces Mesoamericanas 2010.

24. The "Declaración de Cuernavaca," a document created by members of the Zacatecas-based International Network of Migration and Development, contains a critique of the conventional discussion of remittances and development. See Red Internacional de Migración y Desarrollo 2005. While the literature on remittances is too vast to address in this introduction, it is worth noting that researchers have yet to agree on the validity of the official data, the share of the Mexican population that receives remittances, and the degree to which these remittances reach the poorest communities. For an extended discussion of the opposing views to address migration and development from sending regions and a summary of the "Declaración de Cuernavaca" in English, see Castles and Delgado Wise 2008; Portes 2009.

25. In 2006, President Felipe Calderón chose the state of Michoacán as the first site to unveil his strategy against drug cartels. He sent the army to the southern region of the state, an action that quickly brought a wave of human rights violations that captured the

international media and local airwaves. When the First Migrant Summit was inaugurated in Morelia, Michoacán, in May 2006, NPR correspondent Lourdes García Navarro was there ready to cover the entire event until her editor called her and sent her to Apatzingán to cover President Calderón's war against drugs instead. She left Morelia right after the inauguration, and the international media coverage of the event was rather modest.

26. For an overview of the correlations between context of reception and immigrant incorporation outcomes in nine medium-size cities in the United States, see Bada et al. 2010.

27. For a comprehensive national comparison of immigration policy activism in U.S. cities and states, see Varsanyi 2010.

28. Today, Casa Michoacán is located a few blocks from Thalia Hall, and the National Alliance of Latin American and Caribbean Communities frequently uses the restaurant at Thalia Hall for social gatherings. In the early twentieth century, Thalia Hall at Eighteenth Street was a vibrant space for Bohemian music, theater, and transnational political activism to fight for independence from the Astro-Hungarian Empire. The Bohemian National Alliance, an immigrant organization, usually met there to discuss home country politics and eventually merged with other groups to form the Czech-Slovak alliance. The efforts of this group pressured President Woodrow Wilson to propose Bohemian statehood to the Allies in 1915.

29. For an analysis of CASA-HGT ideology in the context of national civil rights Latino struggles, see Pulido 2006.

30. City of Chicago, Office of the Mayor, "Executive Order 85–1," March 7, 1985.

31. On the role of religion in the journey of undocumented Mexican and Central Americans, see Groody 2002; Hagan 2008. For a comparative study of immigrant religious congregations in relation to American identity and belonging, see Levitt 2007. For a cross-national comparison of the role of faith and religious identity among Haitians in France and the United States, see Mooney 2009. For a case study of Chicago immigrant congregations and their moral and social engagement projects, see Kniss and Numrich 2007.

32. For recent ethnographies focusing on the role of the Virgin of Guadalupe in building community and public life among Mexican immigrants in New York City and transnational Mexican migrants in Chicago, see, respectively, Gálvez 2010 and Peña 2011. For a national overview of the Latin Americanization of U.S. Catholicism, see Matovina 2011.

33. On Christian Base Communities in Latin America in the late 1960s, see, among others, Mainwaring and Wilde 1989.

34. The goals of *Las Razas Unidas* were "to provide a vehicle for and to stimulate communication within La Raza, to present a positive cultural image for our people, to develop unity among diversity [and] to promote integration, not assimilation." Richard A. Santillán Collection, Box #2, Newsletters, *Las Razas Unidas, Movimiento Apostólico*, Sterling, Ill. (1974–1975). This newsletter published the biographies of famous Christian Base Community leaders in Latin American, such as Camilo Torres (1929–1966), the guerrilla priest from Colombia, among others. Editors were also active in demanding that the Catholic Church offer masses in Spanish and accept the bicultural nature of Saint Mary's parish in Sterling, arguing that many members of the congregation did not speak English and were being attracted to the Protestant faith. In the mid-1970s, there were no masses in Spanish offered in Sterling, but the Diocese of Rockford provided masses in Spanish in Elgin, Rockford, and Aurora.

35. Today, there are at least four Independence Day parades in Chicago and many more in the suburbs, including Joliet, Cicero, Waukegan, Hanover Park, and West Chicago. For instance, the Independence Day parade in Joliet started in 1962, several years before the

parade in Little Village. However, these parades are not the only ethnic public manifestation of Mexicanness in Chicago, as the city has incubated at least one Emmy-winning migrant-led folk music group (Sones de México) and one internationally recognized migrant-led folk dance group (Mexican Dance Ensemble), which trace their origins to a small church-sponsored Mexican folk dance group in the Back of the Yards neighborhood in the case of the latter and to free rehearsal space opportunities at Casa Aztlán for the former.

36. In 1986, the Movimiento Apostólico invited Baldemar Velázquez, the lead organizer of the Farmworker Labor Organizing Committee (FLOC), to speak to the congregation and urge members to ask Heinz to negotiate a new contract with FLOC.

37. For more details on the rescuing of Saint Francis Church, see Badillo 2006.

38. For an anthropological analysis on the power of nostalgia among Jaliscan migrants for changing the landscapes to include Saint Toribio Romo as an important symbol of belonging in Santa Ana, California, see Hirai 2009. For a historical account of Mexican migrant incorporation to the Lady of Mount Carmel Church in Melrose Park, see Badillo 2006.

39. On the role of faith as one of the main sources of strength for crossing the border, see Massey and Durand 1995.

40. In a recent academic evaluation of the performance of state-level migrant affair offices, the state of Michoacán obtained a score of five, the highest score possible, for its binational advocacy of migrant rights (Ortega Ramírez 2011; Velázquez Flores and Ortega Ramírez 2010).

41. In Mexico, there is no universally agreed-upon inventory of civil society organizations, and these numbers refer to data collected by the Comparative Nonprofit Sector Project of the Center for Civil Society Studies at Johns Hopkins University. Mexican scholars have criticized the data for using a U.S. framework to assess a distinct reality, overemphasizing the formal organizations and missing the majority of groups with no formal legal status, such as faith-based organizations, urban neighborhood associations, and rural public work committees. See Layton 2009.

42. For recent profiles of Illinois nonprofit organizations documenting their expansion in the last two decades, see Lampking and Waringo 2003.

43. For an academic perspective on Chicago's March 10th Movement, see Pallares and Flores González 2010. For a participant testimony written in Spanish by a Chicago leftist activist from Michoacán, see Cortés 2006.

CHAPTER 2 — THE TRANSFORMATION OF MEXICAN MIGRANT ORGANIZATIONS

1. José Vasconcelos had been a visiting professor at the University of Chicago in 1926, teaching a sociology course on Hispanic Americans in Chicago.

2. Sociedad Mutualista Ignacio Zaragoza [sic], meeting at Bowen Hall, Hull House, Chicago, June 2, 1928, Chicago and Calumet Area Field Notes, Paul Shuster Taylor Papers, Bancroft Library Film 2724, Carton 11, Folders 32–34, p. 107.

3. Author's translation of candidate speech (Cárdenas Solórzano 1989).

4. I am thankful to Carlos Arango for sharing his private records about this significant event.

5. For a geographer's perspective on transnationalism and topophilia using Zacatecas and California as a case study, see Nichols 2006.

6. For instance, in Spanish, the word *"paisano"* means fellow countrymen who share same birthplace.

7. Some scholars argue that transnational ties may work against melting into the majority core—predicted by classical assimilation theories—thus leading to more cultural

autonomy and even cultural hybrid identities or "ethnoscapes." See, for example, Appadurai 1996; Chambers 1994; García Canclini 1995.

8. For instance, over 60 percent of Czech fraternal leaders in Chicago and 70 percent of their Italian counterparts previously belonged to mutual aid organizations in their countries of origin and were mostly artisans or small businessmen (Bodnar 1985). This fact should be emphasized because it was not until the 1970s that scholars recognized the premigratory organizational traits of immigrants to the United States.

9. To learn more about different historical periods of Mexican immigration to Chicago from the turn of the twentieth century to the 1970s, see, among others, Amezcua 2011; Arredondo 2008; M. García 2012; Innis-Jiménez 2013.

10. According to the historian Ewa Morawska, "the overwhelming majority of the turn of the twentieth century Slavic and Italian arrivals to the United States, more than 90 percent of whom were of rural backgrounds, came to this country with a group identity and a sense of belonging that extended no further than the 'okolica' (local countryside)" (2001:184).

11. Paul Shuster Taylor Papers, Mexican Labor in the United States, Chicago and Calumet Area Field Notes, Rodrigo's notes. Interview to senor [sic] Angel, vice president of the Mexican Confederation of Societies for the Chicago Calumet area (1926–1927). Indiana Harbor, Ind., August 8, 1928, Bancroft Library Film 2724, University of California, Berkeley, Carton 11, Folders 32–34, p. 3.

12. Edson, George, Bancroft Library Film 2649, Field Reports, Illinois, 1926–1927, p. 5.

13. Membership Applications, Sociedad Mutualista Cuauhtémoc, 1940, (1944–1950), Unión Benéfica Mexicana Records (UBMR), CRA 136, Box 2, Files 5–9, Calumet Regional Archives (CRA), Indiana University Northwest.

14. Bylaws, Sociedad Mutualista Benito Juárez, 1939, UBMR, Series Sociedad Mutualista Benito Juárez, CRA 136, Box 1, File 2.

15. Ernest W. Burgess Papers, Box 188 Series IV, Special Collections Research Center, University of Chicago Library.

16. The Bracero Agreements (1942–1964) were a series of laws and diplomatic agreements, initiated by an August 1942 exchange of diplomatic notes between the United States and Mexico, for managing the importation of temporary labor contracting of Mexican migrants in the United States. For more on the influence of Bracero Agreements on Mexico-U.S. foreign policy related to immigration management and control, see Délano 2011.

17. Correspondence, Sociedad Mutualista Benito Juárez, 1939–1950, UBMR, CRA 136, Files 3–8.

18. Ibid.

19. Ibid.

20. Archivo Histórico Diplomático, Fondo Instituciones Filantrópicas Mexicanas, Files 73–10/523, IV/523 (73–10)/3, and Fondo IV-3399–20.

21. Archivo Histórico Diplomático, Fondo Cónsules, Letter 1027, File (73–10)/514.

22. The Anti-Imperialist Popular Front was created in August 1935. For an extensive analysis of the activities of the Frente Popular Mexicano (Mexican Popular Front), see Flores 2006.

23. Correspondence, Benito Juárez, 1939–1950, UBMR, CRA 136, Box 1, Files 3–8.

24. The Front sometimes engaged in contradictions in their fights against U.S. imperialism, especially when the Front asked President Franklin D. Roosevelt to offer military support to the Loyalists in the Spanish Civil War.

25. Reglamento de las Comisiones Honoríficas Mexicanas, 1930, Archivo Histórico Diplomático, Departamento Consular, Instituciones Filantrópicas Mexicanas.

26. Correspondence, Benito Juárez, 1939–1950, UBMR, CRA 136, Box 1, Files 3–8.

27. Ordinary meeting minutes, 1956, UBMR, CRA 136, Box 1, File 2.

28. By 2006, the Unión Benéfica Mexicana had 95 members. In the late 1980s, the Unión Benéfica Mexicana had 82 members in its roster, down from an estimated total of 1,000 members that the Benito Juárez Society and the Cuauhtémoc Society had in 1948.

29. Community Organizations in Chicago, archive of the Mexican General Consulate in Chicago.

30. *Crown*, February 14, 1976, 5.

31. In an unpublished manuscript, the historian Louise Año Nuevo Kerr describes a Wildcats reunion meeting she attended in 1995 and mentions that many members made trips from Guadalajara, Los Angeles, and Arizona to participate. At the event, all the discussions were taking place mostly in Chicago-accented English although the topics focused on California's Proposition 187, the conflict in Chiapas, and Mexico's peso devaluation. See Año Nuevo Kerr n.d.

32. Annual Report of the Mexican American Council of Chicago 1954–1955, Chicago Historical Society.

33. For a revision of the classical assimilation theory applied to the Mexican case in the United States, see Jimenez 2009.

34. In 2008, a search in the official Illinois Lions Clubs website listed the Chicago Azteca Lions as an active organization meeting every Wednesday. The Mexican Lions Club was not listed, but there is a Chicago Mexica Club.

35. Beauty Pageant Program of 1996, Sociedad Cívica Mexicana, Community Organizations in Chicago, Archive of the General Mexican Consulate in Chicago.

36. To learn more about CLASA presence in Chicago, see Pescador 2004.

37. For more on the process of decentralization of local governments in Mexico, see Grindle 2007.

38. In 2008, more than half (61.5 percent) of Mexican-born adults age twenty-five and older living in the United States had no high school diploma or the equivalent general equivalency diploma (GED) (Passel and Cohn 2009).

39. The Heartland Alliance for Human Needs and Human Rights and the Chicago Community Trust were among the first supporters of Mexican HTAs in the 1990s.

CHAPTER 3 — GENEALOGIES OF HOMETOWN ASSOCIATIONS

1. See, among others, Besserer 2004; Goldring 2002; Smith and Bakker 2008; Smith 2006.

2. Some notable exceptions include Duquette 2011 and Iskander 2010.

3. For more details on this period, see Espinosa 1999.

4. See Alarcón 2002. According to the secretary of migrant affairs in Michoacán, there are currently 217 Michoacano HTAs in the United States organized in seventeen federations of HTAs. Email exchange with Carlos Gamiño, staff member, Secretaría del Migrante Michoacano, November 10, 2011. In Chicago, there are 50 Michoacano HTAs affiliated with the Mexican consulate, representing 23 percent of the total in the United States. Not all Michoacano HTAs are affiliated with FEDECMI due to differences in social, cultural, and political goals.

5. See Portes, Escobar, and Arana 2009.

6. The international migratory patterns of Acuitzio del Canje families to participate in rural agriculture and international wage labor markets as a household strategy to diversify their income was extensively studied in the 1970s by Raymond Wiest (1973).

7. For an overview of DICONSA and Mexican food councils, see Fox 2007.

8. For details on electoral fraud and the dispute for the political control of Michoacán in the late 1980s between the PRI and the PRD, see Zepeda Patterson 1988.

9. For extensive ethnographies of Mexican migrant worker conditions in Chicago, see De Genova 2005; Gomberg-Muñoz 2011.

10. For an excellent discussion about the challenges and opportunities of unionization campaigns led by Mexican immigrant workers, see Apostolidis 2010.

11. For an extended discussion of corn policy since NAFTA, see Fox and Haight 2010. To read a similar ethnography of transnationally engaged migrant men from the municipality of Aguililla, Michoacán, living in Redwood City, California, see the classic study by Roger Rouse (1992).

12. For a comprehensive and interdisciplinary overview of the Michoacán diaspora to the United States, see López Castro 2003.

13. According to Mexican scholars of the Universidad Michoacana de San Nicolás de Hidalgo, family remittances from the United States increased 1,035 percent in the state of Michoacán between 1980 and 2009, going from U.S. $186 million to $2.1 billion (Navarro Chávez and Ayvar Campos 2010).

14. For an interesting journalistic account of the lure to travel to the United States among migrants from Jaripo, Michoacán, and elsewhere, see Quiñones 2007.

15. See INEGI 2006. For an excellent overview on architectural landscape change in rural Mexico as a result of family remittances based on the example of Jalisco, see Lopez 2010.

16. Rosendo is a dual citizen who always votes in U.S. elections and has lived in Chicago for more than thirty years. He came in 1978 without papers. His legal residency was sponsored in the mid-1980s by an electrical company in Chicago who hired him after he graduated with a technical degree in electricity at Chicago's Coyne College.

17. To learn more on the contemporary crisis of Mexico's peasantry and its political consequences for class differentiation and social mobility, see Otero 1999.

18. Personal interview, June 2001, Morelia.

19. Author calculations using official data. I calculated the number using the percentage of people five years of age and older who, between June 2005 and June 2010, left for the United States, regardless of their decision to return to live permanently in Mexico.

20. See Aglietta 1979.

21. The dispersion of Mexican populations outside the traditional destinations in California, Texas, and Illinois has competing explanations. Evidence based on the Mexican Migration Project suggests that the legalization offered by IRCA provided opportunities to explore new labor markets (Massey, Durand, and Malone 2002), while datasets based on labor markets in Los Angeles suggest that the lack of affordable housing and economic crisis in Los Angeles metropolitan area pushed Mexican immigrants out of traditional destinations in the 1980s and 1990s (Light 2006).

22. For a critical analysis of strategies used by the armed forces to recruit minorities in Chicago's public schools, see Pérez 2006.

23. See Consejo Nacional de Evaluación de la Política de Desarrollo Social 2006. During Miguel de la Madrid Hurtado's administration, mandatory basic education was extended to nine years.

24. Personal interview, January 2006. Due to a mix of declining labor opportunities, coethnic overcrowding, and high rents, many Mexican immigrants left California in the 1980s in search of better opportunities in different states, including the Midwest. See Light 2006.

25. These migrant labor portraits and their perpetuation through social networks partly explain the underrepresentation of Chicago's Mexican immigrant population in the

education, health, and social service sector, including public administration, transportation, and public utilities, and in Chicago's high-skilled financial sector. According to an analysis of U.S. 2000 census figures, cooks, construction laborers, grounds maintenance workers, metal and plastic workers, production workers, and janitors and building cleaners occupied the six largest concentrations in a list of the twenty-five largest occupations for foreign-born Mexican men in the Chicago metropolitan area. Professional or high-skilled technician occupations did not appear in this list (Koval 2004).

26. For a classic discussion of the changing social American character since the 1950s, see Riesman, Glazer, and Denney 1950.

27. See, among others, Arias 2009; Espinosa 1998; Goldring 1996; Zamudio Grave 2009.

28. For a classical analysis on the decline of trust and social capital in America measured by membership in formal civil society organizations, see Putnam 1996, 2000.

29. For an analysis of the role played by trust and skepticism for creating democratic values in Mexico and Argentina, see Cleary and Stokes 2006. For a contemporary analysis of the challenges facing Mexican civil society to increase civic participation and improve the quality of democracy, see Olvera 2010.

30. See Fukuyama 1995. In Chicago, Jewish *landsmanshaften* were created as early as 1847, and these organizations later evolved into broad-based providers of medical and burial benefits with their own cemeteries. In the 1940s, there were 130 Jewish organizations, with a few *landsmanshaften* among them. However, by the 1980s the total number of Jewish *landsmanshaften* had shrunk by over 90 percent in the city, as massive Jewish migration to the United States declined significantly.

31. The success of nonprofit ROSCAs in Mexico is widely recognized. Despite recent efforts to increase access to traditional banking systems, for-profit ROSCAs are popular credit options for some mortgage and car sales companies that still appeal to this cultural form of wealth accumulation to acquire more customers. For a comprehensive overview of nonprofit ROSCAS in transnational perspective, see Vélez-Ibáñez 2010. In Mexico, only 40 percent of the population use banks, and *tandas* are a widely popular alternative for savings (Segura 2011).

32. In fact, it is more common to find stories of misappropriation of HTA funds perpetrated by government authorities, unscrupulous priests, and other people living in the community of origin compared to cases where HTA members living in the United States steal collective funds.

33. To learn more about similar examples of shared moral values of civic engagement, bonding social capital, and transnational moral communities among mestizos and indigenous Mexican migrants in Florida's new destinations, see Fortuny Loret de Mola, Solís Lizama, and Williams 2009.

34. The evolution of FEDECMI's bylaws reflects a gradually inclusive language. When the organization was originally chartered in 1997, the language of its bylaws included Michoacanos and their U.S. descendants as main constituents. As the organization evolved and increased its networks with other organizations with similar agendas, its bylaws included more action arenas to defend migrant rights and the inclusion of non-Michoacano and non-Mexican migrants as beneficiaries of its programs, services, and activities.

35. These results are consistent with a study of ninety Mexican, Colombian, and Dominican organizations conducted by Portes, Escobar, and Walton Radford (2007). These authors find that Mexican organizations tend to adopt the HTA format, and regardless of nationality, members of these immigrant organizations tend to be older, to be

better-established, and to possess above-average levels of education, suggesting that it is not incompatible to both assimilate and participate in transnational activities.

36. It is important to stress that mestizo migrants are not subject to "civic death" as is the case in some indigenous migrant communities that follow civil cargo systems for local governance. To learn more on the impact of migration on the civil cargo systems in Oaxaqueño migrant communities, see Gutiérrez Nájera 2009; Stephen 2007.

37. For a good comparison between rural and urban systems of Mexican migrant solidarity, see Hernández-León 2008.

38. For an interesting perspective on the value of cooperative relationships even amid distrust, see Cook, Hardin, and Levi 2005.

39. Intermarriage among HTA members is low, but there are some non-Mexican nationals who attend events due to intermarriage with other Latino groups such as Puerto Ricans, Hondurans, and Salvadorans. In ten years, I observed very few cases of interracial marriage between Mexicans and blacks, Mexicans and Poles, and Mexicans and whites.

40. Interview with Luis Soto, founding member of Taximaroa Club, May 2001, Irving Park, Illinois.

41. For more details on the evolution of this club from soccer to transnational public works, see Pescador 2004.

42. Personal interview, November 2005, Sleepy Hollow, Ill.

43. For a historical account of the process of ethnic identity replenishment in two Mexican communities in Kansas and California, see Jimenez 2009.

44. See Yanún 2011.

45. See Putnam 2000.

46. For an analysis of the role of faith in the social incorporation of Haitian immigrants in Paris and Miami, see Mooney 2009. To understand the role of religion in fostering diverse transnational moral and civic communities in America, see, among others, Kniss and Numrich 2007; Levitt 2007; Williams, Steigenga, and Vásquez 2009.

47. For a detailed analysis, see Hernández et al. 2007; Layton and Moreno 2010.

48. See Duquette and Bada 2009.

49. For an illuminating account of the Catholic Church's participation in the state of Jalisco in the emigration process to the United States, see Fitzgerald 2009. Mario, a member of the first Guadalupano committee formed in Aurora, told me that he paid a fee to a priest from a neighboring municipality to help him arrange his travel to work in Chicago in the late 1950s.

50. For instance, the historian David Badillo finds that "the widespread policy of establishing national parishes for Catholic immigrant groups began to change by the 1920s, when Cardinal Mundelein reversed this policy. Mundelein contended that such parishes increased nativist anti-Catholic sentiment and that the rise of the second generation among many immigrant groups warranted a greater use of English and a more integrationist approach" (2006: 121).

51. Regardless of the difficult start to have their ethno-religious communities accepted, the vast majority of Mexican immigrants share the same religion with the political Irish machine in Chicago, which governed the city during the second part of the twentieth century and the first decade of the twenty-first. The shared Catholicism plays an important positive role for Mexican migrant integration as members of a shared community in some high-ranking power-broker sectors. Mexican HTAs frequently make public remarks of the supportive environment in the city for helping their organizations thrive, especially thanking Mayor Richard M. Daley.

52. In New York City, dozens of Guadalupano Committees have formed to connect Mexican migrants with public spaces of worship and unite around a common cause to fight for immigrant rights across borders. See Gálvez 2010; Rivera Sánchez 2004.

53. The Virgin of Guadalupe has even found a permanent space in a Lutheran church in Aurora.

54. For a comparison of immigrant adaptation processes between Romanians and Mexicans in Aurora, see Palmer 2005.

55. *Las mañanitas* is a happy birthday song of Mexican origin. *Menudo* is a Mexican offal stew usually prepared with dried *guajillo* chilies.

56. The Second Vatican Council (1962–1965) led to the Latin mass being translated into contemporary languages. The first English translation of the mass was published in the United States in 1973, so Spanish masses took longer to take hold in churches with large Latino immigrant congregations, and it was common to bring Latin American priests to spend time addressing the needs of Latino immigrant congregations in the Chicago metropolitan area.

57. For a comprehensive overview of how the Latino majority within the Catholic Church is transforming this institution, see Matovina 2011.

58. Evangelical and Lutheran converts are commonly found in the suburbs, where the lack of Catholic parishes offering mass in Spanish created a fertile ground for proselytizing and inviting Catholic Mexican migrants to convert to other faiths. See Scott 1999.

59. To learn more about the transnational lives of San Juanico families in Chicago and Michoacán, see Farr 2006.

60. During the immigrant mobilizations that took place in Chicago in 2006, many Catholic priests invited their congregations to participate in the marches, providing buses and helping organizers get the necessary city permits. See Davis, Martinez, and Warner 2010.

61. According to Pierre Bourdieu, "the particular strength of male sociodicy comes from the fact that it combines and condenses two operations: it legitimates a relationship of domination by embedding it in a biological nature that is itself a naturalized social construction" (1998: 23).

62. To learn more about interracial relations between blacks and Mexicans in Chicago, see, among others, Arredondo 2008; De Genova 2005.

63. In Chicago, participation in local school councils offers parents an opportunity to engage with school issues. When local school councils work closely with parents and neighborhood grassroots organizations, successful models of parent engagement usually emerge. For a successful engagement model of low-income, non-English-speaking parents in a Chicago public school, see Hong 2011. In Chicago's Local School Councils, approximately 23 percent of parents and community members are Latinos (Bada, Schmit, and Fujimoto 2011).

64. *Pozole* is a soup made from nixtamalized *cacahuazintle* maize with meat, usually pork, chili peppers, and other seasonings and garnish, depending on local culinary traditions.

65. Personal interview, November 2005, Chicago.

66. This is a pseudonym. Due to the candid opinions provided by this volunteer, I decided to protect her identity and omit the time of her appointment.

67. Leadership positions at FEDECMI are unpaid volunteer jobs. Due to the track record of this organization, its limited public and private grant funds are devoted to pay staff salaries.

68. Between 2005 and 2009, more than 35,000 Mexican immigrants naturalized as U.S. citizens in the Chicago metropolitan area, bringing the total naturalized population of Mexican origin in the area to more than 137,000 people (U.S. Census Bureau 2009). For a quantitative analysis on the Latino naturalization gender gap, see Pantoja and Gershon 2006.

69. Similar dual civic engagements among Dominican migrant women had previously been documented. I thank Néstor Rodríguez for bringing this case to my attention. See Singer and Gilbertson 2003.

70. Adrián Félix, in his extensive participant observation of citizenship study groups in Southern California, finds that collective solidarity is helpful to overcome educational barriers and trump the negative emotions that have long discouraged the naturalization process among Mexican immigrants. See Félix 2008.

71. For a legal overview of the changes of Mexican nationality law, see Becerra Ramírez 2000. For a sociological perspective on this topic, see Fitzgerald 2005.

72. For an excellent analysis of the gendered migration process and its effects on land tenure in contemporary rural Mexico, see Arias 2009.

73. For an overview of the significance of topophilic attachments related to space and place, see Tuan 1974.

74. Over time, European American ethnic belongings in Chicago became more symbolic due to, among other things, the lack of ethnic cultural replenishment experienced after western Europe's economic stabilization reduced the incentives to migrate to the United States.

75. In his heterodox analysis of global income inequality, the sociologist Glenn Firebaugh shows that globally, income inequality is increasing within countries but decreasing between world regions mostly as a result of the rapid industrialization of upwardly mobile Asian nations and the end of Communism. See Firebaugh 2003.

76. To learn more about HTA cycles related to binational philanthropy for development, see Orozco 2000, 2004; Orozco and Welle 2005.

77. Children's Day is celebrated on April 30 in Mexico.

78. The Good Weekend was officially established in 2011 close to the anniversary of the Mexican Revolution in an attempt to boost the economy and encourage people to use their Christmas bonus early.

79. For an interesting discussion on the meanings of private and state-sponsored corpse repatriations for Mexican transnational citizenship, see Félix 2011.

80. Illinois schoolchildren lobbied for the monarch butterfly, and in 1975 it became the official state insect of Illinois. A third-grade class from Decatur was the first to suggest the monarch butterfly as state insect for the state (Illinois State Museum n.d.).

81. Personal interview, November 2005, Chicago.

82. While it is hard to assess the type of jobs held by those neighbors, it is important to note that since July 4th fell on a Sunday that year, many employers offered Monday as a vacation holiday.

83. *Las Posadas* is a nine-day Catholic Christmas celebration with origins in Spain, now celebrated in Mexico, some countries in Latin America, and parts of the United States. The nine-day celebration, which begins on December 16 and ends on December 24, symbolizes the nine months of the Virgin Mary's pregnancy.

84. For a recent quantitative assessment of binational civic engagement activities among Mexican immigrants, see Ramírez and Félix 2011.

CHAPTER 4 — MIGRANT CLUBS TO THE RESCUE

1. Mejía Guzmán had previously worked as SEDESOL representative in his home state of Michoacán. Few of Michoacán's municipalities have marginalization levels that are as extreme as those found in Chiapas.

2. For example, see Escobar and Alvarez 1992. For an excellent critique of postdevelopment discourse, see Veltmeyer 2011.

3. Some authors hypothesize that Banco de México changed its methodology to estimate family remittances without explaining the differences with methodologies used in previous decades (Canales 2008; Tuirán, Santibañez, and Corona 2006). One possible explanation of the exponential increase is that these figures include money-laundering activities of drug trafficking and financial transactions among small businesses buying supplies for the nostalgia market. For instance, an alternative calculation estimates that family remittances increased only 30 percent during this period, a number that coincides with the official reports of the U.S. Bureau of Economic Analysis (Canales 2008).

4. In 2006 dollar prices.

5. There is still much work to do to reduce the costs, and above all, the hidden fees in transactions, including disadvantageous exchange rates. After a decade of better regulation and increased participation of financial institutions in remittance markets, the highest share of the market (63 percent) still goes to international money transfer companies, which are the ones with the highest hidden fees and low levels of corporate social responsibility (IADB-MIF n.d.). For example, according to its IRS-reporting 990-PF form, Western Union Foundation offered U.S. $7.7 million in contributions, gifts, and grants paid in 2010, a paltry sum compared to the company's net profit. Western Union community reinvestment efforts are worse than those at Walmart. While Walmart reinvests $2.30 per each $100, Western Union only reinvest 32 cents (United for a Fair Economy 2007: 5)

6. As a case in point, a recent survey found that in states with a historical migratory tradition, including Guanajuato, Jalisco, Zacatecas, and Michoacán, self-employed active migrants are scarce, representing only 6.3 percent of male migrant workers and 7.4 percent of female migrant workers (Papail and Robles 2009).

7. To learn more about the World Bank's dominant perspective on the relationship between migration, remittances, and development, see, among others, Orozco and Wilson 2005; Terry and Pedrodv 2006.

8. Conference panelists included Carla Hills, U.S. trade negotiator; Jaime Serra Puche, Mexican secretary of commerce; Pedro Aspe, Mexican secretary of finance and public credit; and Rainer Steckhan, the World Bank director for Mexico and Central America, among other prominent speakers. In representation of the local Mexican business sector, only Alejandro Silva, an immigrant and president of Evans Food Corporation, appeared as a speaker for a panel.

9. I thank University of Chicago senior lecturer Susan Gzesh for sharing her detailed notes on this forum, the agenda, and the breakfast event. For a discussion of binational resistance efforts organized by civil society against free trade liberalization, see Brooks and Fox 2002.

10. This was a federal social program established in 1991 to distribute funds to highly marginalized communities for infrastructure projects through a matching funds system. When community members were willing to contribute 50 percent of any infrastructure project either with money or labor, the government would fund the other half.

11. In a 1999 note published by Chicago's *Exito!* newspaper, Tinoco Rubí expressed his position on the upcoming presidential elections to his migrant constituents: "I believe that the 2000 elections will be very competitive but I am confident that Mexicans will study their options and will not search any experiments. Our people like assurances. We can't throw away all the experience that our government has accumulated. The opposition

alliance is a fallacy because they never reach any agreements." Author's translation. See Redacción 1999.

12. Chicago's General Mexican Consulate Archive, Fondo Organizaciones Comunitarias, 2000.

13. When Vicente Fox visited Chicago during his presidential campaign in May 2000, his party gave migrants calling cards to talk to their relatives and ask them to vote for the PAN.

14. The letter-writing campaign reached audiences outside Michoacán and Chicago. For instance, Reveriano Orozco, a Michoacano migrant businessman and PRD supporter living in Las Vegas, attentively followed the letters to the editor exchange on the Internet and organized an HTA federation in Nevada to show his support for the nascent migrant movement. In 2004, Nevada-based HTAs would host the Fourth Forum of Michoacano Migrants Living Abroad in a public library in East Las Vegas, and Orozco became a state congress representative representing the PRD three years later. Interview with Reveriano Orozco, the first president of the Asociación de Michoacanos Unidos de Nevada (AMUN), January 2007, Las Vegas.

15. Telephone interview with Gonzalo Badillo Moreno, adviser to the PRD campaign for Michoacán governorship, September 20, 2011.

16. The PAN candidate decided not to visit Chicago.

17. After 2002, Vázquez Mota visited Chicago and Los Angeles several times, including a visit to help Mexican HTAs coordinate relief efforts to victims of Hurricane Katrina in 2005. She also visited HTAs in her position as coordinator for Felipe Calderón's presidential campaign and later as education secretary and congresswoman. During her tenure as secretary of public education (SEP), she donated several computers to Chicago's Instituto del Progreso Latino, a Latino-led educational nonprofit serving Pilsen and Little Village, two of the largest Latino immigrant neighborhoods. During the 2012 presidential elections, Vázquez Mota would reap the benefits of her decade-long close contact with migrants as she won the migrant vote with a comfortable lead, even as she lost her presidential bid at home (C. García 2012).

18. Satélites Mexicanos (SATMEX) is the company that emerged after the privatization of the government-owned satellite services during the administration of President Zedillo. During 2003 and 2004, this company launched a campaign to sell tailored programming for specific cable channel markets in the United States. The company met with HTA leaders to learn about cultural tastes and regional concentrations by states of origin, even commissioning research reports to map the distribution of Mexicans by birthplace across the United States. One of his most successful products is CB Tu Televisión Michoacán, one of the leading cable channels in Michoacán and thirteen additional states. Through Alterna'TV, a distribution network, SATMEX offers a local view of the daily lives of people from the state of Michoacán both in Mexico and abroad. This channel is distributed in several cable markets in the United States and includes spiritual programming, such as live broadcasts of Catholic mass in Morelia's Cathedral to California-based viewers.

19. Created in 2001, Construmex was a branch of the giant cement company CEMEX, which sold construction supplies to migrants in the United States to build new homes in Mexico. Sometimes, it worked with HTAs to organize fund-raisers. For example, "after the devastating hurricane Stan hit Chiapas, the Mexican community in Chicago under the leadership of Construmex raised U.S. $100,000 to replace some 140 homes that were destroyed. Construmex came immediately into play with a significant donation so that the campaign would have a good start" (Hispanic PR Wire 2006).

20. For example, the Association of Producers, Packers, and Exporters of Avocados (APEAM) became an early sponsor of Michoacano HTA activities as a networking opportunity to connect with U.S.-based wholesalers to increase their market-share.

21. President Vicente Fox speech to the Mexican community at Unity Public High School in Cicero, Illinois, June 17, 2004. Author's translation from field notes. The president was probably not briefed sufficiently on the mechanics of the Three-for-One Program, which then did not fund any individual initiatives, only collective proposals with a minimum of two migrants per organization, according to the white book of the program.

22. The main difficulties that IADB found in the Three-for-One Program are: the program does not generate sustainable employment opportunities in the high expulsion regions; the migrants—and not stay-at-home community members—are the only ones proposing projects; communication with migrants is deficient because they do not know the operation rules of the program; migrants perceive that time spent between proposal submission and approval is excessive; there is scarce participation of the community in the supervision, surveillance, and maintenance of finished projects; trust has increased, but there is still room for improvement; and there are no clear mechanisms to guarantee maintenance of finished projects (IADB 2006).

23. Personal communication with SEDESOL consultant hired to implement IADB requirements for the Three-for-One Program, March 1, 2010, Chicago.

24. Email communication with IADB staff member, February 4, 2009.

25. In January 2009, NALACC joined thirty-four NGOs from Latin America and the United States in the organization of several parallel events in Colombia during the fiftieth annual assembly of the IADB governors to protest the bank's policies in the region because, in their view, those policies had failed to eradicate poverty and inequality affecting more than 184 million people in Latin America after more than fifty years of conditional loans to the region.

26. Invitation letter for November 2003 meeting with consultants at the University of Chicago's Human Rights Program.

27. More conservative estimates completed by researchers at El Colegio de Michoacán calculate the exodus of Michoacanos to the United States at about 20,000 per year. See Rodríguez Ramírez 2003.

28. More recently, a policy report on Mexican organized crime groups argues that La Familia, a drug cartel based in Michoacán, "controls around 30 percent of official commerce and that 85 percent of legitimate businesses are in some way or another connected to the organization." See Salazar and Olson 2011. The excessive power concentrated by the drug cartels has made it more difficult for HTAs to negotiate projects directly through their municipal presidents because some state municipal presidents are suspected employees of the cartels. For example, one HTA was in the middle of negotiations with one municipal president when he was arrested along with ten additional municipal presidents, sixteen state government employees, and one state judge, due to their alleged involvement with drug cartels. He was later freed, with all charges dropped, because prosecutors could not provide any evidence, but the HTA had its project delayed because the interim president did not want to respect prior agreements made by an imprisoned president. Once the municipal president returned to his position, the HTA project successfully resumed. For more details on this failed attempt to bring criminal charges on state government officials, read the *Michoacanazo* entry in the blog Desde México 2010.

29. In general, the U.S. government has stricter regulations against pollutants, but illegal exports of waste have increased recently. After NAFTA, the disposal of pollutants by U.S.

companies does not always follow appropriate procedures. With additional standards to get rid of toxic pollutants such as lead, many U.S. companies now resort to Mexico as their toxic dumping ground, taking advantage of low standards and lack of enforcement. See Rosenthal 2011.

30. In a fieldtrip to a cornfield in Tupátaro in 2005, Roberto, a local committee member representative for a soccer field built using Three-for-One funds, explains his relationship with the land, the evolution of his community, and the illusion of free market competition as a solution to lift all boats. He had overstayed several tourist visas until he was caught while attempting reentry at O'Hare airport and was forced to return to his community: "Growing corn is a past time. It is better to use the corn to feed my cows than to sell it because it is more profitable. One thousand Mexican pesos is the guarantee that I have for corn. Since we don't have adobe houses here, the government believes that we are not marginalized and we don't get subsidies for fertilizers. I mainly do this to fight boredom, to show people that I am working. My wife and children are in Chicago. I have been living here three years. In the eighties, people were making a decent living in Tupátaro thanks to pork. Many returned from the U.S. to invest in family pork farms while others stayed in the U.S. and asked their relatives to use the remittances in pork farms. However, in ten years, everyone went bankrupt when we faced competition from imported pork. Many people sold their animals and return to the U.S. to pay their debts."

31. The resource-recycling system is not always successful because it requires the active collaboration of community members and/or local institutions. Fire trucks need firefighters; ambulances need drivers and medical equipment to fully function. Used church pews, school buses, and medical equipment are among the easiest donations to use upon arrival to villages.

32. The 75 percent public cost-sharing scheme for new productive projects financed by individual migrant investors with HTAs in the Three-for-One Program only lasted a few years. By 2008, SEDESOL called a halt to the free financing of productive projects backed by one or two migrant investors and began to offer interest-free financing loans instead, thus making the program similar to the national *Opciones Productivas* model, in which a loan has to be repaid in five years to finance more projects. The operating rules have been constantly modified in the last decade. By 2013, SEDESOL's operating rules for Three-for-One have a formalized loan model in which the federal government would match every dollar invested by any individual migrant affiliated with an HTA for up to MXP 250,000 without requiring support from municipalities and state governments. The model of productive projects financed with Three-for-One matching funds for social cooperatives with at least ten migrant investors affiliated with an HTA is still in place and supports community projects for up to MXP $1 million (Secretaría de Desarrollo Social 2013).

33. Personal interview, July 2005, Atacheo de Regalado.

34. When the turkey project started, several organized groups from neighboring communities became very enthusiastic, especially women. However, they soon grew frustrated with the giant bureaucracy that was needed to obtain government support and also realized that the net profit was going to be less than U.S. $2 per sold animal (interview with female project leader, July 2005, in Francisco Villa, Zinepécuaro).

35. In Mexico, with the exception of Procampo, almost all of many other, less well known farm subsidy programs are biased to favor medium and large-scale producers (Fox and Haight 2010).

36. Interview with Marcos Linares, former Atacheo priest, December 2005.

37. In fact, social production cooperatives in Michoacán do not have an exemplary history of success. Many similar projects were established before and after the economic restructuring of the 1980s with poor results elsewhere in the Ciénega de Chapala, the region where Zamora is located. A pattern of envy and competition among migrants and nonmigrants, along with tensions that arise from the way migration affects the perceived social transformation of the person, had been previously documented in this region (Gledhill 1995).

38. The 4X1 matching fund program added a private investor to the funding sources. In this case, Western Union agreed to finance social infrastructure projects in equal amounts with Mexican HTAs, municipalities, state governments, and SEDESOL.

39. The Transnational Institute for Grassroots Research and Action launched a campaign against Western Union in 2007 to protest its predatory fees and unfair exchange rates and obtained support from numerous immigrant advocacy organizations across the country. However, several Chicago-based HTAs, including FEDECMI, decided to continue the collaboration with Western Union as they believed they had to keep exercising pressure on the company to invest more funds in community development in Latin America and force it to increase its college scholarship funds for Mexican migrant students in the United States.

40. In fact, Mexican businessmen are more accustomed to investing their money outside Mexico. In the aftermath of the controversial 2006 presidential elections, the Mexican well-to-do class and big businesses decided to take their money elsewhere. In the first six months of 2007, wealthy Mexicans sent $15.4 billion to foreign banks and as direct investment to different countries. During the same period, the country only received $19.2 billion as direct investment, thus the capital exodus represented 80.3 percent of the foreign direct investment. Therefore, it is not a surprise that migrant remittance contributions are greatly appreciated because these resources help to stabilize currency losses in Mexico's balance of trade and payments. However, with the more hostile situation facing undocumented workers in the United States, paired with a decline in the construction industry, family remittances decreased in 2007. The total remittance value dropped for the first time since the mid-1980s, confirming the volatility of currency derived from exporting low-paid vulnerable workers (González Amador 2007).

41. Personal conversation with Club Indaparapeo leader in charge of monitoring this scholarship program, Casa del Zacatecano, Chicago, March 2009.

42. In 2011, an estimated 20 percent of Ph.D. graduates born in Mexico lived in the United States, approximately 20,000 persons. A large proportion of those graduates (46 percent) entered the United States in the last two decades (Albo and Ordaz Díaz 2011).

CHAPTER 5 — PARTICIPATORY PLANNING ACROSS BORDERS

1. This committee has representatives of the municipal, state, and federal government, as well as the HTAs, that are involved in the financing of Three-for-One projects. Each committee member has the right to vote in the final project selection. Depending on funds availability, COVAM usually meets twice or three times per year to select the winning projects to receive government matching funds. To learn more about COVAM's genesis, see Iskander 2005, 2006, 2010.

2. For a discussion of municipal presidents' visits to migrants from the state of Jalisco living in the United States, see Fitzgerald 2005a.

3. Binational Michoacán Front (FREBIMICH) Google group communication.

4. For a discussion on market citizenship in the Mexican migrant organization context, see Goldring 2002.

5. A recent estimate calculates economic losses due to corruption to be almost 10 percent of Mexico's GDP. See Reames and Lynott n.d.

6. According to one study done by Enrique Cabrero (1998), only 10 percent of Mexican municipalities reported ever creating a Municipal Development Planning Council, and most of these were dominated by the municipal mayor (cited in Selee 2011).

7. For the most current analysis of the process in which Mexican elites relinquished controls over elections and consented to free and fair elections to avoid general uprising after the 1994 Chiapas Rebellion, see Trejo 2012.

8. A common mechanism employed to solve problems with project implementation such as late delivery, low-quality materials, unfinished or unapproved projects, and so forth is to report the issue directly to the state governor with a respectful yet angry tone of voice during the inauguration of the annual accountability sessions in Chicago. For cases with easy solutions, this mechanism works, but results are less likely for complicated cases. In the eyes of migrant leaders, reporting the problem to the highest authority is easier that sending a formal complaint to the comptroller.

9. Antonio Plaza Urbina, SEDESOL's delegate during a public speech prepared for the Forum on Economic Development of Communities of Origin and Opportunities for Migrant Civic Engagement. Mexican Consulate in Chicago, Presencia Michoacana en el Medio Oeste 2011, June 23.

10. Interview with SEDESOL official, June 2010.

11. Another common corrupt practice documented by SEDESOL is signature forgery by municipal presidents. SEDESOL officials in Chicago learned of that practice when an HTA president from a Durango organization alerted SEDESOL that her signature appeared on a formal Three-for-One proposal that she never signed.

12. This is not a complete list and might not apply to all cases and all states. It is difficult to compare these observations with national trends, but in general, there is a lack of information on approval and rejection criteria and databases with complete information on submitted requests. For instance, in a survey applied by independent evaluators to HTAs in the United States, only 49 percent of interviewees representing HTAs declared to have received information regarding the approval and rejection criteria of project requests for the Three-for-One Program. See Servicios Profesionales para el Desarrollo Económico 2005: 129.

13. Interviews with five municipal presidents. In fact, as a result of complaints by municipal presidents to SEDESOL officials in the first five years of the program, the federal government decided to change national rules. At this time, sponsorship for noncommunitarian small business ventures is done through a 50–50 formula where the municipality is usually exempt and the public funds have to be returned to a communal fund to finance more businesses in the community. This new scheme was implemented in 2009 and tries to encourage investments from small migrant businessmen after SEDESOL realized HTAs were not increasing investments in job-generating projects. In the first ten years of the program, the percentage of individual family productive projects was minimal; 701 projects were implemented, representing 3.7 percent of the total. On the other hand, the number of individual family projects financed is slightly larger than the total of community productive projects sponsored through the Three-for-One Program, 701 versus 635 (Gobierno Federal 2012).

14. Interview with HTA leader from the Bajío Zamorano region, July 2004.

15. Author's calculations using SEDESOL's annual Three-for-One Program datasets and municipal party affiliation.

16. Translation by author. During COVAM meetings, SEDESOL representatives decide the agenda, and fund allocation is privileged toward municipalities with high and very high marginalization indexes because those are less likely to have projects submitted by migrant groups.

17. Total municipal state and federal financing for the years 2004 and 2005 were compared with the total amount invested by migrants in Three-for-One projects. The highest percentage was found in the municipality of Tanhuato, where collective remittances invested in Three-for-One projects were equivalent to 10 percent of state and federal funds received by this municipality.

18. This problem is a national trend. In a survey of fifty HTA representatives from Illinois and California, including leaders from Jalisco, Michoacán, Nayarit, Zacatecas, Sinaloa, and Yucatán, the majority declared to have witnessed approved projects with the participation of "unknown migrants," which suggests that some projects are still being approved for organized stay-at-home citizens or former migrants. See Servicios Profesionales para el Desarrollo Económico 2005: 121.

19. In an independent evaluation of the program conducted in 2005, researchers reported that migrant participants have scarce information about the parallel committees, mostly regarding rights and responsibilities of this organizational structure. See Servicios Profesionales para el Desarrollo Económico 2005.

20. Personal communication with former SMA coordinator of community development projects, January 8, 2006.

21. Interview with SEDESOL officer in Morelia, May 2005.

22. Phone interview with program manager of SEDESO, August 2007.

23. SEDESO changed its name and became SEPSOL during the administration of Leonel Godoy Rangel (2008–2012).

24. The same survey finds that stay-at-home community members have a direct participation in Three-for-One projects through diverse activities: offering support to the parallel committee (18 percent), attending informative sessions (26 percent), project supervision (37 percent), and offering volunteer labor (36 percent).

25. Interview with SEDESOL consultant hired to manage the IADB loan, November 2009, Chicago.

26. For an analysis of the disconnect between development ideas held by migrant organizations and the government's interpretation and execution of those ideas in public policies, see Iskander 2010.

27. Interviews with SEDESO and SEPSOL officials in Morelia, summers of 2004 and 2005 and winters of 2006 and 2009.

28. According to 2010 census estimates, Tupátaro is a small community of 1,581 that experienced a deficit in population replacement between 2000 and 2005 (INEGI 2006, 2010). This community lives from agriculture and small pork farms but has experienced out-migration to Texas, Illinois, and California, especially to the Chicago metropolitan area, where an estimated 70 percent of the Tupátaro community works. However, estimates done using census figures for the municipality register that only 25 percent of the households receive remittances (Rodríguez Ramírez 2003).

29. Interview with submunicipal authority in the municipality of Santa Ana Maya. In 2010, the CODECO program in this village won the state prize as the most successful CODECO.

CHAPTER 6 — EXPANDING AGENDAS AND
BUILDING TRANSNATIONAL COALITIONS

1. Approved in 2011, the Illinois DREAM Act is state legislation designed to make scholarships, college savings, and prepaid tuition programs available to undocumented students who graduated from Illinois high schools. It specifically creates an Illinois DREAM Fund and a nine-member Illinois DREAM Commission, appointed by the governor with Senate consent.

2. Presencia Michoacana in the Midwest is a monthlong celebration to showcase the cultural heritage of the state of Michoacán and takes place every June. Originally inaugurated as the Semana Michoacana in the summer of 2000, it extended the number of activities, and it now offers one-month's worth of civic and political engagement events as well as cultural activities. During the Presencia Michoacana inauguration in 2012, the inaugural mass was offered in P'urépecha and was organized by a satellite P'urépecha HTA from Cobden, Illinois. To learn more about Michoacano P'urépecha migrants and their organizations, see Anderson 2004; Leco Tomás 2009.

3. Skepticism or rejection of the notion of dual nationality, voting in more than country, and multinational civic engagement comes from many disciplines. To read some examples that involve Latino immigrant allegiances and criticisms to supposed contemporary patterns of Latino integration to U.S. society, see, among others, Huntington 2004; López Guerra 2005; Renshon 2005.

4. To learn more about migrant civic engagement and civic binationality practices beyond HTAs, see Fox and Bada 2011.

5. For an excellent comparative analysis of the different scales of transnational migrant organizations in urban, rural, and medium-size cities in different countries, including the United States, see Glick Schiller and Çağlar 2011.

6. In 2007, Puerto Rican–born Thirty-First Ward alderman Ray Suárez introduced a resolution to the city council to recognize the benefits of multilingualism in Chicago.

7. For in-depth analysis of contemporary dilemmas of universal citizenship with a focus on the United States, see Bosniak 2006.

8. The 1.5 generation refers to foreign-born Latinos who migrated to the United States at an early age and were mostly educated in the United States.

9. To encourage the appreciation of Mexican cultural diversity among Chicagoans, Casa Michoacán became a member of the nonprofit Chicago Cultural Alliance to bring diverse programming to mainstream festivals that happen outside of the traditional ethnic neighborhoods of Pilsen and Little Village, joining the cultural heritage organizations of dozens of non-Latino ethnic organizations throughout the city.

10. In the past two decades, leaders of many Michoacán and Mexican HTAs have benefited from some contact with traditional mainstream institutions, charities, and a variety of nongovernmental organizations in Chicago. This trend is more prominent among leaders who came to the United States with at least some college education. Some leaders are now successful business owners, while others have experience as labor union representatives or as executive directors at local mainstream community-based organizations.

11. Inaugurated in 1995, CAPS is an initiative of the Chicago Police Department to increase community participation in crime prevention. Police officers participating in this initiative hold monthly meetings with residents to discuss neighborhood safety issues. For an evaluation of this program, see Fung 2004.

12. After several decades of engagement to find solutions for problems affecting his hometown and his adopted city, Salvador has yet to become a U.S. citizen, a paradox for

someone who has been invested in good citizenship practices to improve the quality of lives of his fellow citizens in Michoacán and his new neighbors in Chicago. Salvador tells me that he wants his wife to pass the exam first because, for his family, it is more urgent to bring the maternal grandparents to Chicago before they die so they can spend quality time with their grandchildren and meet their great-grandchildren. Salvador's wife has applied for citizenship twice but has failed the naturalization test.

13. Recent survey results collected to measure the participation of the Chicago Mexican migrant community in local ethnic artistic events suggests that artistic and cultural engagement both encourage and are encouraged by bilingualism. Bilingual respondents reported higher levels of attendance and participation of their group members (60 percent) than did monolingual speakers of English or Spanish, and Spanish speakers reported higher levels (52 percent) of attendance and participation of their support group members than did English speakers (42 percent). Bilingual individuals tended to be the most culturally and artistically engaged as well as the most active in the public sphere; as a consequence, they enjoyed strong political influence in both Anglo-American-majority and Mexican-majority forums (Wali, Contractor, and Severson 2006).

14. To read a similar analysis of outreach publications among Turkish HTAs in Germany, see Çağlar 2006.

15. Secure Communities is a program initiative of the U.S. Immigration and Custom Enforcement Agency and the Department of Homeland Security aimed at increasing cooperation and partnerships among federal, state, and local law enforcement agencies to expedite the deportation of criminal immigrant offenders. In practice, this program has deported a significant number of immigrants with noncriminal records (28 percent of those arrested by this program in 2010), and some state governments, including Illinois, have publicly challenged this program. See Center for Constitutional Rights 2011.

16. Established in 1972, El Hogar del Niño is a nonprofit day care that offers affordable bilingual/bicultural early childhood education to Latino families in Pilsen.

17. In 2013, Mexican poet and environmentalist Homero Aridjis wrote an editorial to call attention to the dwindling colonies of monarchs visiting Mexico during winter months (Brower and Aridjis 2013). According to recent expert reports, "The American Midwest's corn belt is a critical feeding ground for monarchs, which once found a ready source of milkweed growing between the rows of millions of acres of soybean and corn. But the ubiquitous use of herbicide-tolerant crops has enabled farmers to wipe out the milkweed, and with it much of the butterflies' food supply" (Wines 2013).

18. Due to the recent transition from informal to formal organizational structures, many HTA leaders are learning the ropes of the complex nonprofit world, and few of these organizations are aware that federal legislation allows nonprofits to allocate up to 25 percent of their resources to engage in nonpartisan political activities, among many other challenges to improve their capacity building (Leroux and Goerdel 2009).

19. In May 2006, the Chicago Center for Working Class Studies awarded the prize Democracy in Action to Casa Michoacán in recognition to this important gathering place that united immigrants of all nationalities during the immigrant marches and mobilizations of that year (Piña 2006).

20. For an analysis of CONFEMEX visibility in Chicago's immigration politics and its perilous journey for scaling out and up, see Sites and Vonderlack Navarro 2012.

21. Legal permanent resident is an immigrant status granting foreign nationals the right to reside in the United States permanently and eventually (if the foreign national so chooses) apply to naturalize as a citizen.

22. Other HTAs endorsing this march were the Federación de Clubes Colimenses, Federación de Clubes Zacatecanos del Sur de California, Zacatecanos en Marcha USA, and Club Activo Sinaloa. For an analysis of the 2003 Immigrant Workers' Freedom Ride using Nancy Fraser's concept of counterpublic, see Sziarto and Leitner 2010.

23. Prior to CONFEMEX, in 2000 several Mexican organizations formed the Coalition of Mexican Migrant Organizations in the Midwest (COMMO), an umbrella organization including local branches of Mexican political parties, hometown federations, and civic associations. The model did not work and quickly disappeared, but it was the first time that HTAs crossed the aisle to reach outside of their networks to organize a coalition. In 2000, they believed that it was the right time to scale out since Mexican organizations across the United States had just scored a major victory in late 1999, when the Mexican government attempted to impose a hefty fee to each vehicle that crossed the border during Christmas break and the federations united to stage demonstrations outside the consulates of Los Angeles and Chicago to protest the new law (Leiken 2002). Fortunately, the Mexican government backed off well before Christmas season, and all vehicles crossed without paying any fee during Christmas break. Author's field notes, September 29, 2006, First HTAs Meeting in Chicago, Westside Technical Institute.

24. The First Social Forum on Migration was held during the fifth edition of the World Social Forum. The First World Social Forum took place in Porto Alegre, Brazil, in 2001.

25. The Civil Society Days of the GFMD is a space where civil society has tried to reach out to national governments to advocate for a new framework to understand the relationship between migration and development. This new framework emphasizes that development is far more than economic growth; it must include opportunities for human growth, including access to decent work at home and abroad, health care, education, security, and full participation in political and social processes.

26. The PGA network was established in 2006 with the aim of positioning a human rights framework as fundamental to the migration and development discourse. Now in its seventh edition, the PGA is an annual event and is organized by hundreds of civil society organizations around the world working on immigrant rights and immigration policy reform in their respective countries. The organizations that come together insist on the need to place issues related to migrant communities in a human rights and development context. In this forum, hundreds of delegates of migrant-led organizations, pro-immigrant organizations, unions, faith-based organizations, and academics meet in an independent event aimed at empowering migrant leaders and their constituents to keep fighting for the labor, human, and development rights of all migrants.

27. Recommendations issued by GFMD forums are nonbinding. Therefore, simultaneously held forums organized by transnational networks of human rights activists working on migrant issues are necessary to hold GFMD accountable for the recommendations made to governments every year the forum takes place.

28. Among the sixty-six surveyed Latino-led nonprofits, a large majority (70 percent) have annual budgets of less than U.S. $1 million (Levin and McKean 2009). The insularity of Latino immigrant services organization in Chicago reflects larger national trends. Between 1999 and 2009, foundation dollars *intentionally* designated to benefit Latinos comprised about 1 percent of total foundations' funding at the national level, and the main focus of Latino-serving philanthropies for the past decades were human and health services (Shah, Mukal, and McAllister 2011).

29. All expenditure data for 2009 come from IRS 990 form (Return from Organizations Exempt from Income Tax).

30. American Community Survey 2010, three-year estimates, table C05007.

31. Many of the most active HTA leaders in Chicago had undergone previous political training in their home villages. Due to the long history of one-party rule in Mexico, it is only natural that most of these leaders were affiliated with the PRI. Some were active party members in their youth, belonging to the Revolutionary Youth Front. After their migration to Chicago, some leaders decided to keep their previous political preferences, while others decided to switch party preferences toward the most likely winner in their home state or municipality. In any case, HTAs were capable of mounting a nonpartisan campaign to demand full political rights for Mexicans living abroad through a coordinated national effort with several Mexican organizations across the United States with the support of several Latino organization allies.

32. Ann Marie Tallman remarks during a roundtable discussion on Mexican migrant civic engagement at the Woodrow Wilson International Center for Scholars, Washington, D.C., November 4, 2005. The transcription of her speech was done by the author.

33. Interviews with Michoacano HTA leaders in Mexico City (August 2007) and in Chicago (October 2007).

34. See Redacción 2011.

35. Interview with club president, June 3, 2012, Berwyn, Illinois. Not surprisingly, participation in the Abuelita Visa Program became a serious divisive issue among FEDECMI's board members, leading a small group of clubs to abandon FEDECMI and establish a different umbrella organization.

36. Email communication with Vanessa Guridy, Ph.D. candidate in political science, University of Illinois at Chicago, October 4, 2012.

37. The federation of Jalisco HTAs in Melrose Park, Illinois, has also expanded its binational engagements, although the scaling up of their activities only became visible to the nonmigrant public after 2007.

REFERENCES

Ablanedo Terrazas, Ireri, Michael D. Layton, and Alejandro Moreno. 2008. "Encuesta Nacional sobre Filantropía y Sociedad Civil (ENAFI): Capital Social en México." In *CEPI Working Papers*, edited by Centro de Estudios y Programas Interamericanos, 1–53. Mexico City: Instituto Tecnológico Autónomo de México.

Ackerman, John. 2003. "Co-Governance for Accountability: Beyond 'Exit' and 'Voice.'" *World Development* 32(3): 447–463.

Acuña, Rodolfo F. 2012. "The Failure of National Latino/Mexican American Organizations." In *Dick and Sharon's LA Progressive.* http://www.laprogressive.com/meixcan-american -organizations/.

Aglietta, Michael. 1979. *A Theory of Capitalist Regulation: The US Experience.* London: New Left Books.

Alarcón, Rafael. 2002. "The Development of the Hometown Associations in the United States and the Use of Social Remittances in Mexico." In *Sending Money Home: Hispanic Remittances and Community Development*, edited by Rodolfo De la Garza and Briant Lindsay Lowell, 101–124. New York: Rowman & Littlefield.

———. 2003. "La formación de una diáspora: Migrantes de Chavinda en California." In *Diáspora Michoacana*, edited by Gustavo López Castro, 289–306. Zamora: El Colegio de Michoacán-Gobierno del Estado de Michoacán.

Albo, Adolfo, and Juan Luis Ordaz Díaz. 2011. "Migración mexicana altamente calificada en EEUU y Transferencia de México a Estados Unidos a través del gasto en la educación de los migrantes." In *BBVA Research: Documentos de Trabajo* 25 (11). Mexico City: Servicio de Estudios Económicos del Grupo BBVA. http://www.bbvaresearch.com/KETD/ fbin/mult/WP_1125_Mexico_tcm346–266762.pdf?ts=1392013.

Alejo, Berenice. 2008. "The Latino Landscape: A Metro Chicago Guide and Non-Profit Directory." Notre Dame, Ind., and Chicago: Institute for Latino Studies and the Chicago Community Trust and Affiliates.

American Community Survey. 2010. "Table B05006 Place of Birth for the Foreign Born Population Chicago-Naperville-Joliet-IL-IN-WI Metro Area." Washington, D.C.: U.S. Census Bureau.

Amezcua, Mike. 2011. "The Second City Anew: Mexicans, Urban Culture, and Migration in the Transformation of Chicago, 1940–1965." Ph.D. diss., Yale University.

Anderson, Benedict 1983. *Imagined Communities: Reflections on the Origins and Spread of Nationalism.* New York: Verso.

Anderson, Warren. 2004. "P'urépecha Migration into the U.S. Rural Midwest: History and Current Trends." In *Indigenous Mexican Migrants in the United States,* edited by Jonathan Fox and Gaspar Rivera-Salgado, 355–384. San Diego, Calif.: Center for U.S.-Mexican Studies and the Center for Comparative Immigration Studies.

Andrade Ferreyra, Adriana. 2007. "Ahorro del Migrante: El Caso de la Federación de Clubes Michoacanos y de la Asociación de Clubes Migrantes Michoacanos ubicados en Chicago, Illinois." Paper presented at *Segundo Congreso Internacional de Ciencia, Tecnología, Arte y Humanidades.* Centro de Investigación y Desarrollo del Estado de Michoacán.

Año Nuevo Kerr, Louise. 1976. "The Chicano Experience in Chicago, 1920 to 1970." Ph.D. diss., University of Illinois at Chicago.

———. n.d. "Three Generations of Mexican Migration to Chicago." University of Illinois at Chicago. Unpublished manuscript.

Aparicio, Francisco Javier, and Covadonga Mesenguer. 2008. "Collective Remittances and the State: The 3X1 Program in Mexican Municipalities." Paper delivered to the annual meeting of the American Political Science Association, Boston.

———. 2012. "Collective Remittances and the State: The 3X1 Program in Mexican Municipalities." *World Development* 40(1): 206–222.

Aparicio, Francisco Javier, Claudia Vanessa Maldonado Trujillo, and Brisna Michelle Beltrán Pulido. 2008. "Datos generales de la Evaluación de Consistencia y Resultados 2007 del Programa 3x1 para Migrantes." Dirección General de Evaluación y Monitoreo de los Programas Sociales. Mexico City: SEDESOL.

Apostolidis, Paul. 2010. *Breaks in the Chain: What Immigrant Workers Can Teach America about Democracy.* Minneapolis: University of Minnesota Press.

Appadurai, Arjun. 1996. *Modernity at Large: Cultural Dimensions of Globalization.* Minneapolis: University of Minnesota Press.

Arias, Patricia. 2009. *Del arraigo a la diáspora: Dilemas de la familia rural.* Mexico City: Universidad de Guadalajara-Miguel Ángel Porrúa.

Arredondo, Gabriela F. 2008. *Mexican Chicago: Race, Identity, and Nation, 1916–39.* Urbana: University of Illinois Press.

Arredondo, Gabriela F., and Derek Vaillant. 2005. "Mexicans." In *The Electronic Encyclopedia of Chicago,* edited by Chicago Historical Society. Chicago: Chicago Historical Society. http://www.encyclopedia.chicagohistory.org/pages/824.html.

Ávila, Oscar. 2007. "Seed Money to Grow Jobs: Mexico, Other Latin American Nations Seek to Curb Migration by Investing Remittances from Workers in U.S. to Create Opportunities at Home." *Chicago Tribune Online,* May 10.

Ávila, Oscar, and Antonio Olivo. 2007. "Western Union Boycott Divides." *Chicago Tribune Online,* October 21.

Aylwin, José. 2003. "El acceso de los indígenas a la tierra en los ordenamientos jurídicos de América Latina." In *Mercados de tierras agrícolas en América Latina y el Caribe: Una realidad incompleta,* edited by Pedro Tejo, 163–207. Santiago de Chile: CEPAL.

Bacon, David. 2011. "A Cross-Border Struggle: The Hidden History of Mexico/US Labor Solidarity." *Counterpunch* (Petrolia, Calif.), May 27–29.

Bada, Xóchitl. 2001. "Collective Remittances, Culture, and National Identity: The Reconstruction of Identities among Michoacano Hometown Associations in the Chicago Area." Master's thesis, University of Chicago.

———. 2003a. "La participación cívica comunitaria transnacional de los clubes de michoacanos." In *Diáspora Michoacana*, edited by Gustavo López Castro, 247–285. Zamora: El Colegio de Michoacán-Gobierno del Estado de Michoacán.

———. 2003b. "Mexican Hometown Associations." *Citizen Action in the Americas No. 5.* Albuquerque, N.M.: Interhemispheric Resource Center (IRC).

———. 2004. "Clubes de Michoacanos Oriundos: Desarrollo y Membresía Social Comunitarios." *Revista Migración y Desarrollo* 2:82–103.

———. 2007. "The Binational Civic and Political Engagement of Mexican Migrant Hometown Associations and Federations in the United States." *Iberoamericana* 7(25): 129–142.

———. 2010. "Mexican Hometown Associations in Chicago: The Newest Agents of Civic Participation." In *¡Marcha! Latino Chicago and the Immigrant Rights Movement*, edited by Amalia Pallares and Nilda Flores González, 146–162. Urbana: University of Illinois Press.

Bada, Xóchitl, and Cristóbal Mendoza. 2012. "Estrategias organizativas y prácticas cívicas binacionales de los clubes de oriundos y federaciones mexicanos en Chicago: Una perspectiva transnacional desde el 'lugar.'" *Migraciones Internacionales* 7(1): 35–67.

Bada, Xóchitl, Oscar Chacón, and Jonathan Fox, eds. 2010. *Latino Immigrants in the Windy City: New Trends of Civic Engagement.* Washington, D.C.: Woodrow Wilson International Center for Scholars.

Bada, Xóchitl, Jonathan Fox, Robert Donnelly, and Andrew Selee. 2010. *Context Matters: Latino Immigrant Civic Engagement in Nine U.S. Cities.* Reports on Latino Immigrant Civic Engagement, National Report. Washington, D.C.: Woodrow Wilson International Center for Scholars, June.

Bada, Xóchitl, Joanna Schmit, and Kenneth Fujimoto. 2011. "Does Birthplace Matter? Determinants of Non-Electoral Civic and Political Engagement." *Diálogo* Fall(14): 34–37.

Badillo, David A. 2001. "Religion and Transnational Migration in Chicago: The Case of the Potosinos." *Journal of the Illinois State Historical Society* 94(4): 420–440.

———. 2006. *Latinos and the New Immigrant Church.* Baltimore: John Hopkins University Press.

Bailey, John. 1994. "Centralism and Political Change in Mexico: The Case of National Solidarity." In *Transforming State-Society Relations in Mexico: The National Solidarity Strategy*, edited by Wayne A. Cornelius, Ann L. Craig, and Jonathan Fox, 97–119. San Diego: University of California.

Banco de México. 2013. "La Balanza de Pagos en 2012." Comunicado de Prensa. Mexico City: Banco de México.

Bartra, Armando. 2004. "Rebellious Cornfields: Towards Foods and Labour Self-Sufficiency." In *Mexico in Transition: Neoliberal Globalism, the State, and Civil Society*, edited by Gerardo Otero, 18–36. New York: Zed Books.

———. 2008. "The Right to Stay: Reactivate Agriculture, Retain the Population." In *The Right to Stay Home: Alternative to Mass Displacement and Forced Migration in North America*, 18–25. San Francisco: Global Exchange.

Barvosa-Carter, Edwina. 2001. "Multiple Identity and Coalition Building: How Identity Differences within Us Enable Radical Alliances among Us." In *Forging Radical Alliances across Difference: Coalition Politics for the New Millennium*, edited by Jill M. Bystydzienski and Steven P. Schacht, 21–34. New York: Rowman and Littlefield.

Basch, Linda G., Nina Glick Schiller, and Cristina Szanton Blanc. 1994. *Nations Unbound: Transnational Projects, Postcolonial Predicaments, and Deterritorialized Nation-States.* Luxemburg: Gordon and Breach.

Bate, Peter. 2001. "Un río de oro. El dinero que los inmigrantes envían a sus países sostiene a sus familias y refuerza la economía de la región. Podría hacer algo más?" In *Bidamérica: Revista del Banco Interamericano de Desarrollo*. Washington, D.C.: Banco Interamericano de Desarrollo. October. http://www.iadb.org/idbamerica/index.cfm?thisid=734.

Becerra Ramírez, Manuel. 2000. "Nationality in Mexico." In *From Migrants to Citizens: Membership in a Changing World*, edited by Alexander T. Aleinikoff and Douglas Klusmeyer, 312–341. Washington, D.C.: Carnegie Endowment for International Peace.

Bennett, Larry. 2010. *The Third City: Chicago and American Urbanism*. Chicago: University of Chicago Press.

Besserer, Federico. 2004. *Topografías transnacionales*. Mexico City: Universidad Autónoma Metropolitana–Plaza y Valdés Editores.

Bloemraad, Irene, and Shannon Gleeson. 2012. "Making the Case for Organizational Presence: Civic Inclusion, Access to Resources, and Formal Community Organizations." In *Remaking Urban Citizenship: Organizations, Institutions, and the Right to the City*, edited by Michael Peter Smith and Michael McQuarrie, 109–134. New Brunswick, N.J.: Transaction Publishers.

Bodnar, John. 1981. "Ethnic Fraternal Benefit Associations: Their Historical Development, Character and Significance." In *Records of Ethnic Fraternal Benefit Associations in the United States: Essays and Inventories*, 5–14. St. Paul, Minn.: Immigration History Research Center.

———. 1985. *The Transplanted: A History of Immigrants in Urban America*. Bloomington: Indiana University Press.

Bosniak, Linda. 2006. *The Citizen and the Alien*. Princeton, N.J.: Princeton University Press.

Bourdieu, Pierre. 1998. *Masculine Domination*. Stanford, Calif.: Stanford University Press.

Brinkerhoff, Jennifer M. 2009. *Digital Diasporas: Identity and Transnational Engagement*. Cambridge: Cambridge University Press.

Brooks, David, and Jonathan Fox, eds. 2002. *Cross-Border Dialogues: U.S.-Mexican Social Movement Networking*. San Diego: Center for U.S.-Mexican Studies, University of California, San Diego.

Brower, Lincoln P., and Homero Aridjis. 2013. "The Winter of the Monarch." *New York Times*, March 15.

Burawoy, Michael. 1991. *Ethnography Unbound: Power and Resistance in the Modern Metropolis*. Berkeley: University of California Press.

———. 2009. *The Extended Case Method: Four Countries, Four Decades, Four Great Transformations, and One Theoretical Tradition*. Berkeley: University of California Press.

Burgess, Katrina. 2005. "Migrant Philanthropy and Local Governance in Mexico." In *New Patterns for Mexico: Observations on Remittances, Philanthropic Giving, and Equitable Development*, edited by Barbara Merz, 99–123. Cambridge, Mass.: Global Equity Initiative, Harvard University

———. 2009. "Neoliberal Reform and Migrant Remittances: Symptom or Solution?" In *Beyond Neoliberalism in Latin America? Societies and Politics at the Crossroads*, edited by John Burdick, Philip Oxhorn, and Kenneth M. Roberts, 177–195. New York: Palgrave Macmillan.

———. 2010. "Translocal Networks and Democratic Accountability in Mexico." Paper presented at the annual Latin American Studies Association Conference, Toronto, October 6–10.

Cabrero, Enrique. 1998. *Las Políticas Decentralizadoras en México (1983–1993): Logros y Desencantos*. Mexico, D.F.: Miguel Angel Porrúa.

Çağlar, Ayse. 2006. "Hometown Associations, the Rescaling of State Spatiality, and Migrant Grassroots Transnationalism." *Global Networks* 6(1): 1–22.

Calleja Pinedo, Margarita. 2009. "Los empresarios en el comercio de frutas y hortalizas frescas de México a Estados Unidos." In *Empresarios migrantes mexicanos en Estados Unidos*, edited by M. Basilia Valenzuela and Margarita Calleja Pinedo, 307–343. Zapopan: Universidad de Guadalajara.

Campaña Bid 50. 2009. "50 Años Financiando la Desigualdad." Frente Bid, January 29. http://www.censat.org/articulos/10025-comunicado/216-Declaracion-de-la-Campana-BID50–50-anos-financiando-la-desigualdad.

Campbell, Monica. 2006. "Remittances Help Keep Kids in School—and in Mexico." *Christian Science Monitor Online*, May 15.

Campos-Vázquez, Raymundo, and Horacio Sobarzo. 2012. "The Development and Fiscal Effects of Emigration on Mexico." Washington, D.C.: Migration Policy Institute.

Canales, Alejandro I. 2008. *Vivir del Norte: Remesas, Desarrollo y Pobreza en México*. Mexico City: Secretaría de Gobernación.

Canales, Alejandro I., and Israel Montiel Armas. 2004. "Remesas e inversión productiva en comunidades de alta migración a Estados Unidos: El caso de Teocaltiche, Jalisco." *Migraciones Internacionales* 2(3): 142–172.

Cárdenas Batel, Lázaro. 2004. "Un Día Sin Mexicanos." *MX Sin Fronteras* (9): 30.

Cárdenas Solórzano, Cuauhtémoc. 1989. "Responsabilidad de México para con los Mexicanos en el Exterior." *La Voz del Trabajador Inmigrante* 7(2): 5–9.

Castañeda, Jorge. 2007. *Ex-Mex: From Migrants to Immigrants*. New York: New Press.

———. 2011. *Mañana Forever? Mexico and the Mexicans*. New York: Alfred A. Knopf.

Castles, Stephen, and Raúl Delgado Wise, eds. 2008. *Migration and Development: Perspectives from the South*. Geneva: International Organization for Migration, International Network on Migration and Development, Universidad Autónoma de Zacatecas.

Center for Constitutional Rights, National Day Laborers Organizing Center, and Cardozo School of Law. 2011. "Briefing Guide to Secure Communities." Press release, June 23. http://ccrjustice.org/files/Secure%20Communities%20Fact%20Sheet%20Briefing%20guide%208–2-2010%20Production.pdf.

Chacón, Oscar. 2011. "Globalization, Obsolete and Inhumane Migratory Policies, and Their Impact on Migrant Workers and Their Families in the North and Central American/Caribbean Region." *Journal of Poverty* 15:465–474.

———. 2012. "Reflections About the Recently Concluded 2012 National Latino Congreso." In *Presencia Michoacana en el Medio Oeste*, 22–23. Chicago: Federación de Clubes Michoacanos en Illinois.

Chambers, Iain. 1994. *Migrancy, Culture, Identity*. London: Routledge.

Cleary, Matthew R., and Susan C. Stokes. 2006. *Democracy and the Culture of Skepticism: Political Trust in Argentina and Mexico*. New York: Rusell Sage Foundation.

Cockcroft, James Donald. 2005. *Historia de un pueblo migrante: Los trabajadores de Michoacán*. Mexico, D.F.: Universidad Michoacana de San Nicolás de Hidalgo, Jorale Editores s.a. de c.v.

Cohen, Lizabeth. 1990. *Making a New Deal: Industrial Workers in Chicago, 1919–1939*. Cambridge: Cambridge University Press.

CONAPO. 2010. "Anexo A. Resultados principales del índice de intensidad migratoria México-Estados Unidos a nivel nacional." Mexico City: Consejo Nacional de Población. http://www.conapo.gob.mx/work/models/CONAPO/intensidad_migratoria/anexos/Anexo_A.pdf.

Consejo Nacional de Evaluación de la Política de Desarrollo Social. 2006. "Población total, pobreza por ingresos, indicadores, índice y grado de rezago social, del estado de Michoacán, según municipio, 2005." Mexico City: CONEVAL.

Cook, Karen S., Russell Hardin, and Margaret Levi. 2005. *Cooperation without Trust?* New York: Rusell Sage Foundation.

Cooke, Bill, and Uma Kothari, eds. 2001. *Participation: The New Tyranny?* London: Zed Books.

Cordero-Guzmán, Héctor R. 2005. "Community Based Organization and Migration in New York City." *Journal of Ethnic and Migration Studies* 31(5): 889–909.

Córdova, Rodolfo. 2010. "Migrant Money and Migrant Accountability: The 3X1 Program for Migrants in Tanhuato, Michoacán, Mexico." Unpublished manuscript.

Cortés, Víctor. 2006. *10 de Marzo. La Marcha.* Chicago: Ediciones La Cuadrilla de la Langosta, Misiza.

Crang, Mike. 1998. *Cultural Geography.* London: Routledge.

Cruickshank Soria, Leticia Susana. 2004. "El papel de la Cooperación Internacional para el Desarrollo en el análisis del proyecto 'Capitalización de Remesas para el Desarrollo Económico Local' Nafin—FOMIN/ BID." Master's thesis, Instituto de Investigaciones Dr. José María Luis Mora, Mexico City.

Cruz Hernández, Isabel. 2007. "Hacia un Nuevo Sistema Financiero Rural en México: Acceso Universal a Servicios Financieros en el Campo." Paper presented at the International Conference on Rural Finance Research: Moving Results into Policies and Practice, Rome, March 19–21. Rome: FAO-Ford-IFAD. http://www.fao.org/ag/rurfinconference/documents.asp?lang=en.

Cunill, Nuria. 1999. "Retos de las reformas de segunda generación ¿Mercantilización y neoclientelismo o reconstrucción de la Administración Pública?" *Nueva Sociedad* 160 (March–April). http://www.nuso.org/revista.php?n=160.

Danielson, Michael S. 2011. "Migration as a Democratizing Force in Sending Communities? A Comparative Study of Local Politics in Mexico." Paper presented at the Annual Meeting of the American Political Science Association, Seattle, September 1–4.

Davis, Stephen P., Juan R. Martinez, and R. Stephen Warner. 2010. "The Role of the Catholic Church in the Chicago Immigrant Mobilization." In *¡Marcha! Latino Chicago and the Immigrant Rights Movement,* edited by Amalia Pallares and Nilda Flores González, 79–96. Urbana: University of Illinois Press.

De Genova, Nicholas. 2005. *Working the Boundaries: Race, Space, and "Illegality" in Mexican Chicago.* Durham, N.C.: Duke University Press.

Délano, Alexandra. 2011. *Mexico and Its Diaspora in the United States: Policies of Emigration since 1848.* New York: Cambridge University Press.

Delgado Wise, Raúl. 2004. "Labour and Migration Policies under Vicente Fox: Subordination to US Economic and Geopolitical Interests." In *Mexico in Transition: Neoliberal Globalism, the State, and Civil Society,* edited by Gerardo Otero, 138–156. New York: Zed Books.

Delgado Wise, Raúl, and Humberto Márquez Covarrubias. 2009. "Understanding the Relationship between Migration and Development: Toward a New Theoretical Approach." *Social Analysis* 53(3): 85–105.

Desde México. 2010. "Michoacanazo." Mexican news blog in *Desde México. Escribiendo lo que se tiene que escribir.* Lázaro Cárdenas, Michoacán: Wordpress.

Deufel, Benjamin. 2006. "Trial Membership: Responses to Immigrants in American Communities." Ph.D. diss., Harvard University.

Donner, R. 1994. *The Regulation of Nationality in International Law*. Irvington-on-Hudson, N.Y.: Transnational Publishers.

Drake, St. Clair, and Horace R. Cayton. 1945. *Black Metropolis: A Study of Negro Life in a Northern City*. Chicago: University of Chicago Press.

Duquette, Lauren. 2011. "Making Democracy Work from Abroad: Remittances, Hometown Associations and Migrant-State Coproduction of Public Goods in Mexico." Ph.D. diss., University of Chicago.

Duquette, Lauren, and Xóchitl Bada. 2009. "Continuity and Change in Mexican Migrant Hometown Associations." Paper presented at the Inter-University Program for Latino Research Biennal Conference, University of Illinois at Chicago, September 24.

Duquette-Rury, Lauren, and Xóchitl Bada. Forthcoming. "Continuity and Change in Mexican Migrant Hometown Associations: Evidence from New Survey Research." *Migraciones Internacionales* 7, special issue 1.

Durand, Jorge. 1994. *Más allá de la línea: Patrones migratorios entre México y Estados Unidos*. México, D.F.: Consejo Nacional para la Cultura y las Artes.

———. 2005. "Ensayo teórico sobre la migración de retorno: El principio del rendimiento decreciente." In *Contribuciones al análisis de la migración internacional y el desarrollo regional en México*, edited by Raúl Delgado Wise and Beatrice Knerr, 309–318. Zacatecas: Universidad Autónoma de Zacatecas-Miguel Ángel Porrúa.

Durand, Jorge, and Patricia Arias. 2008. *Mexicanos en Chicago: Diario de Campo de Robert Redfield, 1924–1925*. Mexico City: Miguel Ángel Porrúa.

Durkheim, Emile. 1984. *The Division of Labor in Society*. New York: Free Press.

Embassy of Mexico. 2013. "Consulates of Mexico in the United States of America. Consular Jurisdictions Directory. Carpeta Básica Consular (CIBAC)." Washington, D.C.: Embassy of Mexico.

Escala Rabadán, Luis. 2008. "Migración, formas organizativas y espacio público: La celebración de la guelaguetza en San Diego." Paper presented at the Seminario interno del Departamento de Estudios Sociales. Tijuana: El Colegio de la Frontera Norte.

Escobar, Arturo. 2003. "Actors, Networks, and New Knowledge Producers: Social Movements and the Paradigmatic Transition in the Sciences." In *Conhecimiento Prudente para Uma Vida Decente*, edited by Boaventura De Sousa Santos, 605–630. Porto: Afrontamento.

———. 2008. *Territories of Difference: Place, Movements, Life, Redes*. Durham, N.C.: Duke University Press.

Escobar, Arturo, and Sonia Alvarez, eds. 1992. *The Making of Social Movements in Latin America: Identity, Strategy, and Democracy*. Boulder, Colo.: Westview Press.

Espinosa, Víctor M. 1998. *El Dilema del Retorno: Migración, Género y Pertenencia en un Contexto Transnacional*. Zamora: El Colegio de Michoacán.

———. 1999. "The Federation of Michoacán Clubs in Illinois: The Chicago-Michoacán Project Report." Chicago: Heartland Alliance for Human Needs and Human Rights.

Fábregas Puig, Andrés. 2012. "Chicago: Futbol, identidad, migración." In *Offside/Fuera de Lugar: Futbol y Migraciones en el Mundo Contemporáneo*, edited by Guillermo Alonso Meneses and Luis Escala Rabadán, 47–62. Tijuana: El Colegio de la Frontera Norte.

Faist, Thomas. 2008a. "Migrants as Transnational Development Agents: An Inquiry into the Newest Round of the Migration-Development Nexus." *Population, Space, and Place* 14:21–42.

———. 2008b. "Transstate Spaces and Development: Some Critical Remarks." In *Rethinking Transnationalism: The Meso-link of Organisations*, edited by Ludger Pries, 62–79. London: Routledge.

————. 2009. "Transnationalization and Development: Towards an Alternative Agenda." *Social Analysis* 53(3): 38–59.

Fajnzylber, Pablo, and J. Humberto López. 2007. "Close to Home: The Development Impact of Remittances in Latin America." Washington, D.C.: International Bank for Reconstruction and Development/World Bank.

Farr, Marcia. 2006. *Rancheros in Chicagoacán: Language and Identity in a Transnational Community*. Austin: University of Texas Press.

Félix, Adrián. 2008. "New Americans or Diasporic Nationalists?: Mexican Migrant Responses to Naturalization and Implications for Political Participation." *American Quarterly* 60(3): 601–624.

————. 2011. "Posthumous Transnationalism: Postmortem Repatriation from the United States to Mexico." *Latin American Research Review* 46(3): 157–179.

Fernández, Lilia. 2005. "From the Near West Side to 18th Street: Mexican Community Formation and Activism in Mid-Twentieth Century Chicago." *Journal of the Illinois State Historical Society* 98(3): 162–183.

Fine, Janice. 2006. *Worker Centers: Organizing Communities at the Edge of the Dream.* Ithaca, N.Y.: Cornell University Press–Economic Policy Institute.

Firebaugh, Glenn. 2003. *The New Geography of Global Income Inequality*. Cambridge, Mass.: Harvard University Press.

Fitzgerald, David. 2004. "Beyond 'Transnationalism': Mexican Hometown Politics at an American Labor Union." *Ethnic and Racial Studies* 27(2): 228–247.

————. 2005a. "A Nation of Emigrants? Statecraft, Church-building, and Nationalism in Mexican Migrant Source Communities." Ph.D. diss., University of California, Los Angeles.

————. 2005b. "Nationality and Migration in Modern Mexico." *Journal of Ethnic and Migration Studies* 31(1): 171–191.

————. 2009. *A Nation of Emigrants: How Mexico Manages Its Migration*. Berkeley: University of California Press.

Fletcher, Peri, and Jane Margold. 2003. "Transnational Communities." *Rural Mexico Research Review* 1. http://reap.ucdavis.edu/research/volume1.

Flores, John H. 2006. "Shaping Transnational Identities: Competing Visions of a Mexican American Community between the Frente Popular Mexicano and the University of Chicago Settlement House." Paper presented at the Newberry Library Seminar on Latino and Borderlands History, Chicago, November 18.

Flores-Macías, Gustavo. 2008. "NAFTA's Unfilfilled Immigration Expectations." *Peace Review: A Journal of Social Justice* 20(4): 435–441.

Fortuny Loret de Mola, Patricia, Mirian Solís Lizama, and Philip J. Williams. 2009. "Solidarities among Mexican Immigrants in Immokalee." In *A Place to Be: Brazilian, Guatemalan, and Mexican Immigrants in Florida's New Destinations*, edited by Philip J. Williams, Timothy J. Steigenga, and Manuel A. Vásquez, 80–99. New Brunswick, N.J.: Rutgers University Press.

Fox, Cibelle. 2012. *Three Worlds of Relief: Race, Immigration, and the American Welfare State from the Progressive Era to the New Deal*. Princeton, N.J.: Princeton University Press.

Fox, Jonathan. 2006. "Migration and Development: Encounters and Disconnects." *Grassroots Development* 27(1): 2–4.

————. 2007. *Accountability Politics: Power and Voice in Rural Mexico*. Oxford: Oxford University Press.

Fox, Jonathan, and Xóchitl Bada. 2008. "Migrant Organization and Hometown Impacts in Rural Mexico." *Journal of Agrarian Change* 8(2–3): 435–461.

———. 2011. "Migrant Civic Engagement." In *Rallying for Immigrant Rights*, edited by Irene Bloemraad and Kim Voss, 142–160. Berkeley: University of California Press.

Fox, Jonathan, and William Gois. 2010. "La Sociedad Civil Migrante: Diez Tesis para el Debate." *Migración y Desarrollo* 7(15): 81–128.

Fox, Jonathan, and Libby Haight, eds. 2010. *Subsidizing Inequality: Mexican Corn Policy since NAFTA*. Washington, D.C.: Woodrow Wilson International Center for Scholars, University of California, Santa Cruz, and CIDE.

Fox, Jonathan, and Gaspar Rivera-Salgado. 2004a. "Building Civil Society among Indigenous Migrants." In *Indigenous Mexican Migrants in the United States*, edited by Jonathan Fox and Gaspar Rivera-Salgado, 1–65. La Jolla, Calif.: Center for U.S.-Mexican Studies and Center for Comparative Immigration Studies, University of California, San Diego.

———, eds. 2004b. *Indigenous Mexican Migrants in the United States*. La Jolla, Calif.: Center for U.S.-Mexican Studies and Center for Comparative Immigration Studies, University of California, San Diego.

Fraser, Nancy. 2009. *Scales of Justice: Reimagining Political Space in a Globalizing World*. New York: Columbia University Press.

Fukuyama, Francis. 1995. *Trust: The Social Virtues and the Creation of Prosperity*. New York: Free Press.

Fung, Archon. 2004. *Empowered Participation: Reinventing Urban Democracy*. Princeton, N.J.: Princeton University Press.

Gálvez, Alyshia. 2010. *Guadalupe in New York: Devotion and Struggle for Citizenship Rights among Mexican Immigrants*. New York: New York University Press.

———. 2011. "Resolviendo: How September 11 Tested and Transformed a New York City Mexican Immigrant Organization." In *Politics and Partnerships: The Role of Voluntary Associations in America's Political Past and Present*, edited by Elisabeth S. Clemens and Doug Guthrie, 297–326. Chicago: University of Chicago Press.

Gamio, Manuel. 1930. *Mexican Immigration to the United States: A Study of Human Migration and Adjustment*. Chicago: University of Chicago Press.

García, Carina. 2012. "Josefina gana en voto de Mexicanos en el Extranjero." *El Universal Online*, July 2.

García, Juan R. 1996. *Mexicans in the Midwest, 1900–1932*. Tucson: University of Arizona Press.

García, Myrna. 2012. "'Sin Fronteras' Activism, Identity, and the Politics of Belonging in Mexican Chicago, 1968–1986." Ph.D. diss., University of California, San Diego.

García Canclini, Néstor. 1995. *Hybrid Cultures: Strategies for Entering and Leaving Modernity*. Minneapolis: University of Minnesota Press.

García de Alba Tinajero, Maria, Leticia M. Jáuregui Casanueva, and Claudia Núñez Sañudo. 2006. "Liderazgos y nuevos espacios de negociación en el Programa 3X1 para Migrantes: El caso de Zacatecas." Edited by Rafael Fernández de Castro, Rodolfo García Zamora, and A. Vila Freyrer. Mexico City: ITAM-Universidad Autónoma de Zacatecas.

García Espinosa, Salvador. 2010. "La dinámica migratoria en Michoacán y el sistema urbano estatal." In *Comunidades Mexicanas en Estados Unidos: Diáspora, Integración y Desarrollo en México*, edited by Jerjes Aguirre Ochoa and José Odón García García, 349–357. Morelia: Universidad Michoacana de San Nicolás de Hidalgo.

García García, José Odón. 2006. "Desarrollo Humano y Migración en Michoacán." *Revista de Investigaciones México–Estados Unidos. CIMEXUS* 1(1): 39–58.

García y Griego, Manuél. 1988. "Hacia una nueva visión del problema de los indocumentados en EU." In *Mexico y EU frente a la migración de los indocumentados*, edited by

Manuel García y Griego and Mónica Verea, 139–153. Mexico City: UNAM and Miguel Ángel Porrúa.

García Zamora, Rodolfo. 2006. "Migración Internacional y Desarrollo en México: Tres experiencias estatales." Paper presented at the *Segundo Coloquio Internacional sobre Migracion y Desarrollo: Migracion, Trasnacionalismo y Transformacion Social*. Cocoyoc, Morelos, October 26–28.

Gellman, Erik. 2005. "Pilsen." In *The Electronic Encyclopedia of Chicago*, edited by Chicago Historical Society. Chicago: Newberry Library. http://www.encyclopedia.chicagohistory .org/pages/2477.html.

Germano, Roy Paul, III. 2010. "The Political Economy of Remittances: Emigration, Social Insurance Provision, and Political Behavior in Mexico." Ph.D. diss., University of Texas at Austin.

Gibson, Campbell, and Emily Lennon. 1999. "Historical Census Statistics on the Foreign-Born Population of the United States: 1850–1990." U.S. Census Bureau. Washington, D.C.: U.S. Government Printing Office.

Giddens, Anthony. 1990. *The Consequences of Modernity*. Stanford, Calif.: Stanford University Press.

Ginzburg, Carlo. 1989. "The Inquisitor as Anthropologist." In *Clues, Myths, and the Historical Method*, 156–164. Baltimore: John Hopkins University Press.

Glazer, Nathan, and Patrick Moynihan. 1970. *Beyond the Melting Pot*. Cambridge, Mass.: MIT Press.

Gledhill, John. 1995. *Neoliberalism, Transnationalization, and Rural Poverty. A Case Study of Michoacán, Mexico*. Oxford: Westview Press.

Gleeson, Shannon. 2012. *Conflicting Commitments. The Politics of Enforcing Immigrant Worker Rights in San Jose and Houston*. Ithaca, N.Y.: Cornell University Press.

Glick Schiller, Nina. 2009. "A Global Perspective on Migration and Development." *Social Analysis* 53(3): 14–37.

Glick Schiller, Nina, and Ayşe Çağlar, eds. 2011. *Locating Migration: Rescaling Cities and Migrants*. Ithaca, N.Y.: Cornell University Press.

Gobierno Federal. 2012. "Logros. Programa 3X1 para Migrantes. Power Point Presentation." Mexico City: Secretaría de Desarrollo Social and Secretaría de Relaciones Exteriores.

Goldring, Luin. 1996. "Gendered Memory: Reconstruction of the Village by Mexican Transnational Migrants." In *Creating the Countryside: The Politics of Rural and Environmental Discourse*, edited by Melanie DuPuis and Peter Vandergeest, 303–329. Philadelphia: Temple University Press.

———. 2001. "Disaggregating Transnational Social Spaces: Gender, Place, and Citizenship in Mexico-US Transnational Spaces." In *New Transnational Social Spaces: International Migration and Transnational Companies in the Early Twenty-First Century*, edited by Ludger Pries, 59–76. London: Routledge.

———. 2002. "The Mexican State and Transmigrant Organizations: Negotiating the Boundaries of Membership and Participation." *Latin American Research Review* 37(3): 55–99.

Gomberg-Muñoz, Ruth. 2011. *Labor and Legality: An Ethnography of a Mexican Immigrant Network*. New York: Oxford University Press.

Gómez-Robledo Verduzco, A. 1994. "Derecho Internacional y Nueva Ley de Nacionalidad Mexicana." *Boletín Mexicano de Derecho Comparado* 27(80): 315–345.

González Amador, Roberto. 2007. "Comienza a declinar el ingreso por remesas, advierte el BdeM." *La Jornada Online*, February 1.

González Hernández, José Roberto. 2011. "Rendición de cuentas pública y participación social: El caso del Programa 3X1 en el estado de Zacatecas." Ph.D. diss., Unidad Académica de Estudios del Desarrollo, Universidad Autónoma de Zacatecas.

González y González, Luis. 1995. *Pueblo en Vilo: Microhistoria de San José de Gracia.* Zamora: El Colegio de Michoacán.

Goodman, Gary, and Jonathan Hiskey. 2008. "Exit without Leaving: Political Disengagement in High Migration Municipalities in Mexico." *Comparative Politics* 40(2): 169–188.

Grieco, Elizabeth M. 2004. "Will Migrant Remittances Continue through Time? A New Answer to an Old Question." *International Journal on Multicultural Societies* 6(2): 243–252.

Grindle, Merilee S. 2007. *Going Local: Decentralization, Democratization, and the Promise of Good Governance.* Princeton, N.J.: Princeton University Press.

Grønbjerg, Kristin A., and Curtis Child. 2003. "Illinois Non-Profits: A Profile of Charities and Advocacy Organizations." Chicago: Donors Forum of Chicago.

Groody, Daniel G. 2002. *Border of Death, Valley of Life: An Immigrant Journey of Heart and Spirit.* Lanham, Md.: Rowman and Littlefield.

Guarnizo, Luis Eduardo. 2012. "The Fluid, Multi-Scalar, and Contradictory Construction of Citizenship." In *Remaking Urban Citizenship: Organizations, Institutions, and the Right to the City,* edited by Michael Peter Smith and Michael McQuarrie, 11–38. New Brunswick, N.J.: Transaction Publishers.

Guarnizo, Luis Eduardo, Alejandro Portes, and William Haller. 2003. "Assimilation and Transnationalism: Determinants of Transnational Political Action among Immigrants." *International Migration Review* 108(6): 1211–1248.

Gutiérrez Nájera, Lourdes. 2009. "Transnational Migration, Conflict, and Divergent Ideologies of Progress." *Urban Anthropology* 38(2–4): 269–302.

Gzesh, Susan, Fabienne Venet, and Mario Santillo. 2007. "Human Rights and Migration: Principal Points of Agreement and Recurring Themes." Conference Proceedings of the First Latin American Community Migrant Summit. Unpublished manuscript.

Hagan, Jacqueline. 2008. *Migration Miracle: Faith, Hope, and Meaning on the Undocumented Journey.* Cambridge, Mass.: Harvard University Press.

Hall, Joan. 2011. "Ten Years of Innovation in Remittances: Lessons Learned and Models for the Future." Washington, D.C.: Multilateral Investment Fund, Inter-American Development Bank.

Hernández, Edwin, Kenneth G. Davis, Milagros Peña, Georgian Schiopu, Jeffrey Smith, and Matthew T. Loveland. 2007. "Faith and Values in Action: Religion, Politics, and Social Attitudes among US Latinos/as." Vol. 1. Research Reports. A series of papers by the Institute for Latino Studies and research associates. Notre Dame, Ind.: Institute for Latino Studies. http://latinostudies.nd.edu/assets/95327/original/.

Hernández-León, Rubén. 2008. *Metropolitan Migrants: The Migration of Urban Mexicans to the United States.* Berkeley: University of California Press.

Hilgers, Tina. 2011. "Clientelism and Conceptual Stretching: Differentiating among Concepts and among Analytical Levels." *Theory and Society* 40(5): 567–588.

Hirabayashi, Lane R. 1986. "The Migrant Village Association in Latin America: A Comparative Analysis." *Latin American Research Review* 21(3): 7–29.

Hirai, Shinji. 2009. *Economía política de la nostalgia: Un estudio sobre la transformación del paisaje urbano en la migración transnacional entre México y Estados Unidos.* Mexico City: Juan Pablos Editor–Universidad Autónoma Metropolitana.

Hirschman, Albert O. 1970. *Exit, Voice, and Loyalty: Responses to Decline in Firms, Organizations, and States.* Cambridge, Mass.: Harvard University Press.

Hispanic PR Wire. 2006. "CEMEX'S CONSTRUMEX Celebrates Five Years of Service to the Mexican Community in the U.S." *Hispanic Business.com*. March 28.

Hispanics in Philanthropy. 2011. *Develop Your World: Case Studies*. Promoting Diaspora Support for Local Productive Initiatives Series, edited by the Multilateral Investment Fund. Washington, D.C.: Hispanics in Philanthropy-Inter-American Development Bank.

Hondagneu-Sotelo, Pierette, Genelle Gaudinez, and Hector Lara. 2007. "A Genealogy of the Posada Sin Fronteras." In *Religion and Social Justice for Immigrants*, edited by Pierette Hondagneu-Sotelo, 122–138. New Brunswick, N.J.: Rutgers University Press.

Hong, Soo. 2011. *A Cord of Three Strands*. Cambridge, Mass.: Harvard University Press.

Huntington, Samuel P. 2004. *Who Are We? The Challenges to America's National Identity*. New York: Simon and Schuster.

IADB. 2006. "Proyecto Piloto 3X1 para Migrantes. Innovación y Fortalecimiento. Fase I." Washington, D.C.: Banco Interamericano de Desarrollo and Secretaría de Desarrollo Social. http://idbdocs.iadb.org/wsdocs/getdocument.aspx?docnum=822627.

IADB, MIF, and Bendixen. 2006. "Public Opinion Research Study of Latin American Remittance Senders in the United States." Washington, D.C.: Inter-American Development Bank, Multilateral Investment Fund, Bendixen and Associates. October 18. http://www.cfsinnovation.com/system/files/imported/managed_documents/idb_remittance_study.pdf.

Iglesias, Enrique. 2000. "Palabras del Sr. Presidente con ocasión del acto: 'Las remesas como instrumento de desarrollo: Una conferencia regional.'" Paper presented at *Las remesas como instrumento de desarrollo: Una conferencia regional*, Washington, D.C.: Fondo Multilateral de Inversiones del Banco Interamericano de Desarrollo, May 17–18. http://idbdocs.iadb.org/wsdocs/getdocument.aspx?docnum=563068.

Illinois Government News Network. 2013. "Governor Quinn Signs Sister Lake Pact with Michoacán, Mexico." Springfield: State of Illinois, April 5.

Illinois State Museum. n.d. "State Symbol: Illinois Official Insect—Monarch Butterfly (*Danaus plexippus*)." In *Illinois State Symbols and Their History*. http://www.museum.state.il.us/exhibits/symbols/insect.html.

IME. 2011. "Estadísticas de los Mexicanos en el Exterior: Matrículas Consulares por Circunscripción." Mexico City: Instituto de los Mexicanos en el Exterior.

INEGI. 2010. "Censo de Población y Vivienda 2010." Aguascalientes, Mexico: Instituto Nacional de Estadística y Geografía.

———. 2006. "Resultados Definitivos del II Conteo de Población y Vivienda 2005 para el Estado de Michoacán de Ocampo." Aguascalientes, Mexico: Instituto Nacional de Estadística y Geografía.

Innis-Jiménez, Michael D. 2005. "Organizing for Fun: Recreation and Community Formation in the Mexican Community of South Chicago in the 1920s and 1930s." *Journal of the Illinois State Historical Society* 98(3): 144–161.

———. 2013. *Steel Barrio: The Great Mexican Migration to South Chicago, 1915–1940*. New York: New York University Press.

Instituto Electoral de Michoacán. 2011. "Resultados de la Elección de Ayuntamientos 2011: Proceso Electoral Ordinario." In *Resultados de los Cómputos Municipales de la Elección de Ayuntamientos*. Morelia.

Instituto Nacional de Estadística y Geografía. 2011. "Anuario Estadístico de los Estados Unidos Mexicanos 2011." Aguascalientes, Mexico: Instituto Nacional de Estadística y Geografía.

———. 2012. "Perspectiva Estadística Michoacán de Ocampo." Aguascalientes, Mexico: Instituto Nacional de Estadística y Geografía.

————. 2013. "Producto Interno Bruto Trimestral por Sector 2011–2012." Aguascalientes, Mexico: Instituto Nacional de Estadística y Geografía.

Inter-American Foundation. 2006. *Year in Review. Financial and Statistical Report. Investment by Country*. Washington, D.C.: Inter-American Foundation.

Iskander, Natasha N. 2005. "Social Learning as a Productive Project: Zacatecas and Guanajuato's Cautionary Tales." Paper presented at the International Conference on Migration, Remittances and the Economic Development of Sending Countries, Marrakech, Morocco. February 23–25.

————. 2006. "Innovating Government: Migration, Development, and the State in Morocco and Mexico, 1963–2005." Ph.D. diss., Massachusetts Institute of Technology.

————. 2010. *Creative State: Forty Years of Migration and Development Policy in Morocco and Mexico*. Ithaca, N.Y.: Cornell University Press.

Jiménez, Flavia, Fred Tsao, Lisa Thakkar, and Josh Hoyt. 2008. *Priced Out: U.S. Citizenship— A Privilege for the Rich and Well Educated?* Chicago: Illinois Coalition for Immigrant and Refugee Rights.

Jimenez, Tomas R. 2009. *Replenished Ethnicity: Mexican Americans, Immigration, and Identity*. Berkeley: University of California Press.

Jones-Correa, Michael. 2009. "Latinos in the Washington Metropolitan Area: Findings from the 2006 Latino National Survey." In *Local Goes National: Challenges and Opportunities for Latino Immigrants in the Nation's Capital*, edited by Kate Brick, 19–32. Washington, D.C.: Woodrow Wilson International Center for Scholars.

Kasinitz, Philip, John H Mollenkopf, Mary C. Waters, and Jennifer Holdaway. 2008. *Inheriting the City: The Children of Immigrants Come of Age*. Cambridge, Mass.: Harvard University Press.

Kniss, Fred, and Paul D. Numrich. 2007. *Sacred Assemblies and Civic Engagement: How Religion Matters for America's Newest Immigrants*. New Brunswick, N.J.: Rutgers University Press.

Koval, John P. 2004. "In Search of Economic Parity: The Mexican Labor Force in Chicago." *Interim Reports*. Notre Dame, Ind.: Institute for Latino Studies.

Krauze, Enrique. 2004. "Posdata a Huntington." *Letras Libres* (June): 30–31.

Lampking, Linda, and Stanley Waringo. 2003. "A Portrait of the Non-profit Sector in Illinois." Chicago: Donors Forum of Chicago and Urban Institute Center of Nonprofits and Philanthropy.

Landolt, Patricia. 2008. "The Transnational Geographies of Immigrant Politics: Insights from a Comparative Study of Migrant Grassroots Organizing." *Sociological Quarterly* 49(1): 53–77.

Landolt, Patricia, and Luin Goldring. 2009. "Immigrant Political Socialization as Bridging and Boundary Work: Mapping the Multi-layered Incorporation of Latin American Immigrants in Toronto." *Ethnic and Racial Studies* 32(7): 1226–1247.

Layton, Michael D. 2009. "Philanthropy and the Third Sector in Mexico: The Enabling Environment and Its Limitations." *Norteamérica* 4(1): 87–120.

Layton, Michael D., and Alejandro Moreno. 2010. *Filantropía y sociedad civil en México*. Mexico City: Miguel Ángel Porrúa-Instituto Tecnológico Autónomo de México.

Leal, David L., Byung-Jae Lee, and James A. McCann. 2012. "Transnational Absentee Voting in the 2006 Mexican Presidential Election: The Roots of Participation." *Electoral Studies* 31(3): 540–549.

Leco Tomás, Casimiro. 2009. *Migración Indígena a Estados Unidos: Purhépechas en Burnsville, Norte Carolina*. Morelia: Universidad Michoacana de San Nicolás de Hidalgo.

Lefebvre, Henri. 2006. *Writing on Cities*. Malden, Mass.: Blackwell.

Leiken, Robert S. 2002. "The Melting Border: Mexico and the Mexican Communities in the United States." Washington, D.C.: Center for Equal Opportunity.

Leroux, Kelly, and Holly T. Goerdel. 2009. "Political Advocacy by Nonprofit Organizations: A Strategic Management Explanation." *Public Performance & Management Review* 32(4): 514–536.

Levin, Rebekah, and Lise McKean. 2009. "Así Hacemos, Nuestra Perspectiva: Financial Status and Capacity-Building Needs of Latino Nonprofits in Metro Chicago." Chicago: University of Illinois at Chicago, College of Education.

Levitt, Peggy. 2001. *The Transnational Villagers*. Berkeley: University of California Press.

———. 2007. *God Needs No Passport: Immigrants and the Changing American Religious Landscape*. New York: New Press.

Levitt, Peggy, and Mary C. Waters, eds. 2002. *The Changing Face of Home: The Transnational Lives of the Second Generation*. New York: Russell Sage Foundation.

Light, Ivan. 2006. *Deflecting Immigration: Networks, Markets, and Regulation in Los Angeles*. New York: Rusell Sage Foundation.

Litwicki, Ellen M. 2004. "'Our Hearts Burn with Ardent Love for Two Countries': Ethnicity and Assimilation." In *We Are What We Celebrate: Understanding Holidays and Rituals*, edited by Amitai Etzioni and Jared Bloom, 213–246. New York: New York University Press.

Lomnitz, Claudio. 2001. *Deep Mexico, Silent Mexico: An Anthropology of Nationalism*. Minneapolis: University of Minnesota Press.

Lopez, Sarah Lynn. 2010. "The Remittance House: Architecture and Migration in Rural Mexico." *Building and Landscapes* 17(2): 33–52.

López Ángel, Gustavo. 2004. "Membresía e identidad en procesos migratorios translocales: La experiencia de la Asociación Micaltepecana." In *Clubes de migrantes oriundos mexicanos en los Estados Unidos: La política transnacional de la nueva sociedad civil migrante*, edited by Guillaume Lanly and M. Basilia Valenzuela V., 287–314. Guadalajara: Universidad de Guadalajara.

López Castro, Gustavo, ed. 2003. *Diáspora Michoacana*. Zamora: El Colegio de Michoacán.

López Guerra, Claudio. 2005. "Should Expatriates Vote?" *Journal of Political Philosophy* 13(2): 216–234.

López Zepeda, Leticia. 2011. "Educación, Formación y Capacitación Campesina: La Experiencia de ANEC." *La Jornada del Campo Online* 48, September 17, B1.

Lowrey, Annie. 2012. "An Increase in Barriers to Trade Is Reported." *New York Times*, June 23.

MacLeod, Dag. 2004. *Downsizing the State: Privatization and the Limits of Neoliberal Reform in Mexico*. University Park: Pennsylvania State University Press.

Mainwaring, Scott, and Alexander Wilde. 1989. *The Progressive Church in Latin America*. South Bend, Ind.: University of Notre Dame Press.

Martínez, Anne M. 2003. "Bordering on the Sacred: Religion, Nation, and the United States–Mexican Relations, 1910–1929." Ph.D. diss., University of Minnesota.

Massey, Douglas S., and Jorge Durand. 1995. *Miracles on the Border: Retablos of Mexican Migrants to the United States*. Tucson: University of Arizona Press.

Massey, Douglas S., Jorge Durand, and Nolan J. Malone. 2002. *Beyond Smoke and Mirrors: Mexican Immigration in an Era of Economic Integration*. New York: Russell Sage Foundation.

Matovina, Tim. 2011. *Latino Catholicism: Transformation in America's Largest Church*. Princeton, N.J.: Princeton University Press.

Mauss, Marcel. 1990. *The Gift: The Form and Reason for Exchange in Archaic Societies*. New York: W. W. Norton.

McCann, James A., Wayne Cornelius, and David Leal. 2009. "Mexico's Voto Remoto and the Potential for Transnational Civic Engagement among Mexican Expatriates." In *Consolidating Mexico's Democracy: The 2006 Presidential Campaign in Comparative Perspective*, edited by Jorge Dominguez, Chappell Lawson, and Alejandro Moreno, 89–108. Baltimore: Johns Hopkins University Press.

Merz, Barbara, ed. 2005. *New Patterns for Mexico: Observations on Remittances, Philanthropic Giving, and Equitable Development*. Cambridge, Mass.: Global Equity Initiative, Harvard University.

Migration News. 2007. "Mexico: Migrants, Emigration, Economy." 13(2).

Moctezuma Longoria, Miguel. 2011. *La Transnacionalidad de los Sujetos: Dimensiones, metodologías y prácticas convergentes de los migrantes en Estados Unidos*. Zacatecas: Universidad Autónoma de Zacatecas-Miguel Ángel Porrúa.

Molina Ramírez, Tania. 2005. "El difícil camino de la torre al invernadero: Atacheo, las remesas y los proyectos productivos." *Masiosare* 399. Online edition, August 14.

Monge Arévalo, Marco Antonio. 2005. *El Guerrero de allá . . . Los Guerrerenses Radicados en Chicago, Illinois*. Mexico City: Ediciones Titán.

Mooney, Margarita. 2009. *Faith Makes Us Live: Surviving and Thriving in the Haitian Diaspora*. Berkeley: University of California Press.

Mora-Torres, Juan. 2006. "'Me voy p'al norte (I'm Going North)': The Great Mexican Migration of 1890–1932." Unpublished manuscript.

Morawska, Ewa T. 1985. *For Bread with Butter: The Life-Worlds of East Central Europeans in Johnstown, Pennsylvania, 1890–1940*. Cambridge: Cambridge University Press.

———. 2001. "Migrants, Transnationalism, and Ethnicization: A Comparison of This Great Wave and the Last." In *E Pluribus Unum? Contemporary and Historical Perspectives on Migrant Incorporation*, edited by Gary Gerstle and John J. Mollenkopf, 175–212. New York: Russell Sage Foundation.

Moreno, Alejandro. 2005. *Nuestros valores: Los mexicanos en México y en Estados Unidos al inicio del siglo XXI*. Mexico City: División de Estudios Económicos y Sociopolíticos Grupo Financiero Banamex.

Motomura, Hiroshi. 1999. "Federalism, International Human Rights, and Immigration Exceptionalism." *University of Colorado Law Review* 70:1361–1394.

Moya, José C. 2005. "Immigrants and Associations: A Global and Historical Perspective." *Journal of Ethnic and Migration Studies* 31(5): 833–864.

Mulgan, Richard. 2003. *Holding Power to Account: Accountability in Modern Democracies*. Houndsmills, U.K.: Palgrave.

Navarro Chávez, José César Lenin, and Francisco Javier Ayvar Campos. 2010. "Las remesas en Michoacán y su impacto en la disitribución del ingreso, 2000–2008." In *Trasnacionalismo y Desarrollo en México*, edited by Jerjes Aguirre Ochoa and José César Lenin Navarro Chávez, 173–181. Morelia: Universidad Michoacana de San Nicolás de Hidalgo.

Ngai, Mae M. 2004. *Impossible Subjects: Illegal Aliens and the Making of Modern America*. Princeton, N.J.: Princeton University Press.

Nichols, Sandra L. 2006. *Santos, Duraznos, y Vino: Migrantes Mexicanos y la Transformación de los Haro, Zacatecas y Napa, California*. Mexico, D.F.: Miguel Ángel Porrúa.

Noboyuki, Otsuka, Maritza Vela, Sarah Almonte, Federico Torres, Alberto Bucardo, and María C. Landázury-Levy. 2001. "Capitalization of Remittances for Local Economic Development. Donors Memorandum." Washington, D.C.: Inter-American Development Bank Multilateral Investment Fund. http://idbdocs.iadb.org/wsdocs/getdocument .aspx?docnum=491750.

Ochoa Serrano, Álvaro, and Gerardo Sánchez Díaz. 2003. *Breve Historia de Michoacán*. Mexico City: El Colegio de México-Fondo de Cultura Económica.

Olmedo, Raúl. 1999. *El Poder Comunitario en Tlaxcala: Las Presidencias Municipales Auxiliares*. Mexico City: Secretaría de Gobernación.

Olvera, Alberto J. 2003. "Voice, Eyes, and Ears: Social Accountability in Latin America." Punta Cana: World Bank.

———. 2010a. "The Elusive Democracy: Political Parties, Democratic Institutions, and Civil Society in Mexico." *Latin American Research Review* 45:78–107.

———, ed. 2010b. *La Democratización Frustrada: Limitaciones Institucionales y Colonización Política de las Instituciones Garantes de Derechos y de Participación Ciudadana en México*. Mexico: CIESAS-Universidad Veracruzana.

Orozco, Manuel. 2000. "Latino Hometown Associations as Agents of Development in Latin America." Washington, D.C.: Inter-American Dialogue and the Tomás Rivera Policy Institute. http://www.thedialogue.org/PublicationFiles/Orozco%20Assoc%20-%20HTAs.pdf.

———. 2003. "Worker Remittances in an International Scope." Washington, D.C.: Inter-American Dialogue.

Orozco, Manuel, and Michel Lapointe. 2004. "Mexican Hometown Associations and Their Development Opportunities." *Journal of International Affairs* 57(2): 31–51.

Orozco, Manuel, and Katherine Scaife Diaz. 2011. "Partnerships at Work: Western Union's 4+1 Experience in Mexico." Washington, D.C.: Inter-American Dialogue.

Orozco, Manuel, and Katherine Welle. 2005. "Hometown Associations and Development: Ownership, Correspondence, Sustainability, and Replicability." In *New Patterns for Mexico: Observations on Remittances, Philanthropic Giving, and Equitable Development*, edited by Barbara J. Merz, 157–179. Cambridge, Mass.: Global Equity Initiative, Harvard University.

Orozco, Manuel, and Steven R. Wilson. 2005. "Making Migrant Remittances Count." In *Beyond Small Change: Making Migrant Remittances Count*, edited by Donald F. Terry and Steven R. Wilson, 375–394. Washington, D.C.: Inter-American Development Bank.

Ortega Ramírez, Adriana Sletza. 2011. "Políticas migratorias sub-nacionales en México: Evaluación de las oficinas estatales de atención a migrantes." Unpublished manuscripts, Benemérita Universidad Autónoma de Puebla.

Otero, Gerardo. 1999. *Farewell to the Peasantry? Political Class Formation in Rural Mexico*. Boulder, Colo.: Westview Press.

Pallares, Amalia. 2010. "The Chicago Context." In *¡Marcha! Latino Chicago and the Immigrant Rights Movement*, edited by Amalia Pallares and Nilda Flores González, 37–61. Urbana: University of Illinois Press.

Pallares, Amalia, and Nilda Flores González, eds. 2010. *¡Marcha! Latino Chicago and the Immigrant Rights Movement*. Urbana: University of Illinois Press.

Palmer, Susan L. 2005. "Community-Building Experiences of Mexicans in Aurora, Illinois, 1915–1935." *Journal of the Illinois State Historical Society* 98(3): 125–143.

Pantoja, Adrian D., and Sarah Allen Gershon. 2006. "Political Orientations and Naturalization among Latino and Latina Immigrants." *Social Science Quarterly* 87(5): 247–263.

Papail, Jean. 2005. "Remesas e inversiones de los migrantes de retorno en el centro-occidente de México." In *Contribuciones al análisis de la migración internacional y el desarrollo regional en México*, edited by Raúl Delgado Wise and Beatrice Knerr, 319–332. Zacatecas: Universidad Autónoma de Zacatecas-Miguel Ángel Porrúa.

Papail, Jean, and Fermina Robles. 2009. "Formación de negocios entre los migrantes internacionales de retorno en ciudades medias." In *Empresarios migrantes mexicanos en*

Estados Unidos, edited by M. Basilia Valenzuela V. and Margarita Calleja Pinedo, 271–306. Guadalajara: Universidad de Guadalajara.

Paral, Rob. 2006. "Latinos of the New Chicago." In *The New Chicago: A Social and Cultural Analysis*, edited by John P. Koval, Larry Bennett, Michael I. J. Bennett, Fassil Demissie, Roberta Garner, and Kiljoong Kim, 105–114. Philadelphia: Temple University Press.

Partnership for Prosperity Executive Group. 2002. "Partnership for Prosperity. Executive Summary and Action Plan." Unpublished manuscript.

Passel, Jeffrey S., and D'Vera Cohn. 2009. "A Portrait of Unauthorized Immigrants in the United States." Washington, D.C.: Pew Hispanic Center.

Pear, Robert. 2007. "Little-Known Group Claims a Win on Immigration." *New York Times*, July 15.

Peña, Elaine. 2011. *Performing Piety: Making Space Sacred with the Virgin of Guadalupe*. Berkeley: University of California Press.

Pérez, Gina M. 2006. "How a Scholarship Girl Becomes a Soldier: The Militarization of Latina/o Youth in Chicago Public Schools." *Identities: Global Studies in Culture and Power* 13:53–72.

Pérez-Armendáriz, Clarisa, and David Crow. 2010. "Do Migrants Remit Democracy? International Migration, Political Beliefs, and Behavior in Mexico." *Comparative Political Studies* 43(1): 119–148.

Pescador, Juan J. 2004. "¡Vamos Taximaroa! Mexican/Chicano Soccer Associations and Transnational/Translocal Communities, 1967–2002." *Latino Studies* 2(3): 352–376.

Pfutze, Tobias 2012. "Does Migration Promote Democratization? Evidence from the Mexican Transition." *Journal of Comparative Economics* 40(2): 159–175.

———. 2013. "Clientelism versus Social Learning: The Electoral Effects of International Migration." *International Studies Quarterly* 1(13): 1–13.

Pierre-Louis, François Jr. 2006. *Haitians in New York City: Transnationalism and Hometown Associations*. Tallahassee: University Press of Florida.

Piña, Francisco. 2006. "La Casa Michoacán: Una herramienta del movimiento inmigrante en Chicago." *Presencia Michoacana en el Medio Oeste 2006*, 22–24. Chicago: Federación de Clubes Michoacanos en Illinois.

Portes, Alejandro. 2007. "Migration, Development, and Segmented Assimilation: A Conceptual Review of the Evidence." *Annals of the American Academy of Political and Social Sciences* 610:270–272.

———. 2009. "Migration and Development: Reconciling Opposite Views." *Ethnic and Racial Studies* 32(1): 5–22.

Portes, Alejandro, Cristina Escobar, and Renelina Arana. 2009. "Divided or Convergent Loyalties? The Political Incorporation Process of Latin American Immigrants in the United States." *International Journal of Comparative Sociology* 50(2): 103–136.

Portes, Alejandro, Cristina Escobar, and Alexandria Walton Radford. 2006. "Organizaciones transnacionales de inmigrantes y desarrollo: Un estudio comparativo." *Migración y Desarrollo* 6:3–44.

———. 2007. "Immigrant Transnational Organizations and Development: A Comparative Study." *International Migration Review* 41(1): 242–281.

Pries, Ludger. 2008. "Transnational Societal Spaces: Which Units of Analysis, Reference, and Measurement?" In *Rethinking Transnationalism: The Meso-link of Organisations*, edited by Ludger Pries, 1–20. London: Routledge.

Pulido, Laura. 2006. *Black, Brown, Yellow, and Left: Radical Activism in Los Angeles*. Berkeley: University of California Press.

Purcell, Mark. 2003. "Citizenship and the Right to the Global City." *International Journal of Urban and Regional Research* 27(3): 564–590.

Putnam, Robert D. 1996. "The Strange Dissappearance of Civic America." *American Prospect* 7(24): 34–48.

———. 2000. *Bowling Alone: The Collapse and Revival of American Community.* New York: Simon and Schuster.

———. 2007. "E Pluribus Unum: Diversity and Community in the Twenty-First Century." The 2006 Johan Skytte Prize Lecture. *Scandinavian Political Studies* 30(2): 137–174.

Quiñones, Sam. 2007. *Antonio's Gun and Delfino's Dream: True Tales of Mexican Migration.* Albuquerque: University of New Mexico Press.

Ramakrishnan, Karthick S., and Irene Bloemraad, eds. 2008. *Civic Hopes and Political Realities: Immigrants, Community Organizations, and Political Engagement.* New York: Russell Sage Foundation.

Ramakrishnan, S. Karthick, and Celia Viramontes. 2010. "Civic Spaces: Mexican Hometown Associations and Immigrant Participation." *Journal of Social Issues* 66(1): 155–173.

Ramírez, Leonard G. 2011. "Second City Mexicans." In *Chicanas of 18th Street,* edited by Leonard G. Ramírez, 1–16. Urbana: University of Illinois Press.

Ramírez, Ricardo, and Adrián Félix. 2011. "Transnational Stakeholders: Latin American Migrant Transnationalism and Civic Engagement in the United States." *Harvard Journal of Hispanic Policy* 23:59–82.

Ready, Timothy, Roger Knight, and Sung-Chan Chun. 2006. "Latino Civic and Community Involvement: Findings from the Chicago-Area Survey." In *Latino Research @ ND.* Notre Dame, Ind.: Institute for Latino Studies, University of Notre Dame.

Reames, Ben, and Melissa Lynott. n.d. "Involving Citizens in Public Budgets: Mechanisms for Transparent and Participatory Budgeting." Washington, D.C.: U.S. Agency for International Development.

Redacción. 1999. "Visita Tinoco Rubí a Michoacanos en Chicago." *Éxito,* 8. *Chicago Tribune,* September 16.

———. 2010. "Un cuarto de siglo de Chicago Católico." Suplemento Especial. *Chicago Católico,* 2A. Chicago: Arquidiócesis de Chicago.

———. 2011. "Abuelitos reciben visa especial." *Nuevo Siglo.* Online edition, August 12

Red Internacional de Migración y Desarrollo. 2005. "Declaración de Cuernavaca." *Migración y Desarrollo* 4(1): 1–7.

Renshon, Stanley A. 2005. *The 50% American: Immigration and National Identity in an Age of Terror.* Washington, D.C.: Georgetown University Press.

Reynoso Acosta, Eneida. 2009. "Nueva modalidad del programa 3X1: Inversión en fortalecimiento patrimonial." In *Presencia Michoacana en el Medio Oeste 2009,* 94–95. Chicago: Federación de Clubes Michoacanos en Illinois.

Riesman, David, Nathan Glazer, and Reuel Denney. 1950. *The Lonely Crowd: A Study of the Changing American Character.* New York: Doubleday Anchor Books.

Rivera Sánchez, Liliana. 2004. "Expressions of Identity and Belonging: Mexican Immigrants in New York." In *Indigenous Mexican Migrants in the United States,* edited by Jonathan Fox and Gaspar Rivera-Salgado, 417–448. San Diego: Center for U.S.-Mexican Studies.

———. 2005. "Religious Institutions, Actors and Practices: The Construction of Transnational Migrant Organizations and Public Spaces between Mexico and the United States." Paper presented at the workshop on Mexican Migrant Civic and Political Participation, November 4–5. Washington, D.C.: Woodrow Wilson International Center for Scholars. http://www.wilsoncenter.org/sites/default/files/Rivera%20-%20Religious %20Institutions%20Actors%20%26%20Practices.pdf.

Rodríguez Ramírez, Héctor. 2003. "Migración Internacional y Remesas en Michoacán." In *Diáspora Michoacana*, edited by Gustavo López Castro, 195–221. Zamora: El Colegio de Michoacán-Gobierno del Estado de Michoacán.

Rosales, Francisco A. 1978. "Mexican Immigration to the Urban Midwest during the 1920s." Ph.D. diss., Indiana University.

Rosenthal, Elizabeth. 2011. "Used Batteries from U.S. Expose Mexicans to Risk." *New York Times*, December 9, A1.

Rosenzweig, Roy, and David Thelen. 1998. *The Presence of the Past: Popular Uses of History in American Life*. New York: Columbia University Press.

Rouse, Roger. 1992. "Making Sense of Settlement: Class Transformation, Cultural Struggle, and Transnationalism among Mexican Migrants in the United States." *Annals of the New York Academy of Sciences* 645(1): 25–52.

Ruiz-Durán, Clemente. 2004. "Integración de los mercados laborales en América del Norte." Mexico City: Instituto de Estudios del Trabajo.

Sada Solana, Carlos Manuel. 2006. "El 3X1 en el Contexto de las Comunidades Mexicanas." In *El Programa 3X1 para Migrantes, primera política transnacional en México?*, edited by Rafael Fernández de Castro, Rodolfo García Zamora, and Ana Vila Freyer, 21–44. Mexico City: Instituto Tecnológico Autónomo de México, Universidad Autónoma de Zacatecas, Miguel Ángel Porrúa.

Salazar, Miguel R., and Eric L. Olson. 2011. "A Profile of Mexico's Major Organized Crime Groups." Washington, D.C.: Woodrow Wilson International Center for Scholars.

Santamaría Gómez, Arturo. 2001. *Mexicanos en Estados Unidos: La Nación, la Política y el Voto sin Fronteras*. Mexico: Universidad Autónoma de Sinaloa/PRD.

Santibáñez Romellón, Jorge. 2004a. "Marines y un nacionalismo trasnochado." *La Jornada Online*, July 12.

———. 2004b. "Marines y un nacionalismo trasnochado: réplica." *La Jornada Online*, July 24.

Scott, James C. 1985. *Weapons of the Weak: Everyday Forms of Peasant Resistance*. New Haven, Conn.: Yale University Press.

———. 1998. *Seeing Like a State: How Certain Schemes to Improve the Human Condition Have Failed*. New Haven, Conn.: Yale University Press.

Scott, Lindy. 1999. "La conversión de inmigrantes mexicanos al protestantismo en Chicago." In *Fronteras Fragmentadas*, edited by Gail Mummert, 405–420. Zamora: El Colegio de Michoacán.

Secretaría de Desarrollo Social. 2005a. "Programa de Fortalecimiento Comunitario." Paper presented at the Quinto Foro Binacional del Migrante Michoacano, Morelia.

———. 2005b. "Organizaciones de la Sociedad Civil en Michoacán." Michoacán: Gobierno del Estado de Michoacán de Ocampo. Unpublished manuscript.

———. 2010a. "Cuadro de Inversiones del Programa 3X1 para Migrantes 2002–2010 en el Estado de Michoacán." Morelia: Delegación Michoacán de la Coordinación Estatal de Microrregiones.

———. 2010b. "Relación de Obras Del Programa 3X1 para Migrantes." Morelia: Delegación Michoacán de la Coordinación Estatal de Microrregiones.

———. 2012. "Memoria del Programa 3X1 para Migrantes 2007–2012." México D.F.: Unidad de Microrregiones de la Secretaría de Desarrollo Social.

———. 2013. "Acuerdo por el que se emiten las Reglas de Operación del Programa 3x1 para Migrantes para el ejercicio fiscal 2013." Press release, February 28. Mexico City: Secretaría de Desarrollo Social.

Secretaría de la Función Pública. 2006. "Encuesta de Opinión al Programa 3X1 para Migrantes. Beneficiarios."

Secretaría de Política Social. 2010. "Impartirán Taller a Organizaciones de la Sociedad Civil." Press release, September 24. Morelia: Comunicados de Dependencias del Gobierno del Estado de Michoacán de Ocampo.

SEDESOL. 2005. "Iniciativa Ciudadana 3X1 Michoacán 2002–2004: Approved and Rejected Projects Dataset." Morelia: Delegación Michoacán de la Secretaría de Desarrollo Social.

———. 2006. "Programa 3X1 para Migrantes: Libro Blanco 2002–2006." México D.F.: Secretaría de Desarrollo Social.

———. 2010a. "Cuadro de Inversiones del Programa 3X1 para Migrantes 2002–2010 en el Estado de Michoacán." Morelia: Delegación Michoacán de la Secretaría de Desarrollo Social. Coordinación Estatal de Microrregiones.

———. 2010b. "Programa 3X1 para Migrantes: Annual Databases 2002–2010." México, D.F.: Unidad de Microrregiones.

Seelke, Clare. 2009. "Mérida Initiative for Mexico and Central America: Funding and Policy Issues." Washington, D.C.: Congressional Research Service.

Segura, Lorena. 2011. "¿Por qué no se ahorra en México?" Hoy, 12, December 13.

Selee, Andrew. 2011. Decentralization, Democratization, and Informal Power in Mexico. University Park: Pennsylvania State University Press.

Servicios Profesionales para el Desarrollo Económico. 2005. "Evaluación Externa del Programa Iniciativa Ciudadana 3X1. 2004." México, D.F.: Secretaría de Desarrollo Social.

Shah, Seema, Reina Mukal, and Grace McAllister. 2011. "Foundation Funding for Hispanics/Latinos in the United States and for Latin America." Chicago: Foundation Center and Hispanics in Philanthropy.

Sherman, Rachel. 1999. "From State Introversion to State Extension in Mexico: Modes of Emigrant Incorporation, 1900–1997." Theory and Society 28(6): 835–878.

Siarto, Kristin M., and Helga Leitner. 2010. "Immigrants Riding for Justice: Space-time and Emotions in the Construction of a Counterpublic." Political Geography 29(7): 357–412.

Singer, Audrey, and Greta Gilbertson. 2003. "'The Blue Passport': Gender and the Social Process of Naturalization among Dominican Immigrants." In Gender and U.S. Immigration: Contemporary Trends, edited by Pierette Hondagneu-Sotelo, 359–378. Berkeley: University of California Press.

Sites, William, and Rebecca Vonderlack Navarro. 2012. "Tipping the Scale: State Rescaling and the Strange Odyssey of Chicago's Mexican Hometown Associations." In Remaking Urban Citizenship. Organizations, Institutions, and the Right to the City, edited by Michael Peter Smith and Michael McQuarrie, 151–172. New Brunswick, N.J.: Transaction Publishers.

Slayton, Robert A. 1988. Back of the Yards: The Making of a Local Democracy. Chicago: University of Chicago Press.

Smith, Graham. 2009. Democratic Innovations: Designing Institutions for Citizen Participation. Cambridge: Cambridge University Press.

Smith, Michael Peter, and Matt Bakker. 2008. Citizenship Across Borders: The Political Transnationalism of El Migrante. Ithaca, N.Y.: Cornell University Press.

Smith, Michael Peter, and Luis E. Guarnizo. 2009. "Global Mobility, Shifting Borders, and Global Citizenship." Tijdschrift voor Economische en Sociale Geografie 100(5): 610–622.

Smith, Robert C. 2001. "Comparing Local-Level Swedish and Mexican Transnational Life: An Essay in Historical Retrieval." In *New Transnational Social Spaces: International Migration and Transnational Companies in the Early Twenty-First Century*, edited by Ludger Pries, 37–58. London: Routledge.

———. 2002. "Social Location, Generation and Life Course as Social Processes Shaping Second Generation Transnational Life." In *The Changing Face of Home*, edited by Peggy Levitt and Mary C. Waters, 145–168. New York: Russell Sage Foundation.

———. 2003. "Migrant Membership as an Instituted Process; Transnationalization, the State, and the Extra-territorial Conduct of Mexican Politics." *International Migration Review* 37(2): 297–343.

———. 2006. *Mexican New York: Transnational Lives of New Immigrants*. Berkeley: University of California Press.

Somerville, Will, Jamie Durana, and Aaron Matteo Terrazas. 2008. "Hometown Associations: An Untapped Resource for Immigrant Integration?" *Insight*, July. Washington, D.C.: Migration Policy Institute.

State of Ilinois Trade Mission. 2013. "Illinois-Mexico Business Strength in Numbers." Mexico City office press release, April 3–6. Springfield: Illinois Department of Commerce and Economic Opportunity.

Stephen, Lynn. 2007. *Transborder Lives: Indigeneous Oaxacans in Mexico, California, and Oregon*. Durham, N.C.: Duke University Press.

Suárez, Blanca, and Emma Zapata Martelo, eds. 2007. *Ilusiones, Sacrificios y Resultados*. Mexico City: Grupo Interdisciplinario sobre Mujer, Pobreza y Trabajo, A.C.

Suárez, Víctor. 2011. "El campesinado sin cabeza: Por un referente campesino nacional autónomo y de izquierda." *La Jornada del Campo Online* 48, September 17.

Sulski, Jim. 1980. "Mexican Groups Form Federation." *Daily Calumet, America's Oldest Community Daily Newspaper*, August 1.

Suro, Roberto. 2005. "Mexican Migrant Worker Survey." Washington, D.C.: Pew Hispanic Center, University of Southern California, and Instituto de los Mexicanos en el Exterior.

Tépach Marcial, Reyes. 2011. "Las Participaciones y Aportaciones Federales pagadas y estimadas para las Entidades Federativas de México, enero–diciembre, 2009–2010." México, D.F.: Dirección de Servicios de Investigación y Análisis. LXI Legislatura, Cámara de Diputados.

Terry, Donald F., and Gregory Pedrodv. 2006. "Las remesas como instrumento de desarrollo." Washington, D.C.: Inter-American Development Bank/Multilateral Investment Fund (MIF).

Thelen, David. 1999. "Rethinking History and the Nation-State: Mexico and the United States." *Journal of American History* 86(2): 439–452.

Thomas, William I., and Florian Znaniecki. 1927. *The Polish Peasant in Europe and America*. New York: Alfred A. Knopf.

Tijerina, Edmund S. 1992. "Departing Consul Put People First." *Chicago Tribune Online*, June 25.

Torres, María de los Ángeles. 2004. "In Search of Meaningful Voice and Place: The IPO and Latino Community Empowerment in Chicago." In *La Causa: Civil Rights, Social Justice, and the Struggle for Equality in the Midwest*, edited by Gilberto Cardenas, 81–106. Houston: Arte Público Press.

Torres Delgado, Sergio. 2010. "Denuncia PRI sesgo electoral y clientelar de los programas sociales en Michoacán." *Cambio de Michoacán*, June 14. Morelia.

Trejo, Guillermo. 2012. *Popular Movements in Autocracies: Religion, Repression, and Indigenous Collective Action in Mexico*. Cambridge: Cambridge University Press.

Tuan, Yi-Fu. 1974. *Topophilia: A Study of Environmental Perception, Attitudes, and Values.* Englewood Cliffs, N.J.: Prentice-Hall.

Tuirán, Rodolfo, Jorge Santibañez, and Rodolfo Corona. 2006. "El monto de las remesas familiares en México: ¿Mito o realidad?" *Papeles de Población* 50 (October–December): 147–169.

Tyburski, Michael D. 2012. "The Resource Curse Reversed? Remittances and Corruption in Mexico." *International Studies Quarterly* 56 (2): 339–350.

UNDP. 2008. "Informe Sobre Desarrollo Humano, Michoacán." Mexico City: United Nations Development Programme.

United for a Fair Economy. 2007. "Western Union Pressured on Excessive Remittance Fees." *Fair Play: The Newsletter of United for a Fair Economy* (Summer).

USAID. 2011. "Partnering with USAID: Building Alliances for Sustainable Solutions." Washington, D.C.: U.S. Agency for International Development.

U.S. Census Bureau. 2009. "Table C05007. Place of Birth by Year of Entry by Citizenship Status for the Foreign Born Population." Washington, D.C.: U.S. Census Bureau.

———. 2010. "American Community Survey." Washington, D.C.: U.S. Census Bureau.

U.S. Department of Homeland Security. 2005. "Mexican Legal Permanent Residents (LPRs) by State and County of Intended Residence, Fiscal Year Granted LPR Status, 1985 to 1999 and Naturalization Status by 2004." Washington, D.C.: Office of Immigration Statistics.

———. 2009. "Persons Naturalized during Fiscal Years 2005, 2006, 2007, and 2008 by Core Based Statistical Area (CBSA) of Residence and Selected Characteristics." Washington, D.C.: Office of Immigration Statistics.

Valdés, Dionicio Nodín. 2000. *Barrios Norteños: St. Paul and Midwesterner Mexican Communities in the Twentieth Century.* Austin: University of Texas Press.

Vargas, Jorge A. 1998. "Dual Nationality for Mexicans." *San Diego Law Review* 35 (August): 823–853.

Varsanyi, Monica W., ed. 2010. *Taking Local Control: Immigration Policy Activism in U.S. Cities and States.* Stanford, Calif.: Stanford University Press.

Velázquez Flores, Rafael, and Adriana Sletza Ortega Ramírez. 2010. "Políticas públicas de los gobiernos subnacionales de México en asuntos de migración." In *Perspectivas Migratorias: Un análisis Interdisciplinario de la Migración Internacional,* edited by Jorge Durand and Jorge A. Schiavon, 493–597. Mexico City: Centro de Investigación y Docencia Económicas, A.C.

Vélez-Ibáñez, Carlos G. 2010. *An Impossible Living in a Transborder World: Culture, Confianza, and Economy of Mexican-Origin Populations.* Tucson: University of Arizona Press.

Veltmeyer, Henry. 2011. "The Politics of Language: Deconstructing the Discourse of Post-development." *Canadian Journal of Development Studies* 22(3): 597–620.

Voces Mesoamericanas. 2010. "Relatoría." Conference Proceedings of the *Encuentro Mesoamericano Sobre Desarrollo y Migración.* Cuernavaca, Morelos, September 29–October 1. San Cristóbal de las Casas, Chiapas: Voces Mesoamericanas. Acción con pueblos migrantes.

Voss, Kim, and Irene Bloemraad, eds. 2011. *Rallying for Immigrant Rights.* Berkeley: University of California Press.

Wainer, Andrew. 2011. "Development and Migration in Rural Mexico." Briefing Paper 11 (January). Washington, D.C.: Bread for the World Institute. http://www.bread.org/institute/papers/briefing-paper-11.pdf.

Waldinger, Roger. 2007. "Between Here and There: How Attached Are Latino Immigrants to Their Native Country?" Washington, D.C.: Pew Hispanic Center.

Waldinger, Roger, and David Fitzgerald. 2004. "Transnationalism in Question." *American Journal of Sociology* 109(5): 1177–1195.

Wali, Alaka, Noshir Contractor, and Rebecca Severson. 2006. *Creative Networks: Mexican Immigrant Assets in Chicago*. Chicago: Field Museum.

Wiest, Raymond E. 1973. "Wage-Labor Migration and the Household in a Mexican Town." *Journal of Anthropological Research* 29(3): 180–209.

Williams, Philip J., Timothy J. Steigenga, and Manuel A. Vásquez, eds. 2009. *A Place to Be: Brazilian, Guatemalan, and Mexican Immigrants in Florida's New Destinations*. New Brunswick, N.J.: Rutgers University Press.

Wilson, William Julius. 1999. *The Bridge Over the Racial Divide: Rising Inequality and Coalition Politics*. Berkeley: University of California Press.

Wines, Michael. 2013. "Monarch Migration Plunges to Lowest Level in Decades." *New York Times*, March 15.

Wolf, Eric. 1957. "Closed-Corporate Communities in Mesoamerica and Java." *Southwestern Journal of Anthropology* 13(1): 1–18.

Wong, Janelle S. 2006. *Democracy's Promise. Immigrants and American Civic Institutions*. Ann Arbor: University of Michigan Press.

Wucker, Michele. 2006. "Becoming American." In *Lockout: Why America Keeps Getting Immigration Wrong When Our Prosperity Depends on Getting It Right*, 47–68. New York: Public Affairs Press.

Yanún, Alejandro. 2011. "Tarascos y Mónaco se destacan en la Liga Mexicana." *Hoy*, 40–41, December 13.

Ybarra-Frausto, Tomás. 2006. "Immigrant Imaginations and Imaginaries." In *Caras Vemos, Corazones no Sabemos: Faces Seen, Hearts Unknown, The Human Landscape of Mexican Migration*, edited by Amelia Magalamba-Ansótegui, 6–13. Notre Dame, Ind.: Snite Museum, Institute of Latino Studies, University of Notre Dame.

Zamudio Grave, Patricia. 2009. *Rancheros en Chicago: Vida y conciencia en una historia de migrantes*. Mexico City: Universidad Autónoma de Zacatecas-Miguel Ángel Porrúa.

Zendejas Romero, Juan Sergio. 2003. *Política local y formación del Estado: Procesos históricos de formación de espacios y sujetos sociales en un municipio rural mexicano, 1914–1998*. Wageningen: Wageningen Universiteit.

Zepeda Patterson, Jorge. 1988. *Michoacán: Sociedad, Economía, Política y Cultura*. Mexico City: Universidad Nacional Autónoma de México.

Zúñiga Herrera, Elena. 2004. "Notas demográficas del Estado de Michoacán." Paper presented at the *Ceremonia conmemorativa del 20 aniversario del Consejo Estatal de Población*, June 15. Morelia: Consejo Nacional de Población.

INDEX

absentee voting rights, 11, 24–25, 88, 90, 136, 148, 155–156, 159–160
Abuelita (Grandmother) Visa Program, 157–158
accountability, 110–114
Acevedo, Edward, 146
active organizations, 75
Acuña, Rodolfo, 153
Advisory Commission on Latino Affairs, 14–15
A-Front. See Anti-Imperialist Popular Front
agricultural development projects, 96, 100–102
agriculture, 55, 57, 105–106, 178n30
Alemán, Miguel, 36
Alinsky, Saul, 13
"alternative modernities," 83
American Legion, 43
Anaya, Alfredo, 90
Anderson, Benedict, 34
Anguiano, José, 30, 41
Anti-Imperialist Popular Front (A-Front), 37–39, 168n22
Arango, Carlos, 25
ARISE Chicago, 1
armed forces, migrants in U.S., 164n4
Armijos Suárez, Julio, 70
Arredondo, Gabriela, 29, 40
Arreola, Artemio, 54–55
Arroyo, Gonzalo, 47
assimilation, 39, 44, 138
Association of Community Organizations for Reform Now (ACORN), 146
Association of Social Enterprises (Asociación Michoacana de Promotores de Empresa Social, A.C.), 102

Atacheo de Regalado, 100–102
Azteca Lions Ladies Auxiliary, 45

Badillo, David, 172n50
Bakker, Matt, 6, 54
Balleño, Salvador, 46, 72, 144, 182n12
Banco de México, 9, 83, 175n3
Bartra, Armando, 82
beautification projects, 99, 125, 155
Benito Juárez High School, 25, 147
Benito Juárez Society, 31–32, 35, 36, 38, 41
bilingualism, 183n13
binational agendas of Mexican organizations, 48, 140, 142, 161
Binational Forum of Michoacán Migrants, 2, 22, 91
Binational Front of Indigenous Organizations, 8
binational governing bureaucracies, 77
block clubs, 66, 80, 137, 144
Black Friday celebration (Good Weekend), 76, 174n78
Border Protection, Anti-Terrorism, and Illegal Immigration Control Act (United States, 2005), x, 138, 146, 155, 156
Bourdieu, Pierre, 69, 71, 173n61
Bracero Agreements, Bracero Program (1942–1964), 33, 35, 44, 46, 58, 59, 61, 67, 168n16
budget deficits, 115
Burawoy, Michael, 22
Bush, George W., 10, 93
Byrnes, Dolores, 10

Çağlar, Ayşe, 141, 182n5, 183n14
Calderón, Felipe, 165

Calderón Hinojosa, Juan Luis, 58
campanilismo, 27
Canales, Alejandro, 84
Candelaria's Day celebration, 76
CAPS. *See* Chicago Alternative Police
  System
Cárdenas Batel, Lázaro, 2, 90–91
Cárdenas Solórzano, Cuauhtémoc, 25, 88
Cardinal's Committee for the Spanish
  Speaking, 43
Carmona, Yanitza, 79–80
Casa Aztlán, 13
Casa Michoacán, 5, 16, 70, 90, 136, 145,
  146, 166n28, 183n19
Castañeda, Jorge, 163n3
Catholic Church, 17–18, 37, 69–70,
  166n34, 172n50, 173n56; Latino volun-
  teering in church activities, 17
Ceja, José, 68
celebrations, 76, 77–78
CEMEX, 176n19
Center for Autonomous Social Action—
  General Brotherhood of Workers
  (CASA-HGT), 14
Centro Sin Fronteras, 146
Čermák, Antonín Josef, 15
Cerrito del Tepeyac (Des Plaines, Illinois),
  18, 136
César Chávez Community College (Los
  Angeles), 2
Chacón, Oscar, 56, 148
charitable projects and HTAs, 75
Chávez, Rubén, 72
Chavinda (municipality), 124
Chicago: as city of diversity, 143; civic
  participation of migrants in, 139–140;
  economic opportunities in, 59–62; HTAs
  in, 5–6, 19–21, 45–50, 51–52, 140, 141;
  immigrant incorporation in, 75–77,
  142–143; manufacturing sector in, 59;
  Mexican American identity in, 25–26;
  Mexican American population in, 47;
  Mexican consulate service area, 16; Mexican migrant organizations in, 8–9, 13–
  15; Mexican migrant population in, 3,
  26–27, 33, 40, 164n5; Mexican religious
  associations in, 37; Mexican schools in,
  38; Mexico City as sister city, 15; Michoacán migrants in, 21; naturalization rates
  in, 13, 173n68; religion in, 17–18, 37, 69–
  70; social condition of Mexican laborers
  in, 28; subnational governments in, 19;
  Third City period, 139–140; ties with
  Mexican diaspora, 87–92; as welcoming
  city, 150, 160. *See also* Illinois

Chicago Alternative Police System (CAPS),
  144, 182n11
Chicago Community Trust, 6, 14, 169n39
Chicago Cultural Alliance, 182n9
Chicago Latin American Soccer Associa-
  tion (CLASA), 47
Chicago Mexican Lion's Club, 45
Chicago Religious Task Force on Central
  America, 15
Chicano clubs, 44–45
Children's Day celebration, 76
Christian and Missionary Alliance, 144
Christian Base Communities, 18, 54,
  166n33
churches, 17, 69, 144. *See also* Catholic
  Church
church renovations, 19, 118
Ciclistas S.A.C., 43
citizenship: concept of, 153–154; divided
  meanings of, 140–141; extraterritorial,
  xii, 109–110; as market membership,
  84, 111, 130, 180n4; participatory, 84;
  pluridimensional, multiscalar, and fluid,
  159; reconfiguration of, 159
citizenship, Ecuadorian, 136
Ciudad Hidalgo (city), 1–2, 64, 67; marching band, 67
civic binationality, 7, 51–52, 138
civic engagement, 2–3, 137–138, 139–
  140, 141, 144; dual, 138; networks,
  141–142
civil cargo systems, 172n36
Civil Society Days (Global Forum on
  Migration and Development), 150, 151,
  184n25
civil society organizations, 20; disappearance of, 128; future of, 161; Mexican
  consulates and establishment of, 39;
  numbers of, 167n41; visibility of, 19–21,
  145–146, 151
clientelism, 117, 119, 126, 129
Club 30, 42
Club Chehuayo Grande, 57, 97
Club Deportivo Taximaroa, 47, 67
clubes de oriundos, 5, 63
Club Francisco Villa, xvi, 72, 77
Club Indaparapeo, 104–105
Club La Purísima, 144
Club Miguel Hidalgo, 42
Club Patriótico Mexicano, 45
Club San Luis Potosí, 47
Club San Miguel Epejan, 47
Club Santa Ana Maya, 96
Club Social Latinoamericano, 45
Club Uruapan, 18

Coalition of Mexican Migrant Organizations in the Midwest (COMMO), 184n23
CODECOs. *See* Community Development Committees
Cohen, Liz, 27
Comisiones Honoríficas (Honorary Commissions), 39–40
Comité Guanajuatense de Socorros (Guanajuato's Aid Committee), 33
Commission for Migrant Affairs, 89
Community Development Committees (CODECOs), 112, 128–134, *129, 131*
community development projects, 8, 11–12, 82, 92, 110–111, *122–123*
Confederation of Mexican Federations (CONFEMEX), 20, 50, 81, 148, 150
Confederation of Mexican Societies of the United States of America (Confederación de Sociedades Mexicanas de los Estados Unidos de América), 29
CONFEMEX. *See* Confederation of Mexican Federations
Congress of Industrial Organizations (CIO), 40
Construmex, 92–93, 176n19
consulates, Mexican, 16, 29–30, 35, 39
Cook, Karen S., 159
Cook County (Illinois) Board of Commissioners, 15–16
COPLADEMUN (Planning Committee for Municipal Development), 120
Cornelius, Wayne, 156
Corona, Bert, 14
Corporación Sociedad Amigos Mutualistas, 35
corpse repatriation, 76, 124, 164n4
Correa, Manuel, 79
corruption, 87, 114–115, 180n11
COVAM. *See* Project Evaluation and Migrant Affairs Committee
Cristero War (1926–1929), 37
Crown newsletter, 42
Cuauhtémoc Society, 30–31, *32*, 41
"Cuernavaca Declaration" (2005), 11, 165n24
cultural pluralism, 47
culture, hybridization of, 78
culture, preservation of, 46, 74–79

Daley, Richard M., 4, 20, 140, 172n51
Daniel and Karen May Foundation, 104
Day of the Dead celebration, 76
decentralization of Mexico's foreign policy, 16
decision making, governmental, 111–113

"Declaración de Cuernavaca" (2005), 11, 165n24
de la Cruz, Anita, 60
de la Madrid Hurtado, Miguel, 61
de la Vega, Rosa, 61–62
Delay, Margo, 14
Department of Homeland Security, 15–16, 183n15
deportation drives, 40
devotional capital, 69, 70
Díaz, José, 96
Díaz, Juan, 38
DICONSA (state-sponsored rural store network), 54–55
DREAM Act (SB 2185) (Illinois, 2011), 16, 182n1
drug cartels, 165n25, 177n28
dual citizenship and women, 73–74
dual nationality, 50
Durango Unido, 16
Durkheim, Emile, 63

economic decentralization, 48
economic development, regional, 85
economic opportunities in Chicago, 59–62
economic recession (2008), 9
education, 37–38, 57, 61, 64, 97, 104–105, 169n38
Ejido La Labor (village), 100–102
electoral bias as source of project rejection, 118–119
Electoral Federal Institute (IFE), 136, 156
electoral rights. *See* absentee voting rights
empowered participatory governance, xii, 141
Enlaces América, xvii, 148–149
environmental protection, 96, 177n29
Escobar, Arturo, 7, 83
ethnic succession, 69
Express Workers Mutual Benefit Society, 31
extended incorporation, 49, 50

Fábregas Puig, Andrés, 47
faenas (voluntary communal work), 9, 65, 124, 126, 165n19
faith and solidarity, 68–71
Familia, La (drug cartel), 177n28
families in mutual aid societies, 29
family contacts, nonphysical, 75
Family Focus, 47
family remittance calculations, 9, 83–85, 98, 170n13, 175n3
FEDECMI. *See* Federation of Michoacán Clubs in Illinois

FEDEJAL (Federación Jalisciense del Medio Oeste), 47
Federal Electoral Institute (IFE), 136, 156
Federation of Mexican Organizations, 45
Federation of Michoacán Clubs in Illinois (FEDECMI), 62, 81, 89, 90, 115, 136, 151, 152, 153, 173n67; and Abuelita Visa Program, 157–158; approval of projects through, 118; bilingual annual magazine, 145; bylaws of, 171n34; and civic engagement, 4–5; and monarch butterflies, 76–77; motto of, 14; and women, 72–73
Firebaugh, Glenn, 174n75
First Latin American Community Migrant Summit (2006), 22, 150, 165n25
First World Social Forum on Migration (2005), 149
Flores, John H., 38
flower-growing project, 101
Ford Foundation, 104, 148
4x1 matching fund programs, 103, 179n38
Fox, Vicente, 10, 19, 89, 92, 93–94, 95, 163n3 (chap. 1), 176n13
Francisco Villa (village), 72
Fraser, Nancy, 140, 160–161
FREBIMICH (Michoacán Binational Front), 5
Front (Mexican Popular Front), 37–38, 168n24
Fundamex, 10
funding of migrant organizations, 151–153, 184n28
fund-raising, 97, 112–113
funerals, 76, 164n4

Gamio, Manuel, 59
García, Jesús, 16, 30
García Canclini, Néstor, 78
García Navarro, Lourdes, 165n25
gentrification processes, 143
GFMD. See Global Forum on Migration and Development
Giddens, Anthony, 63
gift giving, 65
Global Forum on Migration and Development (GFMD), 150, 184n25
globalization, technologies of, 63
González y González, Luis, 33
Gortari, Carlos Salinas de, 4, 49, 50, 87, 92
grassroots migrant organizing (action arenas), 7
Great Depression, repatriation of Mexicans during, 15, 40–41
greenhouse cooperatives, 102

gross domestic product (GDP), 9, 83–86, 180n5
Guadalupanismo, 69–70
Guadalupano Club, 69–70
Guadalupano Committees, 70, 173n52
Guadalupe, Virgin of, 18, 69–70, 173n53
Guarnizo, Luis, 159
Guerrero (Mexican state), 87, 92
Guridy, Vanessa, 158
Gutiérrez, José Luis, x
Gutiérrez, Luis, 150
Gzesh, Susan, 175n9

Hardon, Russell, 159
Heartland Alliance for Human Needs and Human Rights, 148, 152
Hernández, Amalia, 25
Hewlett Foundation, 104
Hidalgo (municipality), 89
Hirschman, Albert, 141
Hispanic Federation, 151
Hispanics in Philanthropy (HIP), 104
home, dual meaning of, 74–75
Hometown Associations (HTAs), 5–6; and beautification projects, 125; and binational political rights, 147; in Chicago, 5–6, 19–21, 45–50, 51–52, 140, 141; and Christian Base Communities, 18; and citizenship, 159; and civic binationality, 51–52; civic engagement through, 141; collaboration with CODECOs, 130–132; and community development projects, 11–12, 75, 82, 97; cooperation with Mexican and U.S. governments, 160; definition, 5; emergence of, 26–27; funding of basic infrastructure, 127; growth of, 50; immigrant incorporation into, 142–143; as intermediaries, 144; intervention in state development plans, 110–111; isolation from mainstream U.S institutions, 138; and local problems, 48; mechanical solidarity in, 63, membership in, 20–21, 66–67, 138–139, 171n35; and migrant integration, 80; misappropriation of funds, 171n32; and naturalization, 154, 155; and participatory planning, 111–113; and project selection, 117; and religion, 17–19, 46, 69; and second generation participation, 79; and SMA, 120; and topophilic identities, 147; and trust, 110, 158–159; women in, 71–74; youth participation in, 72, 77, 79, 80, 104, 105. See also clubes de oriundos; Michoacán HTAs
Honorary Commissions (Comisiones Honoríficas), 39–40

hostilities toward migrants, 77–78
Howell Neighborhood House (Chicago), 13
HTAs. *See* Hometown Associations
Hull House (Chicago), 24, 38, 39, 43, 63, 167n2
human rights agendas, 150
Human Work (John Paul II), 18
hyphenated American citizens, 43

IADB. *See* Inter-American Development Bank
ICIRR. *See* Illinois Coalition for Immigrant and Refugee Rights
identity, collective, 21, 76
identity, Mexican American, 25–26
identity, national, 33–35
identity symbols, adoption of, 76
identity through topophilic attachments, 78
Ignacio Zaragoza mutual aid society, 24
Illegal Immigration Reform and Immigrant Responsibility Act (U.S., 1996), 64, 74, 88
Illinois: civil society organizations in, 20; incorporation of Mexicans, 15–16; naturalization of immigrants in, 155; recognition of migrant contributions in, 19–20; trade relations with Mexico, 3; Mexican tourists in, 164n6
Illinois Coalition for Immigrant and Refugee Rights (ICIRR), 77, 136, 146, 148, 149, 151, 152
Illinois Federation of Mexican Americans, 43
Illinois New Americans Immigration Policy Initiative (2005), 12–13, 148, 149–150
Illinois Office of New Americans, 145
Illinois Workers Alliance of Cook County, 37
imagined community, 34
immigrant incorporation, 4, 12–16, 17–18, 75–77, 80, 142–143
immigrant rights, 14–16; and Chicago Catholic Church, 17–18; in Illinois, 150; and transnational agendas, 149
immigrant transplanted spatial patterns, 27, 37, 65, 141
Immigrant Workers Freedom Ride Coalition, 148
Immigration and Customs Enforcement (ICE), 15–16, 183n15
Immigration and Naturalization Service (INS), 40
immigration reform, 46, 64, 74, 88, 149
Immigration Reform and Control Act (IRCA) (U.S., 1986), 46
inactive organizations, 75
inclusiveness condition, 161

income inequality, 174n75
Independent Political Organization in Little Village, 15
Índice Nacional de Corrupción y Buen Gobierno (INCBG), 87
informal economies, 95
informal practices, 142
infrastructure funding, 97, 127
Institute for Mexicans Abroad (IME), 2, 147
Instituto Federal de Acceso a la Información (IFAI), 23
Inter-American Development Bank (IADB), 83, 85, 93, 104, 132, 177n22
Inter-American Foundation, 10, 93
International Solidarity Program, 49, 88
Iraq War (2003–2011), 124
Iskander, Natasha, 95
Italian HTAs, 27
Italian mutual aid societies, 44

Jaliscan HTAs, 19
Jalisco (Mexican state), 92, 99
Jiménez, Trinidad, 36
job-generating projects, 99–100, 105, 180n13
jobs in Michoacán, 58
John Paul II (pope), 18
John Paul II Youth Center, 2
Joliet, Illinois, 16, 166n35
Jones, Robert C., 32
Juárez Club of Chicago, 42

Katz, Friedrich, 87–88
Kirk, Mark, 157

labor, division of, 71–74
labor conditions, 24, 28, 148
Labor Council for Latin Americans Advancement (LCLAA), 151
labor movements, 37–38
Lambda Legal, 151
land inheritance, 62
Landolt, Patricia, 142
landsmanshaften, 171n30
La Purísima (village), 61; La Purísima Soccer Club, 60
Las Cruces (village), 56
Latino Policy Forum, 151
League of United Latin American Citizens (LULAC), 45, 140, 151
Leal, David, 156
legal permanent residents (LPRs), 154, 183n21
Levi, Margaret, 159

Licenciado Benito Juárez Lions Club, 45
Linares, Marcos, 101, 102
literacy instruction, 37–38
Lomnitz, Claudio, 34
loudspeaker factory, 101
LULAC. *See* League of United Latin American Citizens
Lupián, Luis, 30

MacArthur Foundation, 149, 150
Machuca, Linda, 136
MALDEF. *See* Mexican American Legal Defense and Educational Fund
Manuel Pérez Jr. Post 1017, 41–42
manufacturing sector, 59
marching bands, 67
marginalization indexes, 116–117, 118, 120, 174n1, 181n16
Martinez, Ann, 37
Martínez, Juan, 70
Martínez, Refugio Román, 38
Martinez, Virginia, 136
mass media and poverty, 56
matching fund programs, 54, 88, 92, 179n38. *See also* Three-for-One Program
Mauss, Marcel, 65
McCann, James A., 156
Mejia Guzmán, Luis, 81, 174n1
Melrose Park, Illinois, 18, 19 148, 167n38, 185n37
membership in religious congregations, 17
Mérida Initiative, 11–12
meshworks, 7–8
methodology, 21–23
Mexican American Chamber of Commerce of South Chicago, 45
Mexican-American Council of Chicago, 43
Mexican American Democratic Organization of Chicago, 43, 44
Mexican American Legal Defense and Educational Fund (MALDEF), 136, 140, 151
Mexican Catholic League (Liga Católica Mexicana), 37
Mexican Civic Committee, 42
Mexican Community Committee, 45
Mexican diaspora, 4, 51–52, 87–92
Mexican government: cooperation with HTAs, 160; engagement with mutual aid societies, 35–36; and migrant philanthropic organizations, 6; outreach to immigrants, 160; promotion of emigration, 93; relationship with diaspora, 51–52; and subnational governments, 19
Mexican HTAs. *See* Hometown Associations

Mexican Independence Day parades, 43, 166n35
Mexican Movimiento por la Paz con Justicia y Dignidad, 151
Mexicanness, 33–35
Mexican organizations: binational agendas of, 48; and Ministry of Foreign Affairs, 49; in the post–Bracero Era, 44–45; preservation of customs and traditions, 46; topophilia in, 26; transformation of focus, 41–44; unification of, 45. *See also* Hometown Associations
Mexican Patriotic Committee, 42
Mexican Popular Front (Front), 37–38, 168n24
Mexican Relations Committee, 30
Mexican Steelworkers Association, 41
Mexican United Club Council, 43
Mexican Student Movement (1968), 13
Mexico: civil society organizations in, 20; division of labor in, 71–74; as export market, 3; mutual aid societies in, 36
Mexico-U.S. Advocates Network, 148
Michigan and Pátzcuaro's sister lake agreement, 77
Michoacán, 92, 99; absentee voting rights, x, 111, 136, 145; civil society organizations in, 110, 128; decline of rural communities in, 56–58; democratic transition in, 8; development projects in, 95; education in, 57, 104–105; evaluation of economic problems in, 95–96; and *faenas*, 65; interpersonal trust in, 110; jobs in, 58; lack of interpersonal trust in, 63; migrants to the U.S., 86, 95; participatory planning in, 112; population of, 21; remittances to, 86–87; submunicipal authorities in, 130; Three-for-One Program in, 98, 99, 114, 129
Michoacán Binational Front (FREBIMICH), 5
Michoacán HTAs: remittances for community development projects by, 8; and education, 64; fund-raising by, 112–113; and monarch butterflies, 76–77; numbers of, 169n4; project selection in, 116; and Three-for-One program, 98–105; transmission of culture, 74–79; umbrella federation of, 53
Michoacán's Electoral Institute (IEM), 136
microenterprises, 99–100, 104
migrant civil society, 137, 165nn15,22
migrant communities, informal practices of, 142
migrant networks, transnational, 7–8

migrant organizations: in Chicago, 13–15; diversity in, 30–35; funding of, 151–153, 184n28; imagined community of, 34; low membership of, 43–44; monitoring by Mexican consulates, 35; and Sensenbrenner bill, 156. *See also* Hometown Associations; Michoacán HTAs; mutual aid societies

migrants, Mexican: assimilation process of, 44; civic engagement of, 137–138; and context of reception, 12–13; dispersion of, 170n21; and mutual aid societies, 27–30; participation rates in HTAs, 20–21; permanent return to Mexico, 83; population in Chicago, 164n5, 170n25; relationship with municipal authorities, 120–121; self-representation capacity 72, 137, 149, 150; in U.S. armed forces, 164n4

migrant socialization, 75

Migration Policy Institute, 149

migratory phenomenon, attention of the state to, 121, 124

Miguel Hidalgo mutual aid society, 36

Miguel Hidalgo y Costilla Club, 43

Ministry for Social Development (SEDESO), 128, 181n23

Ministry of Foreign Affairs (SRE), 39, 49, 147

Ministry of Social Policy (SEPSOL), 128, 129, 132, 181n23

Minutemen, 146

Mr. and Mrs. Dance and Bowling Club, 42

Mr. and Mrs. Society, 41–42

M & M Society, Inc., 42

monarch butterflies, 76–77, 145, 174n80, 183n17

Money Gram, 15

monopoly capitalism, 59

Morawska, Ewa, 168n10

Morelia (village), 58

Movimiento Apostólico, 18

Mujeres Latinas en Acción, 152

Multilateral Investment Fund (MIF), 85, 93

Mundelein, George, 172n50

municipal authorities, migrant relationships with, 120–121

Municipal Development Planning Councils, 112, 180n6

mutual aid societies, 24, 168n8; crossborder cooperation with, 35; low membership of, 31–32, 43–44; Mexican migrants in, 27–30; in Mexico, 36; and repatriation of Mexicans, 40–41

Nacimiento de la Unidad, El (The Birth of Unity) (play), 149

NAFTA. *See* North American Free Trade Agreement

NALACC. *See* National Alliance of Latin American and Caribbean Communities

National Action Party (PAN), 89, 112, 115, 118–119

National Alliance of Latin American and Caribbean Communities (NALACC), 5, 11, 94, 149, 150–151, 152, 177n25

National Catholic Welfare Conference, 37

National Council of La Raza, 140

National Democratic Front (Frente Democrático Nacional), 25

national identity, 33–35

National Immigration Forum, 149

Nationality Law (Mexico, 1998), 50

National Latino Congreso (NLC), 151

National League of Religious Defense, 37

National Organization for Women (NOW), 151

National Revolutionary Party (PNR), 24

National Solidarity Program (PRONASOL), 49, 88, 175n10

National Survey of Latinos, 17

naturalization, 3–4, 12–13, 42, 73–74, 154, 155, 173n68

Necaxa Soccer Club, 42

neighborhood initiatives, 144–145

Nepantla Soccer Club, 80

New Americans Immigration Policy Initiative (Illinois, 2005), 12–13, 148, 149–150

New Mexican Federalism, 112

North American Free Trade Agreement (NAFTA), 9, 55, 87, 93

Nowak, Stanley, 38

Office of New Americans Policy and Advocacy (Illinois), x

1.5-generation community advocates, 142, 182n8

Orlandi Valuta, 15

Ortiz Rubio, Pascual, 24

Our Lady of Mount Carmel church, 19

out-migration, 9

PACME. *See* Program of Attention for Mexican Communities Abroad

Packard Foundation, 104

PAN (National Action Party), 89, 112, 115, 118–119

Pan American Games Committee, 43

Panindícuaro (municipality), 124

parallel committees, 125–126, 133–134, 181n19
Park, Robert, 44
participation, cross-border, 35–40
participatory citizenship, 84
participatory parity, 161
participatory planning and HTAs, 111–113
Partnership for Prosperity, 10, 93
Party of the Democratic Revolution (PRD), 89, 90, 112, 115, 118
Patronato Pro-Juventud Mexicana en el Extranjero (Mexican Youth Abroad Sponsoring Committee), 36
Peggy Notebaert Nature Museum (Chicago), 76
Peña, Elaine, 69
People's Global Action on Migration, Development, and Human Rights (PGA), 150, 184n26
philanthropic organizations, migrant, 6, 106
Pilsen (Chicago's neighborhood), x, 5, 13, 25, 42, 77, 163n3
Pilsen Neighbors Community Council, 13
Polish immigrants, 34
political rights, binational, 147
posadas celebration, 1, 18, 78, 163n2, 174n83
poverty, 9, 56, 81
prayer, 70; prayer groups, 5, 21, 46
PRD. *See* Party of the Democratic Revolution
Presencia Michoacana in the Midwest, 136, 182n2
PRI (Revolutionary Institutional Party), 25, 89, 90, 185n31
priests, 68, 69, 70
productive projects, 98, 99–100, 118
profit-generating projects, 118
Program of Attention for Mexican Communities Abroad (PACME), 47, 54, 147
Project Evaluation and Migrant Affairs Committee (COVAM), 108, 109, 115, 116–117, 118, 179n1
Pro-Mexico Benefit Society (Sociedad de Beneficencia Pro-México), 37
Pro-Mexico Committee, 37
PRONASOL (National Solidarity Program), 49, 88, 175n10
protectionism, national, 96
Protective Society for the Benefit of Latin American People, 41
public policy making: and collective remittances, 9–10; unequal access to, 143
public sphere, legitimacy of, 160–161

Purcell, Mark, 143
Putnam, Robert, 66

Quinn, Pat, 15, 16, 77

Rainbow/Push Coalition, Chicago Latino Chapter of, 148
Razas Unidas, Las (newsletter), 18, 166n34
reception, immigrant contexts of, 12–13, 47, 51, 139, 141–142, 166n26
reciprocity, norms of, 65
regidores de pueblo (village delegates), 130
religion, 17–18, 46, 68–71. *See also* Catholic Church; churches
reminiscing, 77
remittances: beneficiaries of, 85, 165n24; collective, 8–11, 54, 80, 83–84, 95, 103–104, 106, 111, 114, 127, 130; for community development projects, 8, 95; declining value of, 179n40; evaluation of, 85–86; and immigration reform, 88; to Michoacán, 86–87; noneconomic impact of, 87; and poverty, 9; and public policy design, 9–10; and regional economic development, 85; for social reproduction, 82–83; socio-political effects of, 84; volume of, 83–84, 175n3
remittance transfer companies, 15, 88, 92–93, 103, 175n5, 179nn38–39
repatriations, Mexican, 15, 40–41
resource recycling systems, 178n31
reunification of families, 157–158
Revolutionary Institutional Party (Partido Revolucionario Institucional [PRI]), 25, 89, 90, 185n31
Revolutionary Youth Front (PRI's youth training program), 185n31
"right to stay home," 82
"right to the city," 143
Rincón de Dolores Club, El, 1, 76
Rivera Sánchez, Liliana, 68
Rosales, Arturo, 33
ROSCAs (rotating savings and credit associations), 63–64, 171n31
Rotary clubs, 66, 71
rural communities, 8–9, 11, 34, 54–58, 74
rural cooperative models, 102

Saint Francis Church, 18, 167n37
Saint Francis Crier, 43
Saint Francis Girls Club, 43
Saint Francis University, 16
Saint Joseph Church, 70
Saint Mary's Catholic Church, 18
saints, 69

Salinas de Gortari, Carlos, 4, 49, 50, 87, 92
Sánchez, Rosendo, 57, 97, 170n16
sanctuary city law, 14
sanctuary movement, national, 15
San Miguel Epejan (village), 60
San Rafael (village), 89
Santa Ana Maya (municipality), 89, 103
Satélites Mexicanos (SATMEX), 92–93, 176n18
Save Ethnic Studies movement, 153
scalar analysis, 6
Schiller, Nina Glick, 82, 141
scholarships, 97, 104–105
school councils, Chicago, 173n63
Scott, James, 106
Second Binational Forum of Michoacán Migrants, 2, 91
Second Vatican Council (1962–1965), 17, 173n56
Secretariat for Migrant Affairs (SMA), 98, 113–114, 120, 121
Secretariat of Social Development (SEDESOL), 8, 81, 82, 88, 98, 99, 104, 113, 132, 165n17; objectives, 125; productive projects through, 178n32; project selection, 116, 118; regulation of COVAM meetings, 109; and Three-for-One Program, 94, 165n17
Secure Communities Program, 16, 183n15
SEDESO (Ministry for Social Development), 128, 181n23
SEDESOL. See Secretariat of Social Development
self-employed active migrants, 175n6
Senate bill 1557 (Illinois, 2009), 15
Sensenbrenner bill (U.S., 2005), 138, 146, 155, 156
SEPSOL (Ministry of Social Policy), 128, 129, 132, 181n23
Service Employees International Union (SEIU), 146
services, societal exchanges of, 65
service sector, 95, 170n25
Sherman, Rachel, 35
Siervo de la Nación prize, 81
SMA. See Secretariat for Migrant Affairs
Smith, Michael Peter, 6, 54
Smith, Robert, 6
soccer clubs, 67
soccer leagues, 47
social clubs, 42, 144
Social Development Ministry. See Secretariat of Social Development (SEDESOL)
social entrepreneurs, philanthropic organizations as, 106

social gatherings, 76
social heterogeneity of HTAs, 66–67
social infrastructure financing, 97
social mobility through family remittances, 84
social networks, 63
social production cooperatives, 179n37
Sociedad Cívica Mexicana de Illinois, 46
Sociedad Mexicana Cuauhtémoc, 41
Sociedad Unida de Artesanos de Durango (Durango's United Society of Artisans), 33
solidarity, 63, 67–71
Sotelo, William, 42
Southwest Voter Registration and Education Project (SVREP), 151
sports and solidarity, 67–68
sports clubs, 43, 47, 51, 67, 68
state-centered framework, 9–10, 141, 165n22
state-society relations, 3, 8, 52, 92, 106, 108, 110, 111, 114
stay-at-home citizens, 181n18, 181n24
Stephen, Lynn, 8
submunicipal authorities, 119–120, 130
submunicipal rural governance, 110, 119, 120
subnational government management and offices in U.S. territory, 16, 19
Suro, Roberto, 42
symbolic capital, 69

Tallman, Ann Marie, 155–156
tandas (ROSCAs), 63–64, 171n31
taxes, voluntary, 94
Taximaroa Club, 79
telephone connections, 48
Tepeyac Association of New York, 163n1
Thalia Hall (Chicago), 166n28
Third Binational Forum of Michoacán Migrants, 2
Thomas, William, 34
Three-for-One Program, 8, 11, 81, 87, 93–95, 111, 165n17, 181n17; absence of private businesses and philanthropies in, 103; budget allocation, 99; comparison with CODECO projects, 130, 131; concentration in few states, 9; corruption in, 114–115, 180n11; creation of sustainable development projects, 10; decision-making process for, 126; electoral bias in, 118–119; evaluation of, 94, 132, 177n22; evolution of, 95; fundraising for, 113; in geographically isolated communities, 119–120; job-generating projects

Three-for-One Program (*continued*) through, 180n13; and local groups, 127–134; and marginalization, 116–117; in Michoacán, 98, *99*, 114, *129*; in Pan-indícuaro, 124; policy guidelines for, 91; productive projects through, 98, 99–100, 178n32; project allocations, 108; project criteria, 180n12; project selection, 109, 116–117, 124–125, 179n1; rejection rates, 115, 117–119; and remittances, 9; for scholarships, 97; target population of, 99; transparency of, 113, 115

Three Kings Day celebration, 76

Tinoco Rubí, Víctor Manuel, 53, 89, 175n11

Tlaxcala (Mexican state), 130

tomato export markets, 102–103

topophilia, 26

topophilic identities, 26, 32, 34, 46, 47, 51, 78, 147

Toribio Romo, Saint, 18–19

Torres, Rubin J., 42

Tovar, Luis, 105

traditions, 79–80

Transmitters of Money Act (Illinois, 1995), 15

transnational action, legitimacy of, 161

transnational citizenship, second face of, 54

transnational communities, 164n14

Transnational Institute for Grassroots Research and Action, 179n39

transnational migrant action, 7

transnational moral communities, 64, 171n33, 172n46

transnational political citizenship, 6

transnational public spheres, 140

transnational theories on grassroots organizing, 134

Transparencia Mexicana, 87

Transversal Programs Directorate, 114

trust: building of, 126; and HTAs, 110; networks of, 62–67; and priests, 68

Tuan, Yi-Fu, 26

Tupátaro (village), 133, 181n28

turkey husbandry projects, 101, 178n34

Unión Benéfica Mexicana (UBM), 41, 169n28

United Nations Development Program (UNDP), 63

United Network for Immigrant and Refugee Rights (Red Unida por los Derechos de Inmigrantes y Refugiados), 25

United Packinghouse Workers, 37

United States: civil society organizations in, 20; manufacturing sector in, 59; Mexican-born population in, 46; as welcoming environment, 160

United States Agency for International Development (USAID), 11–12

United States government: cooperation with HTAs, 160

University of Chicago Settlement House, 38

urban revitalization project, 56–58, 139–140

"U.S. and Mexico, The: Threshold of a Trade Revolution" (1991 forum), 87–88

Vaillant, Derek, 40

Vasconcelos, José, 24

Vatican Council II (1962–1965), 17, 173n56

Vázquez Mota, Josefina, 91, 176n17

village delegates (*regidores de pueblo*), 130

Virgin of Guadalupe, 18, 69–70, 173n53

visibility of migrant civic organizations, 19–21, 145–146, 151

Vivanco, Pablo, 60–61

volunteerism, 17, 65, 70–71

Voz de Michoacán, La (newspaper), 89

Washington, Harold, 14–15

welfare services, decrease in, 64

Western Union, 15, 92–93, 103, 104, 175n5, 179nn38–39

Western Union, Money Gram, and Orlandi Valuta class-action lawsuit, 15, 103

Wildcats of Saint Francis, 43

William C. Velazquez Institute (WCVI), 151

Wolf, Eric, 34

women, 62, 68, 70–74

worker rights, immigrant, 148

World Bank, 85

"Year of Mexico" (Chicago, 2010), 20

Zacatecano HTAs, 72, 92, 126

Zacatecas (Mexican state), 99, 115

Znaniecki, Florian, 34

ABOUT THE AUTHOR

Xóchitl Bada is an assistant professor in Latin American and Latino studies at the University of Illinois at Chicago and affiliate guest professor at El Colegio de Michoacán. She is coeditor of the series on Latino Immigrant Civic Engagement, published by the Woodrow Wilson International Center for Scholars.

www.ingramcontent.com/pod-product-compliance
Lightning Source LLC
Chambersburg PA
CBHW022309280326
41932CB00010B/1039